A. Gruar Forbes

The Empires and Cities of Asia

A. Gruar Forbes

The Empires and Cities of Asia

ISBN/EAN: 9783743309364

Manufactured in Europe, USA, Canada, Australia, Japa

Cover: Foto ©ninafisch / pixelio.de

Manufactured and distributed by brebook publishing software (www.brebook.com)

A. Gruar Forbes

The Empires and Cities of Asia

THE EMPIRES AND CITIES OF ASIA.

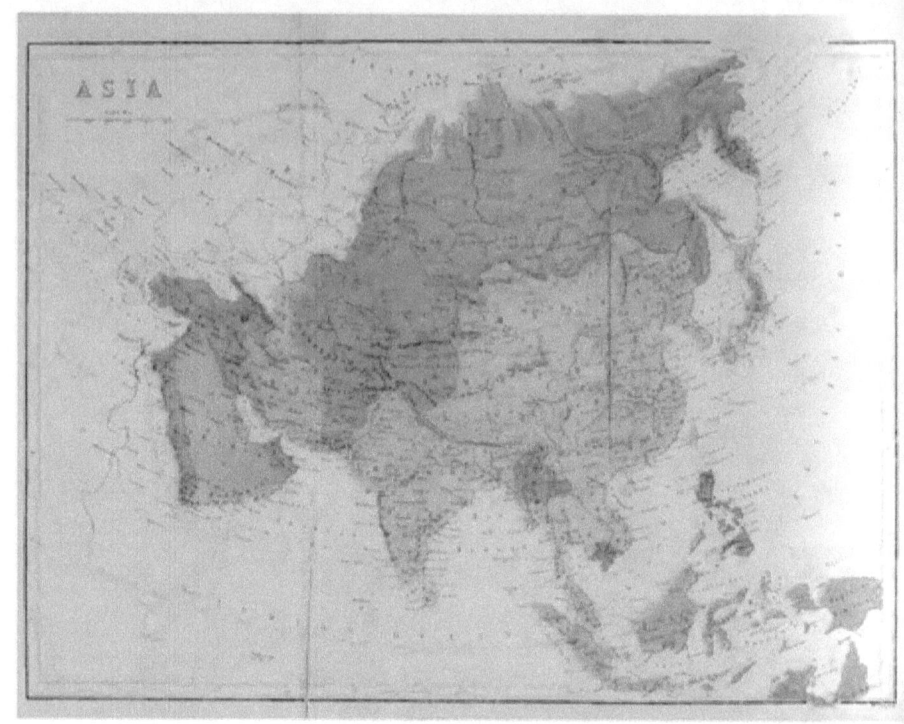

THE EMPIRES AND CITIES OF ASIA.

By A. GRUAR FORBES,

AUTHOR OF "PIONEERS OF THE CHRISTIAN FAITH, &c., &c.

WITH A MAP.

LONDON:
VIRTUE AND CO., 26, IVY LANE,
PATERNOSTER ROW.

[*The right of Translation is reserved.*]

LONDON:
PRINTED BY VIRTUE AND CO.,
CITY ROAD.

PREFACE.

IT is the design of the following pages to supply a concise record of the History of Asia, that shall be more entertaining, because less ambitious, than historical documents generally; and at the same time to put before the reader such a view of that great Continent as may contribute to a distinct conception of it in its ancient condition and also in its present state. The latter cannot properly be apprehended without a knowledge of the former. As space would permit, the geographical boundaries and divisions have been traced, and the more note-worthy localities and remarkable events in the history of the various nations which have occupied the soil have been indicated. The dominions of the great Powers at present bearing rule in Asia have not been so fully dwelt upon, inasmuch as separate books have supplied ample information in respect to each of them. But even of these, and of their several countries, a distinct if not enlarged view has been sought to be presented. Central Asia has more especially been contemplated as not so generally known, and also on account of the importance of present political and military movements in that section of this immense territory. At the latest moment of our writing intelligence reaches England to the effect that Khiva has fallen before the armed menace of Russia; but the reports are indefinite and confused, and require confirmation. Whatever the fact may now be, the alleged event is imminent, and may be regarded as accomplished. This was the last remaining of the independent Khanates. If others have the reputation of being self-ruled, their freedom is but nominal. The Khan of Khiva has been a robber-king, and his overthrow and subjection can only be regretted for political reasons. But now Asia is occupied only by wandering tribes, small tributary states, and the great Powers. Such being the fact, intelligent observers cannot but feel that matter is being largely and quickly accumulated for the history of the future.

In the composition of this picture of Asia many authorities have been consulted as to the lands, the people, and the state and prospects of this interesting portion of the world, although it has not been deemed expedient to burden the page or distract the attention of the reader by means of many quoted references. Grateful acknowledgment is hereby made for the assistance which has been obtained from Malte-Brun, Laurie, Ritter, Niebuhr, Botta, Layard, Kitto, Edkins, Legge, Atkinson, and others, as well as from the Journals of the Asiatic Society, and Government Despatches.

London, June, 1873.

CONTENTS.

	PAGE
PREFACE	V

CHAPTER I.
TOPOGRAPHY, LANGUAGES, AND NATURAL HISTORY. . 1

CHAPTER II.
TURKEY IN ASIA 72

CHAPTER III.
TURKEY IN ASIA.—(*Continued.*) 154

CHAPTER IV.
ARABIA 208

CHAPTER V.
PERSIA 222

CONTENTS.

CHAPTER VI.
Russia in Asia 237

CHAPTER VII.
The Tartars 281

CHAPTER VIII.
Britain in India 299

CHAPTER IX.
China 327

CHAPTER X.
Japan 341

Conclusion 346

Frontispiece . . . . Map of Asia.

LIST OF ILLUSTRATIONS.

Map of Asia	*Frontispiece*
Natives of Arabia	*face p.* 208
Ruins at Petra	,, 220
Calcutta	,, 298
Delhi	,, 308
Madras	,, 312
Bombay	,, 320

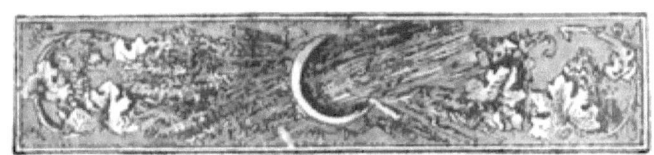

ASIA.

CHAPTER I.

TOPOGRAPHY, LANGUAGES, AND NATURAL HISTORY.

THERE are many circumstances which make this part of the world an object of special interest. It was here that the Creator planted the Garden of Eden; it was here that the first sin was committed. The ark was here. It was in Asia that God placed his own peculiar people, the Hebrews. The great work of redemption was accomplished in this part of the world. The patriarchs, prophets, and apostles lived and laboured here. The light of the Gospel first shone in this land. The first Christian Churches were here planted, and the truth first sealed by the blood of martyrs. The first great edifices in the world were built here, their ruins being still the wonder of mankind. The first great empires were here founded, while the rest of the world was but thinly populated by a few scattered barbarians wandering from place to place. In Asia the first associations of human beings into societies were formed, and the first cities built that men might gather themselves together for the sake of progress, or manufacture, or defence. Here the light of science first shone; the seeds of knowledge first sprung up and flourished; commerce, agriculture, and other useful arts were invented; and from this centre they were transmitted into all the neighbouring countries. On such accounts, as well as for its importance in a political, philosophical, and commercial point of view, it must at once be acknowledged that Asia has special claims on our attention.

The centre of Asia consists of a great plain, or tableland, which extends thousands of miles in every direction. This great tract of upland is probably the highest region in the old hemisphere, and forms the largest extent of elevated land in the world. It contains the countries of the Kalmucs, the Mongols, Thibet, and Eastern Turkestan, or the original country of the Turks. From the borders of this tract in the centre of Asia the great rivers of the continent flow towards the ocean in different directions. The Oxus and Jaxartes are on the west, the Amur on the east, the Ganges and Burrampooter on the south, and the Oby and Janisea on the north. The countries that surround this elevation are naturally inclined planes or slopes, hanging upon it.

On the south are the immense countries of India, gradually coming down to the level of the Southern or Indian Ocean. These are exposed to the fiercest force of the tropical sun. They are sheltered from the north winds by the rocky front of the high lands behind them. On the west of this high country are the territories of the ancient Persian empire. On the east is China, with its vast territory, its rivers flowing towards the great Pacific, or Eastern Ocean. On the north is Siberia, sloping gradually down to the Icy Sea. The rivers of Siberia are bound up in ice during half the winter. The rivers which flow towards the south, from the high centre of Asia, through countries subject to periodical rains, have, by carrying down immense quantities of mud and earth, formed great fertile plains near the sea coasts, similar in their nature to the Delta or rich valley of Lower Egypt.

Therefore, in the southern parts of Asia, from Persia to China, near the mouths of the Indus, the Ganges, and other rivers, there are large tracts of level country which are periodically overflowed, and this, with the heat of the climate, leads to a most exuberant vegetable production, of which, in temperate zones, we can have little conception.

The great central high ridge of mountains is of much importance as regulating the temperature, and for other reasons. It was called Imaus by the ancients. It is the Indian Caucasus. Its modern name is Hindoo-kho. The northern front, which overlooks Lake Baikal and the southern parts of Siberia, is of great extent; it is called the Altaic ridge or chain.

In all known ages the inhabitants might be divided into the barbarous and the civilised. Those who lived in cities, towns, and villages, and those who subsisted by agriculture, or commerce, or manufacture, were, to a considerable degree, qualified for taking their place among their fellow-men; but those who depended on their flocks, on the chace, or on depredation, were far otherwise. Selfishness and self-will ruled them, and they were rude in the extreme.

The ridge known under the general name of the Mountains of Taurus was one of the most remarkable features in the ancient Greek and Roman conception of Asia. To them it was thought of as a line of separation between two worlds—the civilised and the barbarous; or two climates—the warm and fertile, and the cold and barren. In this chain of mountains there are, however, several breaks. Among others, there is a vast chasm, opposite to the south end of the Caspian Sea, which was of importance with the ancients as being supposed to be in a direct line with Issus and Rhodes. This remarkable passage is now called the Strait of Khoward. Alexander the Great passed through it on his way from Rages towards Aria and Bactria. It is eight miles long, and not more than forty yards in breadth. There are various other ridges of mountains, Amanus, Lebanon, and others. This high country lies to the south, inclining to the west. Having passed the

Mediterranean and the southern border of Palestine, it goes onwards to the Red Sea, where it extends and becomes the centre of Arabia, terminating in what is usually named Arabia Felix, on the southern part of the Arabian peninsula.

Another ridge goes towards the south; it was called Zagros by the Greeks, and it proceeds towards the Persian Gulf. Between it on the east, and the Syrian ridge of which we have spoken last, and Taurus on the north, is a great valley which formed the territory of the ancient Assyrian empire. That empire was thus guarded by a wall of mountains on three sides, and by the Persian Gulf and the Arabian desert on the other side. The Tigris and the Euphrates, upon which Nineveh and Babylon formerly stood, water this vast plain. These regions are of great importance in ancient history. They are the original seats of civilisation and power, though they are now sunk into obscurity—a prey to barbarians, who live in tents, and wander over the sites of empires with their flocks and herds. The eastern part of the countries formerly known as Asia, or as the Persian Empire, still retains that name. To the west of the Euphrates Asia belongs to Turkey, with the exception of the part called Arabia; to the north and north-east lies the dominion of Russia; while to the east and south-east stretch the great Empire of China, and the territory of the British rule in India; there are also different independent tribes in various parts whose localities and characteristics we shall have subsequent occasion to notice. To enter into particulars:—

Asia lies between 1° 20′ and 78° N. latitude, and between 26° and 190° E. longitude. The greatest length from north to south, in the direction of the meridian, or from Cape Roumania, in Malaya, to Cape Taimura, in Siberia, exceeds 5,300 miles; and the greatest breadth from west to east, along the 40th parallel of N. latitude, or from Baba Burun, in Asia Minor, to the east coast of Japan, is about 5,600 miles. The superficial area is about 17,500,000 square English miles, or four times the extent of Europe, and 650,000,000 is the number given as its population. The boundaries are—on the north, the Arctic Ocean; on the south, the Indian Ocean; on the east, the Pacific Ocean; and on the west, the Ural mountains and the river Ural, the Caspian Sea, the range of Caucasus, the Strait of Yenikaleh, the Black Sea, the Channel of Constantinople, the Sea of Marmora, the Dardanelles, the Archipelago, and the Levant, all of which separate it from Europe; and the Isthmus of Suez and the Red Sea, which separate it from Africa.

We learn from Homer that, before the war of Troy, there was intercourse between the inhabitants of Europe and Asia. Such intercourse was, however, but restricted, and even the Phœnicians appear to have known but little of Asia as a whole. The establishment of the Persian monarchy, B.C. 550, advanced the knowledge of this part of the world. States which had hitherto been divided were incorporated under one sovereignty, and their commerce was widely extended. The Persian empire being established, Darius, the son of Hystaspes, seems to have required a geographical and statistical account of his entire dominions to be prepared, and this more distinctly and fully revealed territories which hitherto had been but partially known. Information continued to be extended, as we learn from Herodotus, and from Xenophon's Anabasis, or "The Expedition of the Ten Thousand." The conquests of Alexander enlarged greatly the knowledge of Asia among the Greeks. He attempted, with but small success, to pass the boundaries of the Persian empire to the north and south, gaining some amount of acquaintance, however, with the country and the nomadic tribes beyond the Jaxartes (*Sir-Daria*, Yellow River), which at that time wandered, as at present, over those extensive deserts. His attempts on the south and east were attended with more substantial results. He crossed the Indus and four of the rivers which traverse the Punjaub, and advanced nearly to the banks of the Jumna and the valley of the Ganges. Returning to Persia, he gave orders to his admiral, Nearchus, to sail along the coast from the Delta of the Indus to the mouth of the Euphrates. The geographical information acquired during the expeditions of Alexander was incorporated in a map by one of his companions in arms, Dicæarchus, a pupil of Aristotle. Most of the Greek kingdoms in Asia were overthrown by the Romans. The extreme eastern boundary of the Roman empire was formed by the Tigris, the Euphrates, and the mountains of Armenia; but the military expeditions of the Romans being conducted in countries previously known, there was but little added by their means to the knowledge of the world respecting those countries. In ancient times the curious and inquiring were indebted for much of their information in regard to the Asian continent to Strabo, Pliny, Ptolemy of Alexandria, Nearchus, and Arrian, as well as to Herodotus and Xenophon.

Much later there was inaugurated an epoch of greatly enlarged acquaintance with Asia. The Emperor Justinian II., in the year 569 of the Christian era, sent one of his governors to one of the wandering tribes of the Turks in the steppes, on the west and south of the Altaic Mountains, with the view of inducing them to attack their common enemy, the Persians. By this means, these countries came to be better known. An Egyptian merchant, named Indicopleustes, who had long traded with India, and had frequently visited it, composed his "Topographia Christiana;" in which he gives much information respecting Ceylon and the roads of Upper Asia. The Arabs, by their commercial intercourse with India by the Red Sea and the Gulf of Persia, did much to unveil the obscurity of these parts. But none have done more in this direction than the Chinese. From the historical records of their empire it is clearly proved, that two hundred years before our era they were anxious to collect geographical knowledge respecting the extensive provinces and tributary kingdoms of their dominions; and they have continued this work to the present day. Europeans began to renew their acquaintance with the countries of Asia, on the shore of the Mediterranean, in the eleventh century by pilgrimages, and soon after by the Crusades (1096-1272), undertaken for the deliverance of the Holy Sepulchre. Marco Polo, a Venetian of great enterprise, resided among the Mongols from 1275 to 1292; and, notwithstanding the extremely pictorial style of his writing, he has added to our knowledge of this continent. The Mongol empire is principally the subject of his descriptions. After Marco Polo, and the romance of his narrative, the number of travellers in Asia increased. Still there was no great extension of the boundaries of trustworthy knowledge supplied by their means.

Explorations along the coasts of Africa have given us information in regard to Asia. And to this information additions have been made by science, and travel, and commerce, on the part of the European nations—all which it will be proper to remark upon as we proceed to look in detail on the several countries, and the enterprises and conflicts of different times. From the industry and commerce of the English in modern times, as well as from the success of the British arms in various parts of the continent, our acquaintance with it has been increased. The Russians, also, have so pushed their way into hitherto obscure territory that we know better than before the peculiarities of the countries of Asia.

Asia is distinguished by mountainous ranges, table-lands, and great valleys or plains. There are many islands which lie near the continent, and which ought to be considered in regarding it or describing it. The Sundas, for example, form the most extensive archipelago of the globe. The highlands and lowlands and islands furnish a great variety of natural features in the countries, and of widely diversified character in the populations. Such countries, in the very centre of the civilised world, must have vast influence on the whole human family, and that influence must have told in all past periods of the world's history.

When we turn our attention to the Himalayas, and restrict the name to the region which lies between India and Thibet, we are met at once by the fact that not more than a fifth part is well known to Europeans. This portion of the great Himalaya range includes the high country near the sources of the Ganges, the Jumna, a tributary of the Ganges, and the Sutledge, a tributary of the Indus. There are here many varieties of mountain scenes, natural productions, tribes of men, and wider diversities of political constitution than can be found in any other hill country in the world. The length of this range is about 1,300 miles; and, in Europe, it would cover all the countries between the Pyrenees and the Sea of Azof. The breadth of it is from 250 to 350 miles. The whole chain, reaching from the high pinnacles of the Hindu Coosh, near Cabul, to the most eastern valleys of Assam, near the source of the Brahmapootra, is surmounted everywhere with snow—and this fact is the reason for the Indian name Himálaya, which means "the dwelling of snow."

The entire range is divisible into three sections. The most eastern is less known than the others. The central part includes the mountains of Nepaul, and the capital of Nepaul, a city situated in one of the valleys, and standing 4,784 feet above the level of the sea. The White Tower, one of the mountain peaks of this division, rises to the height of 25,261 feet. Here, also, is the Dhawalagiri, or the White Mountain, 28,000 feet, the highest known pinnacle in the world. The western region comprehends the ridges which traverse the countries of Kamaoon, Gherwall, Bissalin, and Sirmore.

Along the lowest southern slopes there is a flat country, scarcely a thousand feet above the level of the sea, with bogs and forests, and sultry heat, which make it the continual home of many diseases. This country is called Tariyana. There are numerous hills running across these great mountain systems, though sometimes they lie in the same direction with the loftier elevations; and among these are many deep valleys and ravines. The trade between India and Thibet is carried on by means of these mountain passes—the lowest of them being, probably, not much below the height of Mont Blanc—none of them being less than 14,000 feet above the sea-level, and some of them rising even to 18,000.

There are four great rivers which take their rise on the mountain ranges which surround the table-lands on the north of the Himalayas. These are the Irtish, the Yenesei and the Tuguskas, the Lena, and the Amur. They are, respectively, 2,000, 2,500, 2,000, and 1,900 miles in length. The Irtish, with its tributaries, drains upwards of 1,300,000 square miles, the Yenesei about 1,000,000, the Lena nearly 800,000, and the Amur about 850,000—all taken together, a space much more extensive than the whole of Europe. The greater part of this extended surface belongs to Siberia. These rivers abound in fish, have plenty of water at all times, and are navigable to the extent of two-thirds of their courses. The lower part being northern is, for six months of the year, covered with ice. In the spring the waters in the upper tributaries become swollen and tear off their banks, and great masses of rock and earth are carried down and strewed over the flats below. The navigation on the principal water-courses is, therefore, inconsiderable, but is of greater importance in their tributaries running east and west, by means of which a water communication is established through the greater part of the countries lying between the Ural Mountains and Obhotzk.

From the mountains bordering on the highlands of Eastern Asia there are two terraces, with appended slopes, which descend to the Pacific Ocean. There are besides, many inferior declivities, following the same direction, which are watered by smaller rivers. The two former terraces give rise to the two great river systems of the Ho and Kiang—the former running upwards of 2,000, and the latter more than 2,900 miles. Each of them carries off the waters of a surface of upwards of 700,000 square miles. The Chinese call these the Sons of the Ocean, probably because the tide rises in them for more than 400 miles—by which means they are rendered inland seas, and are navigable for a great distance from the coast. The space between these two rivers forms an immense delta, and the rivers themselves, as a double river system, formed on the most colossal scale, skirt the most fruitful and best cultivated country in the world, Central China, which is indebted to these rivers for its commerce, its civilisation, and its canals.

In Southern Asia the rivers form three distinct groups. In India, east of the Ganges, there are six or seven of these, their course lying from north to south, or S.S.E. The Irawaddy is probably the largest. At some points it is about eighty yards wide. Within the Ganges, the rivers run in quite a different direction from that of the rivers beyond the Ganges. The Ganges and the Indus take a diverging course, and enter different parts of the sea; but their tributaries, especially the Jumna and the Sutledge, approach one another, and facilitate the commercial intercourse of the nations which inhabit the countries through which they flow. The advantages which result from the flowing of these rivers into different gulfs is very great. The Gulf of Bengal brings the inhabitants of the peninsula into communication with the nations of Malay origin, and with the Chinese; while the Gulf of Malabar opens to them the coasts of Persia and Arabia. It is principally on account of this direction of the rivers that India within the Ganges has enjoyed such opportunities of civilisation over India beyond the Ganges.

The river system of the Ganges and the Brahmapootra extends about 1,300 miles in length, and drains a surface of nearly 650,000 square miles. The Ganges rises in the Himalayas, which being covered with perpetual snow, there is always an abundant descent of water, which is carried off by many great rivers, some of which exceed the Rhine, both in volume and in length of course. These rivers enter the Delta of Bengal, which is twice as large as that of the Nile, and presents an extensive and intricate system of rivers and canals, both for irrigation and navigation. By its junction with the Brahmapootra, which descends through the valley of Assam, the river system of the Ganges becomes double, and not unlike that of the great Chinese rivers. The Ganges and Brahmapootra descend from regions different in natural advantages, of which only that adjacent to the Ganges has attained a high degree of civilisation.

The river system of the Indus has a special historical interest, in part because it contains the Punjaub, the country of the five rivers which descend from the eastern mountains; and in part on account of its geographical position. The sources of the Indus, as well as those of its great tributary, the Sutledge or Satadru, were discovered only in 1812. Both of them rise in the high table-land of Thibet—the Indus on the slopes of the Kailasa Mountains, and the Sutledge in the sacred lake of Manassarovara. These rivers, not originating on the southern slopes of the Himalayas, but on the north, pierce the range in its entire breadth, and pass through large clefts in the mountain mass before arriving at the low plains of Hindustan. The course of the Indus is upwards of 1,500 miles long, and it drains a surface of more than 400,000 square miles.

There are, by this arrangement of nature, ten or twelve great terraces in Eastern Asia, differing from each other in many particulars. They are partly divided from one another by passes, and partly flanked by low lands. Sometimes mountains rise in the middle of these low lands, but in no case do they attain to the height of those of Central Asia. In Southern China, there is the mountain region of Yun-nan, Su-Chan, and Kuang-si; beyond the Ganges, it occupies the country of Laos; and on the peninsula within the Ganges, is the table-land of the Deccan. The plateau of Deccan rises at an average from 3,000 to 4,000 feet above the level of the sea, the greatest part of the peninsula lying between the Arabian Sea and the Bay of Bengal.

In Western Asia, the highlands are of smaller extent; but they form a principal feature in the formation and character of this great continent. This part of Asia is not only nearer to Europe, but is also more like it in natural formation, and is more closely connected with it. In Western Asia are the highlands of Iran, flanked by the deep plains called Turan, on the north-east. These elevations and depressions extend from the Upper Indus, throughout the whole of Western Asia to the shores of the Grecian Archipelago. The central portion is occupied by Persia; over the western parts is exercised the dominion of the Turks; and over the eastern that of Afghanistan. This division of Asia is materially different from the highlands of Eastern Asia, inasmuch as, generally, it is better capable of being cultivated, and, in reality, exhibits extensive tracts which are under cultivation at the present day, or were so in former times. As to the fact of a former cultivation, there are many ruins of great towns, and other monuments of architecture existing even in those districts which are at present neglected; as on the north-east in Khorasan, the ancient kingdom of Bactria, towards the south in Karmania and Persis, and also in the western districts, as in Kurdistan, which formerly lay in ancient Media. This is not the fact, however, in the south-eastern corner of these highlands, which include the ancient provinces of Gedrosia and Arachosia, which now form part of Beloochistan, and attain their greatest height in the table-land of Kelat, which rises to 7,000 feet above the level of the sea. The eastern descent, towards the valley of the Indus, is extremely rapid. It is formed by steep rocks, and feeds no rivers. It is entirely without cultivation, and has no roads, except one, namely, that from Candahar, through Pisheen, Quetta, and Baugh, to Shickarpoor. It is inhabited only by stray tribes of Afghan origin, which have no historical records.

The northern edge of this highland, which extends along the southern shores of the Caspian Sea and the deep plains of Bucharia, is historically famous, as containing the Bactrian, Parthian, Hyrcanian, and Caspian mountain passes, which are narrow defiles, affording a passage for the armies of the conquerors descending from Iran to Turan. This country has for many centuries been the abode of warlike mountain tribes, whose chiefs, by holding possession of the mountain passes on the north, have extended their dominion over the extensive plains of the table-land. This was the policy of Nadir Shah and of Fet'h Ali Shah, who, sensible of this peculiar circumstance, fixed their residence at Teheran, a town built near one of the passes, on the high table-land. The caravans which travel eastward to India and Bucharia, and westward by Tauris (Tabreez) to Armenia and Asia Minor, are obliged to pass along the southern side of this mountain-girdle, and near the openings of the passes. Along the great road, which is invariably fixed to this tract by the nature of the surface on the northern boundary of the table-land, there rose great emporiums. Here we find the towns of Cabul, Candahar, Herat, Meshed, Nishapoor, Teheran, Rai (the ancient Rhagae), Casbin, and Tauris.

The southern border of the table-land of Iran is still more distinctly marked by nature, separated as it is from the low and narrow coast and the wide plains watered by the Tigris and the Euphrates, by a broad mountain tract, which, beginning at the mouth of the Indus, extends to the point at which the rivers of Mesopotamia break through the rocky masses of the high table-land, and enter the low plains. This mountain tract consists of from three to seven ridges, running parallel to each other, and separated by a corresponding number of longitudinal valleys, which sometimes extend many days' journey in length. The ridges themselves are, like the Jura mountains in France, composed of limestone, and rise like terraces from the low coast higher and higher. Beyond them extend the wide table-lands. There are but few mountain passes leading through this natural entrenchment of Persia, a country which, on this account, may be considered as a fortress erected by nature for the defence of the nations which inhabit it. Among the narrow mountain passes which lead from the sultry low coast, called the Gurmsir (warm region), and through the great staircase of mountain terraces, to the cool table-land in the interior, called Sirhad, three roads have acquired celebrity in history—the eastern, the middle, and the western mountain road.

The eastern mountain road begins at the harbour of Bender Abassi or Gambroon, near the entrance of the Gulf of Persia, and leads northward to Kirman, the ancient Karmania, situated on the cool table-land, in a spot which abounds in springs, and is covered with fruit-trees, though on all sides surrounded by desert plains, in which it lies like an oasis in the midst of the Libyan desert or Sahara. The middle mountain road begins at the town of Aboushehr or Bushire, on the shores of the Persian Gulf, and leads first over a lower ridge to Kazrun, near Shahpoor, the residence of the Sassanidae (of king Sapor I. A.D. 240), which is situated in the first valley. From this point it crosses a rocky mountain to Shiraz, the former residence of the Arabian caliphs, which stands in a wider and richer valley. It then proceeds through winding courses among the mountains, and by deep and narrow ravines, to the valley in which are found the deeply interesting ruins of the ancient Persepolis. From these ruins, and in a northern direction, it again lies in narrow passes, among high rocks, which are full of monuments of the early ages of Persia. At last it issues from the mountain region, and enters the extensive table-land on which Ispahan, the residence of the Sufi dynasty, is built. The capitals and great towns of these different dynasties are built on the fields of battle where signal victories were obtained, and are placed at the openings of the most difficult mountain passes, full of narrow defiles. The Arabs had to pass through this difficult road on their way to Persepolis, and this has also been the route of modern travellers who have entered the inland provinces of Persia from the Persian Gulf. The Macedonians, under Alexander, and afterwards Timur, passed from the banks of the Karoun to Persepolis, up the valley of the Jerahi, and by the pass of Kalat-i-Sefid.

The western mountain road, which lies to the north-west of the former, may be called the Median, in opposition to the Persian, which passes through Persepolis. It begins at or near the modern Bagdad, and goes through the Mediae Pylae of the mountain range called Zagros, and passes by Kermanshaw, Besittoon, and the ruins of the temple at Kungavar, terminating at Hamadan, the ancient Ecbatana, in Media. This road also reveals many historical monuments. It crosses the upper course of the rivers which flow through the lowlands of Susiana.

There is thus a series of towns and cities, the capitals of the ancient kings, and now the sites of interesting ruins, beginning with Kerman and including Persepolis, Parsagadae (or Parsagarda), Ispahan, and Hamadan, and terminating again at Tauris; it lies along the internal slope of the mountain ridges which border the table-land of Iran on the south, and which is analogous to that which forms the northern girdle of these mountains. By these towns is marked the boundary which separates the region of the natural fastnesses, of the mountain passes, of the battle-fields, of the pastures, and of the country adapted to the chase, which is formed by the mountain terraces, from the interior table-land, which is more level and uniform in its aspect. But in the table-land itself are some ridges of hills which, lying mostly in a general direction east and west, attain only a moderate height. There are also a few valleys, of no great depth, covered with green meadows, or scanty pasture lands or steppes, and in a few places with sandy deserts, or a soil impregnated with salt.

Abushehr is on the shore of the sea in the valley Gursmir, and has a climate favourable to the growth of palms. Kazrun lies on the first mountain terrace, and is 2,772 feet above the level of the sea. The highest point of the pass Desht-i-Arjun, above Shiraz, rises to 7,200 feet. The town of Shiraz itself, which is built on the second mountain terrace, is 4,284 feet above the sea. Its climate is favourable to the vine. Rose-bushes grow to the size of trees; but the palm does not succeed. The highest point of the pass over the third mountain ridge above Persepolis rises to 6,666 feet. Ispahan, lying in the plain which forms the third terrace, is 4,140 feet above the sea. From this level the mountain passes lying farther north towards Kohrood, rise nearly 2,000 feet higher. Near Koom there is the greatest depression in the table-land. The surface sinks here to the extent of 2,046 feet. In the plain it rises again in the direction of Teheran, which has an elevation of 3,786 feet. The mountain pass which leads to the Caspian Sea past Kishlac, rises to 4,572 feet; and the entrance of the Hyrcanian pass at Shahrood to 3,414. The Demawend is the highest mountain peak in these parts, and attains an elevation of 10,000 feet, most of the adjacent summits not rising more than 7,000 feet. The slope of this range towards the Caspian Sea is very steep and abrupt, the distance from the crest of the mountain to that immense lake being very short.

The most remarkable feature in the physical geography of Persia is the absence of considerable rivers, though this country is at least as large as the whole of Germany. This fact is not occasioned by the want of springs, which are found almost everywhere, at no great depth, rendering the country cultivable in most districts; but there are no extensive valleys to furnish channels for running waters. This natural characteristic of the country has deprived it of one of the most efficient means of extensive civilisation. The nations inhabiting Iran have never, therefore, quite emerged from the condition of pastoral life, combined with the frequent change of abode, although, from time to time, they have exhibited a considerable amount of mental culture.

In Iran, at the western extremity, between the innermost corners of the Gulf of Persia and of the Caspian Sea, at about the fiftieth meridian, the table-land narrows to nearly half its former extent, and increases in height. Extensive plains lie beyond towards the east, but to the west the hilly region becomes higher and higher. The elevated region of Persia and Kurdistan begins in this locality; and here are the sources of the Zab, the Tigris, the Aras, and the Euphrates, with the lakes of Urmia and Van. The table-land is replaced by mountains, which rise to an enormous height, with elevated valleys between them. Azerbijan, the fire region, is one of these, and is famous as the native country of Zoroaster. The mountain ranges and the table-lands are again united in the mountains of Armenia, Azerbijan in relation to them being only a lower terrace. The Asian countries to the west of Armenia resemble in their structure those of Europe rather than those of Eastern Asia. There are no longer the same compact masses, rising to a great height, and swelling out to large dimensions, the masses are more separated and distinct. There are four divisions of this kind.

The first is the highland of Armenia, which, as a triangle, occupies the space between the three seas—the Caspian, the Black Sea, and the Gulf of Alexandretta. The plains on which the town of Erzeroum is built rise to 7,000 feet above the level of the sea, and the highest summits of the Ararat, which overtop the plains, attain the height of 17,260 feet. The second great division is formed by the Caucasus, united as it is by hills of moderate height, which in part cover the Caucasian isthmus. This mountain region is remarkable for its isolated position and its entire independence of the table-lands of Asia, and also by the fact of its double descent to the north and the south, which makes it much more like the mountain regions of Europe than those of Upper Asia. It resembles the mountainous region of Switzerland, and, as in that country, it is peculiar in its natural productions and in the character of its inhabitants. But the rivers which rise in these mountains—the Kur, Phas, Kuban, Terek—cannot be compared with those of Europe either in length or in other respects of importance. On the western border of the highlands of Asia is the peninsula of Anatolia, the third of these elevated masses, which is surrounded by seas, and is joined on the east to Persia by the mountain system of the Taurus. The interior is occupied by a table-land which, on the average, rises to about 2,000 feet above the sea-level, and descends with steep slopes towards the north and the south. The descent is gentle towards the west, and is formed by long fertile valleys with abundant streams. It terminates on the shores of the Ægean Sea in a coast full of promontories and indentations, marking the termination of the ranges which run from east to west in this peninsula. It extends like a bridge for the passage of nations between Asia and Europe. The fourth region is formed by the mountains of Syria, which, running towards the south, contain Mount Libanus, and thence continue to the lofty cone of Sinai, an elevated mountain mass, which is a rare occurrence in Asia.

Though Western Asia is indented by gulfs and arms of the sea, making peninsulas and headlands, there are no great river systems such as occur on the eastern side of Asia. It presents forms of smaller dimensions, like those of Europe, and better adapted to the use and dominion of man. There is only one extensive river system in this country, and it consists of only two large rivers, a feature which is especially characteristic of Asia. This is the river system of the Euphrates and Tigris, or of the Shatt-el-Arab. The north branch of the Euphrates comes from the neighbourhood of Erzeroum, and the east branch from the western extremity of the table-land of Iran, where the country rises to a great height, forming a complete mountain system, with lateral hills and intervening elevated valleys. The Tigris rises on the south side of the high range, and along the north side flows the Euphrates. The Euphrates has a winding course of nearly 1,800 miles. When these rivers have forced their way through the Taurus, the Euphrates to the north of Rumkala, and the Tigris above Mosul, they begin to converge and to surround Mesopotamia, till they approach the ancient Babylonia, but they do not unite in it. Their waters form a great delta, and then enter the Persian Gulf by the same channel.

This double river system in Asia is one of its most remarkable features. In the valley of the Nile, civilisation descended along the banks of the river from one royal city to another, from Meroë to Thebes, and thence to Memphis and Sais. But in the valleys of the double rivers of Asia we meet with double royal residences, double civilisation, and double political systems, as Babylon and Nineveh respectively on the Euphrates and Tigris; Delhi and H'Lassa, with Brahminism and Buddhism, on the river system of the Ganges; and on the double river systems of China, the Southern and the Northern Empire, Ma-chin and Khatai. When in the progress of time civilisation descended these streams, and met at their conflux, or where they approach near each other, the different degrees of perfection which it had attained, and the different turn it had taken, must have produced, as the nations came into contact with one another, a beneficial effect. The same is the fact in regard to the fourth great system of double rivers, the Sir and the Gihon, on the banks of which, in the centre of Asia, similar circumstances are repeated in respect to the cities of Samarkand and Bokhara.

The highland of Eastern Asia is formed by the Deccan, which is an independent and isolated limb of the mountain system to which it belongs. In like manner the peninsula of Arabia projects from the highland of Western Asia, and may be considered as entirely independent. As the Deccan is separated from the highland region by the lowland of Scinde, so Arabia is divided from the mountain system of the Taurus by the lowland of Syria, which extends to the south-west of the Euphrates. The country again rises to the south of this lowland, and has quite a different character. This forms the highlands of Arabia, which contain the tableland of Nejd, the country of the Wahhabites—a cold country, connected on the south with the elevated Yemen or Arabia Felix, which descends in terraces towards two seas. The descent towards the west is steep, and formed by parallel mountain ridges, with well-sheltered valleys between them, in which are situated the famous towns of Mecca and Medina. This part of the country is better known than the corresponding steep descent towards the south between Aden and Hadramaut, and thence to Muscat. The eastern declivity falls with a gentle slope towards the Gulf of Persia, and surrounds the islands of Bahrein, which are noted for their pearl banks. The cold Nejd is the native country of the Arabian horse and the Arabian camel. Coffee grows on the terraces which border it on the west, and the low and narrow coast, with its sultry air, produces also the date-palm.

In Arabia there are features which entirely differ from those which mark the other parts of Asia. As already indicated by its geographical position, it forms a point of contact between Asia and Africa, and has the distinguishing qualities of both. Even the population, the original Arabs, resemble no nation so much as the mountaineers of Abyssinia, who occupy the upper country on the opposite side of the Red Sea, speak a language resembling that of Arabia, are equally well formed, and nearly equal in mental quality. Confined to their own territory by the nature of their country, and separated from the rest of the world by seas and mountains, the Chinese feel no inducement to leave their fertile and extensive home. They have, therefore, remained in ignorance of other nations, and formerly excluded foreigners from their soil. The Hindoo is born for his own Indian world, and is fit for no other, and is placed in a country in which all the advantages of Asia are concentrated. Here, in this territory, there is in many particulars an advanced civilisation; but the Hindoo is not migratory, has seldom left the boundary of his native land, and with stolid indifference has received foreigners—some as conquerors, others as merchants or colonists, or missionaries. The Arabs, whose original country lies between two great divisions of the globe, have assimilated themselves to both of these, and, at one period of their history, extended their dominion to the most western point of Africa, as well as to that of Asia. In these parts there are still to be found lingering remains of the former occupation. The larger number of Arabs are to be found beyond the peninsula, which is the native country of their nation, but which prepared them for the endurance of every climate. Its sultry coasts resemble the arid deserts of Lybia; the moderate climate of the terraces approaches that of Iran, the Deccan, and Catalonia; and the cold Nejd differs little in its character from the highland of

Central Asia, on which we find the Arabs in many parts at a great distance from their native country.

The lowlands of Asia are everywhere situated within the highland regions and the valleys which are formed by the terraces which are connected with them. These hills and terraces probably cover a space of not less than 4,300,000 square miles, or more than a fifth part of the whole extent of Asia. There must, therefore, be 6,000,000 square miles for the surface of the lowlands. These lowlands are spread around the most elevated parts of the interior, and form the countries which lie along the sea, the lower course of the great river systems traversing them with many windings and but little fall. It was in these plains that the great empires of antiquity attained their greatest power, and continued for the longest period of time. These plains are six in number, and, unconnected with each other, are different in their individual characteristics.

The great Chinese lowland is the first, and lies on the eastern shore of Asia, along the Pacific Ocean, beginning at Pekin, and extending along the Yellow Sea southwards by Nankin to the province of Kiang-si. It is south of the fortieth parallel, and reaches nearly to the tropic. The climate is temperate; the agriculture is advanced in its extent and manner; the system of canals is most extensive; and this is the richest granary in the world.

The second is the Indo-Chinese lowland, lying

between the Gulf of Tonkin and that of Siam, and which extends from the tenth degree of north latitude to the tropic, comprehending the Kingdoms of Camboja and Siam. It has the advantage of being south of the tropic, and, being plentifully supplied with water, is well suited to the cultivation of rice. There are in it large spaces covered with standing water as well as several lakes.

The third is the lowland of Hindostan or Scinde. It includes the northern part of India, and lies between the Gulf of Bengal and that of Gujerat. It is bounded by the two river systems of the Ganges and the Indus, and is overlooked by three table-lands,—those of Thibet, Iran, and the Deccan. Situated out of the torrid zone, but near the tropic, it has all the advantages of a tropical climate, with but few of its disadvantages. In the richness and variety of the natural scenes which surround it, it is unequalled by any of the others. It is as populous as the lowland of China, and much exceeds it in the number of the nations which occupy it, and also in that of the great cities and centres of civilisation which it includes,—as Agra, Delhi, Benares, Calcutta, Lahore, Mooltan, Ajmeer and others. The western half, however, is a desert covered with sand.

Syria and Arabia constitute the fourth of these great lowlands, the boundary being the innermost corner of the Gulf of Persia on the east; on the west the mountains of Syria; on the south the table-land of Nejd; and on the north and north-east Iran. The northern half only is watered by the river system of the Euphrates and the Tigris, the southern portion suffering much from the absence of moisture, being arid and desert.

There are thus two lowlands which may be called maritime, and two which may be called continental. The Chinese and Indo-Chinese lowlands are generally surrounded by seas, exposed to the action of high tides, and frequently drenched by the moisture brought by the winds from the east and south-east. The lowland of Hindostan, and that of Syria and Arabia, on the contrary, only border on narrow bays, and on the south and the north are over-topped by high table-lands which have always a dry atmosphere. It follows, consequently, that in these last-named lowlands there is great dryness in the air, as in the former there is much moisture. They are therefore, respectively, distinguished by all the corresponding variations of animal and vegetable life. In China and the peninsula beyond the Ganges, the inhabitants approach in their manners and customs the inhabitants of islands; but in India and Babylonia they resemble the population of inland countries. The southern half of the lowland of Syria and Arabia resembles the African Sahara, and is therefore called the Arabian Desert. It is characteristically tropical, although situated beyond the tropics; and, divested of many of the peculiarities of Asia, is more like Africa in many of its natural productions, as well as in its climate.

The fifth of these lowlands is that of Siberia, which is

the most extensive, and occupies more than the half of the area of all the lowlands of Asia, and extends along the Polar Sea the whole length of the continent from the Ural Mountains to the Pacific Ocean. It is traversed by extensive river systems, but it derives little advantage from that fact, inasmuch as it contains only in the southern third of its surface (between 50° and 60° N. lat.) habitable and cultivable land. In all parts this district has been colonised by Europeans. Here are the most numerous European settlements in Asia. The northern and most extensive division, lying either within the polar circle or near it, is beyond the bounds of cultivation, and belongs rather to the polar regions than to that division of the globe which has been called the East. The lowland of Siberia, though its maritime boundary exhibits no great variety, has, by its elevation above the level of the sea, a great influence on the whole continent of Asia, which no doubt would have presented quite a different aspect if great mountains had occupied the northern shores of Siberia, and formed its boundary towards the Polar regions.

Bucharia occupies the sixth lowland, and it is entirely continental, without contact with any part of the ocean, and watered by inland seas, the Caspian and the Lake of Aral. Its greatest extent is in the direction of the double rivers which traverse it. Beginning at the innermost angle formed by the western edge of the table-land of Thibet, and the northern edge of that of Iran, this greatest of all the depressions on the surface of the globe extends to the north-west over the countries adjacent to both banks of the Volga, up to the river Don and the boundary of Europe, between the mountain ranges of the Ural and of the Caucasus. It may, therefore, be considered as the means of connection between Central Asia and Europe. Its great plains are but scantily watered, the surface being mainly formed of gravel. Agricultural enterprise has consequently but little encouragement. These spaces are commonly called steppes—or plains covered with grass, without trees, and having only here and there a few tracts of cultivated land. In such a country nomadic tribes find a natural home. Although deprived of all the riches of nature, except in a few places in which agriculture is carried on by artificial irrigation and immense labour, this lowland is historically remarkable. As it is in the centre of very extensive countries, and surrounded by various nations, it has been concerned in all the great historical events. It was here that the conquerors,—such as Cyrus and Alexander, who proceeded from the west, or those of China, who came from the east, the Bactrians, Ghazuarides, and Great Mogols, from the south, and the Russians from the north,—met with a stop to their further progress.

The country being naturally poor, and the lands surrounding it being comparatively rich, the various political changes in the neighbouring countries have frequently induced its inhabitants to pass beyond their own boundaries, the more especially because they had no fixed abode, but led a nomadic life. The Chinese and Hindoos never left their country, but took root there, and grew into settled nations; but the inhabitants of this lowland have been nations of change and migration for centuries, and, since the times of the Scythians, Goths, Alans, Uzes, Comanes, Petsheniges, Turks, and Tartars, till nearly our own times, have repeatedly inundated Europe, destroying and impairing and retarding its civilisation. Great changes, meanwhile, occurred in their own country, in regard both to the population and the dynasties which ruled over it. In our own times, it exercises a great influence on political events, by the geographical position which it occupies, and the obstacles which it presents to the progress of the three great Empires of Asia—the Chinese on the east, the Russians on the north, and the British on the south.

We thus find that in Asia there are six great lowlands, different in their character, and independent of one another. They spread below and around two highlands which occupy an immense space, and which are themselves surrounded by seven or eight less extensive and separated mountainous or table-land regions—those of Southern China, the peninsula beyond the Ganges, the Deccan, Arabia, Syria, Armenia, and the isthmus of the Caucasus, each having its own peculiar features. To these must be added ten or twelve intermediate formations, terraces—and, putting all together, we have in Asia nearly a score and a half of great natural divisions, subject to individual natural laws. Their mutual connection and reciprocal influence alone can afford us a true view of the great variety and combination of the natural phenomena, with the historical events of this great division of the globe.

The SOCIAL CONDITION of Asia presents a most varied scene. Peculiar to this continent is the transmission of institutions, usages, and manners unaltered from the earliest ages. The life of the patriarchs, as described in the earliest of existing historical records, is still found unchanged in the Arab tent. The courts of Babylon and Nineveh appear to have been marked by features of pomp similar to those of Ispahan and of Delhi before it fell. Asia, even before the beginning of the historical period, seems to have made considerable progress in civilisation; but then she stopped short, and has allowed herself to be far outstripped by the originally less advanced nations of Europe.

The despotism to which the people of Asia are generally subjected has, no doubt, much to do with this absence of change and of progress. A republic, an aristocracy, a representative assembly, political liberties and privileges, regular control of the community in any such mode as we should call constitutional, are ideas altogether foreign to the mind of an Asiatic. Still, although the general principles of government remain the same from age to age, the change of ruler and of dynasty is much more frequent than in Europe. As the ideas of hereditary right and of primogeniture are much less deeply rooted, a younger son, or even an uncle, of the reigning sovereign, if more able and popular, finds it easy to dispute the sceptre with him, and even to wrest it from his hands. Oriental sovereigns still maintain the primitive institution, not excepting the greatest of them, of sitting and administering justice in person. The seat of residence and rule is not usually unalterable, as are the maxims and modes of the administration. Every successive prince may select some favourite city, which he either has originated, or which he means to raise from insignificance by lavishing his wealth upon it in the way of adornment. The abodes of his ancestors are neglected, and hence Asia is covered all over with decayed capitals and ruined palaces.

In many parts of Asia a system of plunder is systematically carried on. Communities, chiefs, and even princes, do not scruple to share in it. There is nothing clandestine in it. It is avowed, sometimes boasted of, as a calling which is respectable. If, however, they have accepted a composition similar to the old "black mail" of this country, or if they have pledged their faith, they inviolably abide by their agreement. The numerous tracts of mountain and desert afford them holds in which to shelter themselves, and these are seldom far from some rich plain, or great commercial route, on which to exercise their depredations. Arabia, from time immemorial, has been a hive of such plunderers.

The *attire* of the Orientals, we need scarcely say, is

widely different from that of Europeans. Instead of our short tight garments, they wear long flowing robes, wrapped loosely round the body. Instead of the hat they wear a light turban, and for shoes have sandals. In entering a house, or when wishing to show respect, they take off the sandal, when we would remove the hat. They do not use chairs, tables, plates, knives, forks, or spoons. At meals, they seat themselves cross-legged on the floor, and eat out of a large wooden bowl placed in the centre, and filled, not with solid joints, but with stews or sweetmeats. This dish is common to the whole company, and each thrusts in his hand without ceremony, and carries the morsels direct to the mouth. They are very scrupulous about washing their hands. They do not use beds. An Oriental going to sleep merely spreads a mat for himself, adjusts his clothes, and lies down. The amount of household furniture, for the reasons which have just been specified, is small, and consists of little more than carpets covering the room and sofas set round it, of which some are of peculiar beauty and fineness. Their garments are also simple, though composed among the rich of fine materials, and profusely ornamented with jewels and precious stones. Their arms and the trappings of their horses are objects on which they make a studied display of magnificence. All over the East the beard is allowed to grow, and is regarded with reverence.

In *disposition* and *temper* the people of Asia are grave,

serious, and recluse. They have no balls, theatres, or large assemblages. They regard that lively social intercourse in which many Europeans delight as weak and frivolous. Except when roused by strong excitement, they remain stretched or seated on their sofas and divans, and look with pity on those whom they see walking about for recreation or amusement. We cannot easily estimate their moral qualities as compared with those of Europeans. Their domestic attachments are strong, and they have much reverence for their ancestors. Their ordinary deportment is mild and courteous; and they show themselves capable of generous and benevolent actions. Yet, among the subjects of the great empires, the obligations of truth and honesty were habitually disregarded. At the present day, the chiefs and principal men are usually designing, treacherous, and inhuman—devoid of honour, and capable of the most enormous crimes. The smaller tribes, although they display greater manliness, as being frequently called upon for self-defence, are rude and coarse. Towards women the conduct of the Asiatics is always degrading. Polygamy is probably the source of this evil. Women are systematically excluded from society. The Mahometan doctrine which declares them to have no souls; the Hindoo practice of prohibiting them from reading, writing, and being present at religious services; are parts of a system which is manifestly intended to reduce them to a lower level. It is true, there is one local example (in Thibet) which is of an opposite character. There, there is female sway, and a plurality of husbands; but this is only an exception to the general rule, and is manifestly the result of mere caprice in former times.

RELIGION is professedly in high regard among the Asians. The Divine Name is continually on their lips. But their creeds are all marked by a deep tincture of superstition, such as seems naturally to connect itself with a crude and imperfect knowledge. The most savage and degrading rites are practised in many parts of the continent; and, in all of them, the favour of the Deity is expected to be obtained rather by munificent donations, costly temples, and elaborate worship, than by purity of heart and life. Christianity, although it was at first revealed in Asia, and spread in parts of it, has not maintained its ground there against those superstitions. There are two systems of faith which divide Asia very much between them. The one is that of Mahomet, which, by the arms of his followers and of the conquering Tartars of Central Asia, has been thoroughly established over all the western parts as far as the Indus. Even in India, it became, for centuries, the ruling religion, and has many adherents even now; but it was never there the religion of the body of the people. The other is the religion of the Hindoos, which is divided into two great sects—those of Brahma and Boodh; the former occupying the whole of Hindostan, and the latter having its head-quarters, or rather its centre, in Thibet, fiillng the whole of the east of Asia and Tartary, and reaching northwards even beyond the Altaï.

Agriculture is carried on in many parts with industry and care, though generally with less skill and with ruder implements than in Europe. There is much less capital, particularly in live stock, employed upon the land. The cultivators rise very slightly above the rank of the peasantry. The principal expense is in irrigation. Crops without watering would, in many districts, be impossible. There are also several manufactures in Asia which are not equalled in richness and beauty by those of any other part of the world, although they are conducted with small capital and simple machinery. The carpets of Persia, the muslins of India, the porcelain and the lacquered ware of China are unrivalled. Commerce is fettered by the jealousy of the greater rulers, and yet it is not inactive. In Europe commerce is chiefly maritime, in Asia it is principally inland, while, at the same time, there is much accomplished by means of the sea. The interior caravan trade is still large, although it has been diminished since Europe ceased to be supplied in this way. There is a considerable amount of trade by sea on the southern coasts; but it has now been partly reduced, so far as foreign exports are concerned, by the direct intercourse of England with India and China. It has been converted in a great degree into a coasting trade.

The ASIATIC LANGUAGES are capable of being classed into seven groups:—1. The Semitic; 2. The languages of the Caucasus; 3. The Persian; 4. The languages of India; 5. The languages of the region beyond the Ganges; 6. The Tartar tongues; and 7. The languages of Siberia.

The *Semitic* languages may be divided into five branches:—1. The Hebrew; 2. The Syriac, or Aramean; 3. The Median; 4. The Arabic; 5. The Abyssinian. The Hebrew includes the Hebrew, the Phœnician, and the Punic. The ancient or pure *Hebrew* was used up to the time of the Babylonish captivity. The Jews use it for all sacred purposes even now. In this language most of the Old Testament is written. The *Chaldee* is almost identical with the Syriac; it was brought with the Jews from Babylon. The oldest work in it is the book of Daniel. This was the language spoken at the courts of Nineveh and Babylon. The *Rabbinical* dialect is a mixture of the Chaldee with the pure Hebrew. The *Phœnician* was formerly spoken along the whole coast of Syria; it differed but little from the Hebrew. The *Punic, Carchedonic*, or *Carthaginian,* was one of the dialects of the Phœnicians. The *Syriac*, or *Aramean*, was formerly used in parts of Persia, and even in Tartary and Central Asia, where it came to be known through the merchants and the religious sect of the Nestorians. The *Median* was spoken, as the name implies, in ancient Media. It is the Pehlvi, or Phelvy, formerly in use in Western Persia. The *Arabic*, one tongue, is yet divisible into three sections :—The *ancient* Arabic, which has long been extinct; the *literal* Arabic, common to the whole Arabian nation. It is the written and literary language of most of the nations subject to the vast empire founded by Mahomet. The Koran was written in it. It is still used in the Mahometan worship. The *vulgar* Arabic is the language spoken in Arabia, and in the greater part of Syria and Mesopotamia, and in part of Khusistan, or Fars, along the Persian Gulf, in the Kingdom of Persia, in some parts of the Malabar and Coromandel coasts, in all parts of Egypt, in Nubia, especially along the Nile, in all the towns of the Barbary States by the Moors and Arabs, and in a part of their plains by the Beduin Arabs, in a part of Beled-el-jereed, and in some of the oases of the African deserts. There are slight diversities of dialect observable in this wide sphere of use for the Arabic, but in all the language is essentially the same, and can be understood by all without much difficulty. The *Abyssinian* belongs strictly to the Semitic branch of tongues, but has been much corrupted.

The *languages of the Caucasian region* are several:—
1. The *Georgian*, which consists of the ancient and modern Georgian, the Mingrelian, the Suane, and the Lasian; 2. The *Armenian*, including the ancient Armenian, now extinct except in books and in worship, and the vulgar Armenian, which is the modern language spoken by the Haikans in Turkish and Persian Armenia, in part of Georgia and Shirwan, and in the government of Istchil; 3. The *Lesghian* languages, including the

Awar, the Kazikumuk, the Akusha, and the Kura; 4. The *Mizdjedghi*, spoken by the people of that name, in Southern Circassia, and comprising four principal dialects; 5. The *Circassian*, spoken by the Circassians, or Cherkasses, whose true name is Adije, probably the Zyges of Strabo, and the Ziches of the Byzantine writers; 6. The *Abassi*, spoken by the Abassi, who are now subjects of Russia. All the languages of the Circassian region are extremely harsh, and are remarkable for an extraordinary assemblage of consonants, and an accumulation of vague and diphthongal sounds, many of them guttural. The Armenian and the Georgian are the only written languages; those who speak the others use in writing either the Arabic, the Georgian, or the Turkish.

The Persian languages consist of:—1. The *Zend*, formerly spoken in Bactriana, where it ceased to be in common use before the Christian era. The Zend-avesta, the sacred book of the fire-worshippers, is written in this language. The Magi, or priests, spoke it; 2. The *Parsi, Farsi*, or ancient *Persian*. This was a language which had surpassed the Zend in copiousness, accuracy, and elegance, long before it became the language of the court and of public business in Persia. It is not now in use; 3. The *Modern Persian*. This is derived from the Parsi, and was formed during the prolonged domination of the Arabs in Persia, and is a mixture of Arabic and Turkish with Parsi. It is spoken in Persia, and in part of India, especially among the Mahometans in Agra and Aurungabad. It had long been the language of the court of the Great Mogul. A dialect of it is spoken in Bukharia, in some towns of Asiatic Russia, and in some provinces of China; 4. The *Kurde*, or Coord, spoken in Kurdistan and Lauristan. The Kurdish differs but little from the Persian in words, but much in grammar. It is harsh, and much less polished. 5. The language of the *Ossetes*, inhabiting the high valleys of the Caucasus. It bears an affinity to that of the modern Arabs. 6. The *Pooshto*, or Afghan. It has much analogy with the Persian, and but little with the Semitic tongues. Its literature is very poor; 7. The *Beluch* is spoken by the dominant nation of Beluchistan and Scinde. It much resembles the Persian. It is written in the Arabic character, with some additional letters.

The languages of India. India has come to be a great empire in itself. We are not now much accustomed to deal with it as part of Asia; therefore our notice of its tongues may here be all the more brief. Of the languages of India—1. Is *the Sanskrit*. It is a dead language, though formerly spoken throughout a great part of India. The sacred books are written in it; 2. The *Bali* or *Magada*. It is a sister tongue to the Sanskrit. It is not now spoken; but is continued as the liturgic, hieratic and literary language of Ceylon, Bali, Madura, part of Java, throughout Indo-China, and Malacca. Among the living languages of India there are many derived from the Sanskrit, such as Hindustani, the Punjaube, the Cashmerian, the Caubal, the Scindee, the Zinganee, and many others; while there are many tongues not affiliated with the great parent Sanskrit at all, the Touppah, the Garow, the Choomeas, the Cattywar, the Gond, the Cottesghur, and the Wadasse.

The *languages of the regions beyond the Ganges* are divided into five branches:—1. The *Thibetan;* 2. The *Indo-Chinese;* 3. *The Chinese,* and this last again separates itself into varieties.—1. The *Kou Wen,* or ancient Chinese, which is perhaps the most monosyllabic language in the world, and which contains the greatest number of monophonous words. 2. The *Kouan Kou,* or modern Chinese. 3. The *Ching Cheu,* spoken by the inhabitants of Fo Kien; 4. The *Corean,* spoken in the kingdom of Corea; and 5. *The Japanese,* which is in use not in Japan only, but also in the Foo Choo islands, distinguished as being inhabited by perhaps the only people in the world unacquainted with the use of warlike weapons.

The Tartar languages are divisible into three families:—1. The *Tungusian.* This is common to the ancient and modern inhabitants of Mandshuria, and to several tribes inhabiting Eastern Siberia. There are two languages combined in it,—the *Mantschew,* spoken in the Chinese Empire by the Tunguses, who have been the dominant nation since 1644, when the ancestor of the now reigning family was placed on the throne; and the *Tungus,* spoken by the Tunguses, who live in the Russian Empire, scattered over more than a third of

Siberia, from the Yenesei to the Sea of Okhotsk; 2. *The Tartar* or *Mongol*, comprises all the idioms used by the Tartars properly so called, subdivided as they are into many communities dispersed over Mongolia, as also in part of Thibet, in the Chinese Empire, and several parts of the Russian Empire. These idioms form a family composed of at least three languages, the Mongol proper, the Calmuck, and the Bouriet; 3. *The Turk* family, including the *Turkish*, the *Yakoute*, and the *Tchouwache*. There are many dialects of the Turkish. The *Osmanli*, or Turkish proper, is spoken by the Osmanlis, Ottomans, or Turks; the *Kaptchak* by the pure Tartars as they call themselves, who live in the Russian Governments of Kasan, Simbirsk, Penza, and Saratov, and by the pretended Tartars of Astrachan and Orenburg; the *Turcoman*, which is used by the nomadic nation of Turcomans, split up into many sections; the *Caucaso-Danubian*, which is spoken in three dialects by the Basians, the Koumuks, and the Nogais, who are dependent on the Russian Empire; the *Kirghis* and the *South Siberian*, spoken by various Turkish tribes inhabiting that region; *the Yakoutes*, who speak the language so named, are the most northern and most eastern of all the Turkish tribes; the *Tchouwaches*, called by the Russians the Mountain-Tartars, are most numerous in the governments of Kasan and Wiatka. Their language differs only by many provincialisms from that of the Yakoutes.

The *Siberian* languages are several :—1. *That of the*

Samoides. This nation is still nomadic, and is to be found principally in the centre of Asia; but is scattered over the whole of the northern region, from Olensk to the Straits of Warjatz, and in Europe from the Straits to the White Sea; 2. *The Yenesei,* so called from the river Yenesei. The people who speak these languages live in the government of Torusk, and separate the Samoides of the south from those of the north; 3. *The Youkhagire* is spoken by the Youkhags, or Adon Dommi, a much reduced nation, few in number, and who have generally embraced the Christian religion; 4. The *Koryeke*, which includes dialects spoken in the north-east of the government of Irkutsk by several communities called Koryekes, and some others, comprised under the denomination of Tchuktches. These tribes occupy the territory to the east of Youkhagires, and are surrounded by real Tchuktches, by the Kamtchadales, and the Tunguses; 5. The *Kamtchadale* is spoken in the peninsula of Kamtschatka by people who call themselves *Itulmen.* Small-pox ravaged this district in 1768, 1784, 1800, and 1801. Those who escaped have generally embraced Christianity, and adopted the Cossack mode of living; the *Kurilian* includes the speech of the Ainos or Kurilians, the aborigines of the Kurilian archipelago, the isle of Taraiki, and part of Mandshuria. The languages comprised in it are the Kurilian proper, the Jesso, and the Tarakas.

We may divide Asia into these parts:—*Southern Asia,* which consists of Asia Minor, Syria, and the other

Asiatic parts of the Turkish Empire; Arabia, Persia, Hindostan, India beyond the Ganges, and China. To this division are appended the great Oriental Archipelago, which forms the empire of Japan. *Middle Asia* consists almost exclusively of the vast regions of Tartary, divided into Chinese and Independent Tartary. To this may be added the Caucasian territory, situated between the Black Sea and the Caspian. *Northern Asia* consists wholly of an immense plain, subjected to the sway of Russia, and bearing the name of Siberia.

Many questions may be asked respecting the POPULATION of Asia. Was this continent ever more fully occupied than it is at present? How many of its inhabitants were destroyed during the wars of the Mongols? How far has its population decreased, owing to the despotism exercised by the Turks in the western countries? How many nations have already become nearly extinct, or have quite perished, as the Philistines, the Phœnicians, the Parsees, the Babylonians, the Lydians, the Bactrians, the Medes, and the Sogdians? More than forty nations were destroyed in the middle ages by the Mongol wars, according to the statements of the annalists of that time; and some have become nearly extinct in our own times, as the Doms in the Himalaya range, the Miao-tse in Southern China, the Tata in Northern China, the tribes of the Tunguses, Eastern Turks and Samoiedes in the mountains of Sayansk, and others in Mount Caucasus. These questions can be answered only with approximate probability. But the people still remaining, some of them in immense multitudes, and others in smaller numbers are these: the *Semites*. The *Jews* are a principal portion of this section of the human race. They are scattered over a great part of Asia, and are most numerous in the Ottoman territory, and in Persia and Arabia. There are also many of them in India, Turkestan, and China. The *Arabs* are probably the most numerous of this branch of the world's population. They occupy nearly the whole of Arabia, the greater part of Syria and Mesopotamia, with parts of Khusistan and Fars in Persia. They have also settlements on the coasts of Malabar and Coromandel, in Turkestan, and in the regions of the Caucasus.

The *Georgians* occupy the country, Georgia, whose name they bear, and are also to be found in Imeritia. The Mingrelians, the Suanes, the Lazes, at the eastern extremity of the Black Sea, also belong to the same race.

The *Armenians* are a people who form the great mass of the population of Armenia. They are also numerous in Georgia, Shirwan, and Azerbijan. They are scattered through all the commercial cities of Turkey, Persia, India, Turkestan, and even in some parts of China. Related to them are the Abasses or Absue, who inhabit Abakssethi, or the great Abassie, several tribes of whom are vassals of Russia. The Natoukhashi are also of the same race essentially, and speak a language much like that of the ordinary Armenian.

E.

The name *Persian* covers several divisions of men. The *Persians*, *Parsees*, or *Guabers* are settled in the largest numbers in and about Gujerat, in India, and in Yezd in Iran. They are also found in Kerman, Moultan, and at Baku in Shirwan. They are better known under the name of *Iranee* than by that of Persians. These are admitted to be the descendants of the original Arab conquerors who overspread Persia during the most brilliant period of Islam prosperity. They form the great mass of the population of Iran, and are also the most numerous and polished members of this family of nations. The *Bukharians* are the indigenous inhabitants of Great Bukharia, and of the principal towns of Chinese Turkestan. In the large towns of Siberia, Central Asia, and China, they are very numerous, and many are engaged as merchants. In Kurdistan and Louristan are to be found the *Kurds* and *Lourees*. The *Affghans* or *Poushtaneh* are in Affghanistan, and the north-western parts of India, and in Rohilcund in the north-east of India. The *Belootshees*, who possess the south-eastern parts of ancient Persia, occupy also the country of Scinde, on the lower part of the Indus.

The *Hindoos* are the most numerous of all the tribes in the world. Their habitat extends over the whole of India to the north of the Tuptee and Godavery. The principal branches of the race are—The *Moguls*, originally composed of Turks, Bukharians, and Persians who speak the Hindustani language. They originally formed the leading class in the Mogul empire. They are to be found chiefly in Hindostan or Northern India; the *Sikhs* are the principal people of North-Western India; the *Bengalees* form the mass of the population of Bengal, and of some parts of the bordering provinces; the *Mahrattas* principally occupy the western part of the Deccan, and portions of Khandeish, and Gujerat; the *Singalese* are in Ceylon; the *Maldives* also belong to the same race; and so do the *Zinganees* or *Gipsies*, who are spread over Europe and Western Asia, and who are also to be found in some parts of Northern India.

The *Malabar* family comprehends the people who inhabit that part of India which lies between Cape Comorin and the Tuptee and Godavery. The leading branches are the *Malabars*, the *Tamul* who inhabit the Carnatic, and the *Telinga* or *Telooyoo*, who extend from Pulicat to Orissa. The Garrows, the Kathes, the Gonds, the Bheels and other tribes, who have lived from remote ages in India, do not belong to those families which form the great body of the people of the country. They are more or less distinguished by the savage and barbarous character of their customs.

As to numbers, the *Chinese* compete with the Hindoos. They form nearly the whole population of China. They are settled along the coasts of Hainan and the west coast of Formosa, in Siam, Malacca, Singapore, Penang, Ceylon, Calcutta, Mauritius, and have even found their way to Brazil, and are now to be met with in newly-discovered parts, and in fresh fields of enterprise opened up by recent gold and diamond discoveries; the *Mianmai*, or *Miajamma*, or *Birmans*, are the principal occupants of the basin of the Irawaddy; the *Maons*, or *Peguans*, inhabit Pegu. The *Tai*, or *Tai-nai*, called also *Laos*, *Shyans*, *Shans*, and *Siamese*, are the ruling people of Siam, and occupy the whole of Laos. Here there are also the *Annamites*, subdivided into *Tongkinese*, who are most numerous, and the *Cochin-Chinese*, who have obtained sway in the empire of Annam; here too are the *Sian-pi*, or *Coreans*.

The *Japanese* are spread over the whole empire of Japan, and are almost the only population. In power and civilisation they rank high among Asiatics. The Loochooans are part of the same race. The *Miaotees*, the *Tolos*, and the *Mientings* are numerous tribes found in China; but they do not belong to the Chinese stock. The savage tribes of Hainan, the *Kemoys* in the mountains which separate Laos from Cochin-China, and the *Karens* in Birmah are unconnected with the more civilised peoples among whom they live.

The *Tunguse* are subdivided into *Mantchoos* and the *Tunguse* proper. Since 1664 the former have been the ruling class in China, and, in many particulars, are far advanced in civilisation. They form one-half of the population of Laiotung, and the entire community of the Mandchusia, as far as the confluence of the Oussuri and the Amur. The proper Tunguses are inferior to the others in their civilisation, and are to be found chiefly in the Russian Empire, in which they spread over a third part of Siberia, from the Yenesei to the sea of Okhotsk. The Mantchoos furnish a remarkable fact in the history of civilisation. It is only about 250 years since they were nomades, ignorant of the arts of reading and writing, but they now possess a rich literature, especially valuable for its acquaintance with the learning of China, which has been communicated through the medium of translations. It is the Mantchew, and not the Chinese, which is the language of the court at Pekin.

The *Mongolians.*—This general name includes the *Mongols*, the *Kalmucks*, and the *Buriates*. The Mongols, subdivided into *Mongols* properly so called, *Khalkas*, and *Sharaigol*, or Mongols of Thibet, occupy Mongolia and a part of Thibet, as well as Hohoner in the Chinese Empire. There are also some of them to be found in Chinese Russia. The *Kalmucks*, or *Olet*, inhabit a great part of Soongaria. The Buriates are in the government of Irkutsk.

The *Turks.*—The *Osmanlee*, or *Othmanlee*, or *Ottoman Turks*, are the dominant people in the Ottoman Empire. They are the principal and most civilised portion of the race to which they belong. They are most numerous in Asia Minor. The *Usbecks*, or *Ouzbecks*, or *Usbegs*, are predominant in Independent Turkestan. The *Turks* of Siberia, or *Tomalians*, who are the pretended *Tartars* of Siberia, or *Tomaliun Tartars*, are spread over the governments of Tobolsk,

Tomsk, and Jenisseisk. The *Turcomans* are subdivided into many stocks and branches, and are found in Affghanistan, Turkestan, Ottoman, and Russian Asia. They have for more than a century been very numerous in Persia. Here also are the *Kirghiz*, subdivided into *Bourouts*, or Eastern, and *Kazak*, or Western. A part of the Bourouts are tributaries to China; the greater part of the Kazaks are vassals of Russia; the rest are independent. These numerous tribes speak the Turkish language. Dialects of the same language, more or less varied, are also spoken by the *Sokha* or *Yakoutes* in Jenisseisk and Yakoutsk—these being the most eastern and northern of all such tribes, and also the least civilised. The *Tchouwaches*, sometimes called *Mountain Tartars*, wander over a part of Orenburg.

The *Samoiedes.*—The *Tawghi*, a part of this family, extend from the Jenissei to the Lena, and are the most northern people of the old world. The *Ouriangkhai* are the most southern section of this race. Most of them are found within the Chinese Empire, between the Syanian Mountains and those of Altaï and Khangai. The rest are in Russia.

The *Jenisseians.*—These tribes are chiefly confined to the government of Jenisseisk. They are divided into the *Denka*, the *Imbazk*, the *Poumpokolsk*, the *Kottes*, and the *Assanes*.

The *Koriaks* comprise only the small and savage tribe of this name, and it is found at the north-east of Asia, in the districts of Okhotsk, Kamschatka, and the country of the *Tshouktshi*.

The *Youkaghires* are a scattered and scanty race, whose tribes inhabit the country between the Yakoutes and the Koriaks, along the Icy Ocean.

The family of the *Kamschatka* are few in number, and occupy the country which bears their name. They are chiefly fish-eaters.

The *Kurilians* or *Kuriles* inhabit the Kurile islands and the southern part of Kamschatka. The *Ainos*, or *Jesso*, occupy the island of Jesso. The *Tarakai* or *Ainos*, are in Tarakai, or Segkai, or Seghalien; the *Giliaki* occupy that part of Mandchuria to the east of the Oussouri, and are called *Fiaka*, or *Kedjen* by the Mantchoos.

The *Ursalians* or *Tschudes* include the people called *Mansi*, who are found between Kourgan and Beresov, in the government of Tobolsk, and the *Ostiaks*, distinguished as the As-Iakh, or Ostiaks of the Obi, the Ostiaks of Kersov, of Jougan, of Narym, and others.

The *Malaisians*.—These are the aboriginal inhabitants of Formosa, including the *Malays*, who form the principal portion of the population of the peninsula of Malacca, and the neighbouring islands. We must, however, except the mountains in the interior of the peninsula, which are inhabited by a negro race of an entirely different origin.

Besides these native Asiatic families, there are many colonies of Europeans in most parts of Asia: *Greeks* in the Ottoman Empire; *Russians* in Siberia; *English*,

Scotch, *Irish*, *Portuguese*, and a few *French* and *Danes* in India; *Dutch* in Ceylon, Java, and the Moluccas; and *Spaniards* in the Philippines.

CIVIL GOVERNMENT is traceable, generally, in these nations, to patriarchal and paternal authority. There was a sort of Republicanism at first, in most of them. But the great monarchies were formed by conquest. The conquerors ruled over the subjected nations. There is readily observable, in respect to all the nations of Asia, he fact that religion greatly affected their whole polity. The farther back we trace the history of any nation the greater appears to be the influence of religion upon the civil government. In the smallest republics even, the sentiment of a common religion was necessary as a bond of union among the citizens. The bitterest political opponents acknowledged that they were the children of one mother, when they assisted at the customary rites of their gods, and worshipped in the temples erected by their ancestors. Religion was, especially, the principle of unity in all the confederations of antiquity, and infused into them a spirit of nationality. Thus the temple of the Tyrian Hercules became the centre of the Phœnician league; that of Jupiter Latialis of the Latin confederacy; and the Greeks, notwithstanding their perpetual contests, felt that they were one people, when they were assembled to celebrate the festival of the Olympian Jupiter. In the great monarchies, which were composed of a mixed multitude of nations of different religions, religion could not be a bond of union; still it was of the greatest importance, inasmuch as it interposed the only description of legislation which could moderate the despotism of the rulers. It frequently happened that, among the sovereign people, before they issued as conquerors from their own abodes, peculiar veneration had been paid to some sacerdotal caste; and, though the inevitable effect of foreign conquest was to elevate the military order and its chiefs above the priestly order, the priests yet retained sufficient influence to act as a wholesome check upon the monarch, and their power might thus be beneficial not only to their own people, but indirectly to the most remote subjects of the empire.

The COMMERCE of the ancient nations is an important point in judging of their civilisation. Modern commerce is chiefly carried on by sea; but the ancient commerce was generally by land. The continents of the Old World were contiguous. They made, in fact, but one great continent; and communication between the most distant parts of them was possible by land. If an inland sea separated some of them, the separation was but a narrow space, and might easily be crossed. The traffic of the Mediterranean was, in general, only an appendage to the land traffic, which brought to its shores the produce of remote regions. The land traffic of Asia, and such countries, must be regarded in its peculiarities. The merchant must prepare himself to encounter the desert, and the dwellers in the desert. He cannot travel alone. The caravan must be mustered at a fixed place, on a stated occasion. The route must have its springs, its palm-trees, and its islands of verdure, however far these may change or lengthen the course of the journey. Naturally, if any of the resting-places can support a fixed population a town is built, and it grows into a depository of wealth from distant nations, and is one of the centres of their exchange. It may come to be a mighty city, and, when the stream of commerce changes into another channel, the modern traveller marvels at the splendour and the desolation of Palmyra or Baalbec. We have abundant kindred illustrations in the development in England of the railway traffic, as compared with that of the ancient and neglected roadways. In these Asian commercial journeys the camel was the unwearied servant of the merchant.

As to Central Asia, of which we would more especially speak, having referred to its topographical outline and physical characteristics, let us look at the habits of the people of its different regions. The great empires of Asia all seem to have been formed or founded by mountaineers or nomade tribes, who issued from their barren fastnesses, and overran the more wealthy and less warlike countries around them. Such was the origin of the Chaldean Empire, the Persian, the Parthian, and the Saracen. It was also so with the conquests of the Mongol Khans, and such was the origin of the dominion of their descendants in India and China.

In all these instances the nomade conquerors have become settled peoples, and, in large measure, have adopted the manners and customs and habits of the conquered nations. But conquest is not the best of means for the origination of a new community or nation. The essentially military character of the great empires which have succeeded one another in Asia, is a principal reason why despotism has so long reigned in that part of the world. The spirit of political liberty seems everywhere to be crushed; the people are held in awe and ruled by fear. Yet it must be owned that the temper of self-indulgence, so prevalent everywhere and standing aloof from any recognition of the claims of the community, must have largely contributed to the continuance of such despotism.

In regard to the commerce of Asia, the inland traffic is carried on by the same routes which have been used in all ages, and the advantages of position which made certain localities the scenes of a busy commerce and the common marts of nations are still the same. Bactria was the point to which the routes converged from the banks of the Indus, from Thibet, and through the great desert of Cobi from the extreme regions of the east, and of Northern China. Babylon was the great centre at which all three united streams met the commerce of the Indian Ocean and the Persian Gulf, and from which the wealth which they brought was dispersed in different directions to the countries of the west. Some portion of it was diverted to Asia Minor and the shores of the Euxine; but the main stream flowed across the desert to the cities of Phœnicia. It was augmented there by all the commerce of Arabia, by the productions of the peninsula itself, and by the still more precious fruit of its maritime intercourse with India and Southern Africa. From Phœnicia the wealth of the eastern world was spread over all the countries which bordered on the Mediterranean, and distributed to Egypt, to Carthage, and to Greece. Among the articles of this commerce were the cotton fabrics of Southern India, and the woollens of its northern regions of Cashmere and Belur. Silk was imported from Serica; furs were also drawn from the central and northern parts of Asia; spices and aromatic resins, for use in sacrifice chiefly, formed part of the merchandise; frankincense from Africa; cassia and cinnamon from remote regions of India, or from Ceylon and the Indian islands—these all had their place in the caravan; precious stones from the northern parts of India; pearls from the Persian Gulf, then as now; gold, procured from the African continent, it being used in Asia with magnificent profusion; all of them were the material of trade at the stations and cities of the great roadways in Asia.

There is no such interference on the part of the civil rulers in Asia with the personal liberties, the domestic life, and the commerce of the people, as some have supposed. If we understand by a despot an absolute monarch, who disposes of the property, the honour, and the lives of his subjects, employing them with indefinite and uncontrolled authority, we do not find any such governments in Eastern Asia, although many have believed that they existed there. Manners, ancient customs, prevailing opinions, and even popular errors, form everywhere a more embarrassing restraint on rulers than could possibly be imposed by any limitations of the statute-book. It is only in some Moslem tribes, and particularly in Persia, that we meet with the despotism and the servility which some have attributed to the whole of Asia. The kings of Asia have been accounted despots because they are approached on the bended knee, and their modes of speech, and the style of their courts, seem clearly to indicate the possession by the sovereign of a power which is unrestrained; but, with exceptions such as those which have been named, it is not so. The sovereigns do, indeed, assume to themselves the titles of gods; they are the vicegerents of Allah, brothers of the sun and moon, and asylums of the universe; and they have been treated as if all this were true, their pride being flattered, and no opposition being offered to their will; and yet the most despotic sovereign in Asia understands well that there are means by which the people may relieve themselves of him, if he should go too far in opposing the cherished customs and sentiments of the community. The Governments of Ottoman Asia, Persia, Russia, Bukharia, and others in Turkestan, India, Chin-India, China, Japan, and some of the islands, are despotisms, differing in degree.

Besides the ancient republics, established in the Greek cities of Asia, and in Syria and Palestine, we find, in the centre of the continent, tribes whose political institutions are pre-eminently republican. The principal of these are the Affghans, between India and Persia.

In Asia there are also many nations whose governments may be compared to those of the European kingdoms of the Middle Ages. Such were the Mahrattas before the downfall of the Peishwa, and the Affghans before the subversion of the Kingdom of Cabul; and such are still the Belootshees, the Mongols, the Kalmucks, the Mantchoos, several mountain tribes of the Caucasus, particularly the Circassians and Abassians, as well as some Turkee communities. The empire of Japan is, properly speaking, a feudal monarchy, ruled by a prince. Some nations are entirely free,—for example, the Bedouin Arabs, the Kurds, and several sections of the inhabitants of the Caucasus and of Syria. The small nomadic nations of Syria, and many of the Arab tribes have a pastoral and patriarchal form of government, which is generally hereditary in certain families. Others are ruled by the elders, and, in reality, are republics. Thibet, Boutan, and parts of Arabia, have a kind of theocratic government. The Imaums of Sanaa and Muscat are a sort of political high priests, invested with the temporal power. The rulers of Thibet and Boutan are absolute pontiffs, bearing the titles of Dalai-lama, Bogdo-lama, and Dharma-lama, and are held to be emanations of the Deity himself. We may affirm, in general, that Asia affords examples of every possible kind of government, from the freest republicanism to the most absolute despotism.

Of MINERALS there is considerable variety,—Rock-crystal and amethysts in the Altaï, Himalaya and Ural mountains; cornelians and agates in India; onyxes in Mongolia; jasper in the Altaï; pearl on the shores of the Gulf of Okhotsk; beryl near the lake of Baikal; lapis lazuli in the same mountains, and on the banks of the Oxus; topazes in the Ural mountains; sapphires in Ceylon; turquoises in Khorasan; and diamonds in Deccan, Borneo, and the Ural mountains. There are *volcanic products* in the Sunda Islands. Various *metals* are met with in different parts:—Gold in Japan, Thibet, Yun-nan, Cochin-China, Tonkin, Siam, Malacca, Borneo, Assam, Ava, and in the Ural mountains. Many rivers bring down gold in their sands. Silver is found in China, Da-uria, Japan, Armenia, Anatolia, and the Ural mountains; tin in Malacca, Anam, the Sundas, and in the empire of Burmah; mercury in China, Japan, and Thibet; copper in the Ural and Altaï mountains, Japan, China, Nepaul, Azerbijan, Armenia, and Mount Taurus; malachite in China and Siberia; iron in the Ural mountains and through Central Asia as far as the peninsula beyond the Ganges, as well as in Japan and Persia; lead in Da-uria, China, Siam, Japan, Georgia, and Armenia.

There are extensive layers of *fossil shell-fish* found on

the highest table-lands of Thibet, from 16,000 to 18,000 feet above the sea, and the strata of the tertiary formation of Siberia are full of the animal remains of the old world,—as the elephant, mammoth, rhinoceros, and others.

Of the BOTANY of Asia we must treat sparingly. There is an irregular line from west to east, beginning at Mogadore, and reaching to the Hydraotes of Alexander, and which, in this vast extent, passes along the crests of the Atlas near Cairo, by the summit of Mount Tabor, Bagdad, Shiraz, Kelat, and Moultan. This represents the southern or inferior limit of the zone in which it lies. The olive is here at the northern limit of its healthy and productive growth. Northwards it languishes, and at last ceases to grow. It is said to grow on the coasts of Macedonia, but it is not seen anywhere about the Sea of Marmora. It appears again at Sinope, and along the shores of the Black Sea as far as Gourich. In lat. 45°, in the southern part of the Crimea, and a degree further down on the western border of the Caspian, it is also to be found. The river Terek marks the limits of its progress. The mean annual temperature of the plains in this zone, from the lower boundary, is 22° to 23° of Reaumur. For the higher boundary it is 14°. In the Mediterranean portions of this district there are at least six herbaceous plants for one of the woody species. The greater number of the trees, shrubs, and under-growths of the equatorial zone are not divested of their foliage at any season of the year. The temperate zone has only about forty species with continuous leaves, the arctic zone about twenty-four, and the southern limit not more than ten.

In the Mediterranean, the temperate transition zone, the Compositæ and the Leguminosæ are most numerous; they constitute about a fourth of the entire vegetation. Among the vegetable products are the Cruciferæ, Gramineæ, Labiatæ, Caryophyllaceæ, and Umbelliferæ; after them the Scrophularieæ, Rosaceæ, Boragineæ, Ranunculaceæ, and Cyperaceæ, and, finally, the Liliaceæ. The plants which hold the highest rank among the productions of the temperate transition zone are the Amentaceæ and the Coniferæ; and, after them, the Rosaceæ, Leguminosæ, Terebinthaceæ, Rhamnaceæ, Jasminaceæ, Coprifoliaceæ, Cistaceæ, Ericaceæ, and Labiatæ. But the peculiarity which gives the transition zone its distinguishing characters is the combination of the productions of different other parts of the world. From the lowly vegetation which composes the Arctic flora, to the gigantic and generally luxuriant vegetation of the Indian regions, we find in Asia every intermediate kind. The extremes sometimes seem to exist in the same country. For example, the Himalayas present an Arctic vegetation in their higher regions, and not far below is the vegetation of warmer climates in full luxuriance. Still, most of the countries of Asia have a homogeneous and characteristic vegetation of their own.

Of all the productions of the vegetable kingdom none has been a greater favourite than the vine. But it is not a wide-spread plant. The cultivation of it is restricted to narrow limits. Excess of heat is unfavourable to its growth, as well as too much cold. Its southern limit is where the mean temperature is between 69° 8′ and 70° 6′ Fahrenheit; and its northern boundary is 47½° or 48°, and where the lowest temperature at any season of the year is not below 34°. It is only within the middle regions of the temperate zone that the vine comes to perfection, but within those limits it is found throughout Western Asia. The finest grapes are produced in Asia Minor, Syria, and Palestine; but the vine is still found in its wild and native state in the forests of the ancient Colchis (at the eastern end of the Black Sea), climbing to the tops of the loftiest trees. Farther east, the grapes and the wines of Shiraz and Mazanderan have the highest repute in Persia. Native vines are also found along the upper banks of the Oxus, in Kashgar, to the east of the Belur; in Kunawar, in the British portion of Little Thibet; and also in Malwah, or Central India. They are also cultivated in the gardens of H'Lassa, in Great Thibet; and in China, on the shores of the Eastern Ocean, the vine is plentiful.

Next to the vine in repute is the olive, which is also confined to temperate climates, and is indigenous to Syria, along the eastern shores of the Black Sea, and at Tukh-ti-Suleiman, near the Indus. The cultivated olive is easily produced in all parts along the shores of the Levant which are free from frosty winds.

Tea is produced abundantly in the southern provinces of China. The best is grown upon the hills of Foki-en. It is also indigenous in Assam, within the limits of the British territories.

Rice is the staff of life to the Hindoos, Indo-Chinese, and Chinese, who value it so highly that they pity the Europeans, who grow no rice at home, and wonder how they can do without it. It is produced abundantly in all the well-watered plains of those countries, and requires great heat as well as much moisture to bring it to perfection.

We shall have occasion to take notice of the vegetable products of the separate countries as those countries are brought under review.

In respect to the ANIMALS of Asia, it is to be observed that, in the continent there are three zones, and this fact, of course, affects the character and habitat of every description of animal to be found within its bounds. In the central zone we find the Bactrian, or double-humped camel, the tarpan, or wild horse, the jaghatai, another species of horse, very fleet of foot; several kinds of horse-tailed oxen, antelopes, and other species of the deer family. Panthers are found in the western division—also a singular species of cat, the manal, the original of the Angora cat. The Indian tiger has been seen in Siberia. Tigers abound in China. Troops of dogs of different kinds, jackals, and wolves prey upon the antelopes, asses, and wild horses. The musk animal is to be found in all the mountains. The Altai are inhabited by the argali, or rock-sheep; the southern mountains by the egagre, or wild goat; and Caucasus by the egagre and the chamois. The western prolongation of this zone, which extends through Persia and Arabia, is overrun by antelopes and gazelles. There are also lions, panthers, caracals, and other sorts of cats, jackals, and monkeys. The mountains and tablelands are also inhabited by the onager, or wild ass, beautiful and fleet, and much esteemed in the East. The single-humped camel is native to Arabia only, but is also found wherever the Arabs have settled.

In the northern zone, on the river banks, and in the vast forests of Siberia, there are innumerable troops of reindeer, elks, brown, blue, and black foxes, bears, gluttons, and several kinds of martins and squirrels. Along the shores of the Arctic Ocean, the great Polar bear preys on every living creature. In the waters of the ocean are found seals and various kinds of Cetacea. Notwithstanding the fact that its water is fresh, and that it is distant from the sea, the Lake Baikal, like the Caspian, abounds in a particular species of seals.

In the southern zone every region teems with life. In India are several species of antelopes and deer, which, till a few years ago, were unknown in Europe. In Thibet are swarms of blue antelopes, whose horns, which fall annually, have more than once reminded English authors of the fabulous unicorn. There are also found the chitkaru with four horns. In Bengal is the white-spotted axis; in the forests of Orissa is found the jungle-cow, the wild original of the domestic beeves of India. There are few lions in India; but there are numerous tigers, which are very fierce. Over the same regions is spread the black-skinned, half-naked buffalo, with horns turned back, both wild and tame, delighting in the muddy banks of the seas, lakes, and rivers. Between the Ganges and the Indus the forests abound with squirrels, peacocks, pheasants, and jungle-cocks. Several species of bears inhabit the forests among the Ghauts. The elephant and the one-horned rhinoceros live in the forests, but it is in the south-east of India that these animals attain their largest size. There is also found the two-coloured tapir, which ranges from Malacca to the southern provinces of China; ourangs, gibbons, and various kinds of monkeys are also to be found in these parts. In the Ganges there are 250 kinds of fish described by Buchanan, and these furnish food for the alligators with which its waters abound.

In every zone the birds are very various. They are generally adorned with rich plumage. Great vultures tyrannise over all other birds on the banks of the Indus. There are also found large numbers of eagles, falcons, buzzards, and screech owls. Swarms of paroquets, of every variety of colour, inhabit the continent and the neighbouring islands. Among the domesticated animals the elephant claims the pre-eminence, and is to be found chiefly in the lowlands of India, in Birmah, and in Siam, being seldom seen in the mountainous region to the north. The camel is to be met with everywhere over a large extent of country. There are two varieties, as we have already had occasion to mention, one with two humps, and the other with only one. The former is usually called the Bactrian camel. It is more rare than the other, and seems to belong to the great deserts of North-Eastern Asia and the table-land of Pamer. It is sometimes called the dromedary, but is a true camel, and is spread over Arabia, Persia, Western India, and Northern Africa. The dromedary, or racing camel, is only a variety of the species. It is generally of lighter form, and is better adapted for travelling or flight. The other domestic animals of southern and western Asia are horses, mules, asses, buffaloes, beeves, sheep, and goats. Of the central and eastern parts, the domestic animals are chiefly horses, cattle, goats, and sheep; there are also the yak of Thibet and Pamer, and the bushy-tailed bull of Thibet. In the severer climates farther north the cattle are stunted in size, and can scarcely subsist. Their place is supplied by the reindeer, which furnishes the people with food and with the means of transport. During part of the year they live upon its flesh and milk. Its skin supplies them with the principal part of their dress, and its horns with various utensils. In Kamschatka, and the other north-eastern regions, dogs are trained to draw sledges in winter over the frozen snow.

In the southern countries of Asia there are many REPTILES, some of which are armed with the most deadly poisons. They are all hideous in their appearance, and some are of great size and strength; but they are seldom found beyond the Altaï. Mosquitoes, gnats, ants, and flies swarm in the southern regions. Even in the short summer of Siberia, mosquitoes and other troublesome insects abound. But the locust is the most destructive of all these winged creatures. It appears occasionally in the sandy regions of the north-west of India, and is found in countless swarms in Arabia and Syria. It also abounds to the north of the Altaï, at the sources of the Irtish, whence it extends its destructive flight as far as the Crimea and the southern provinces of Russia in Europe.

CHAPTER II.

TURKEY IN ASIA.

TURKEY in Asia lies between 30° and 42° latitude, and 26° and 49° longitude. It is bounded on the north by the Black Sea and the Russian province of Imeritia; on the south by Arabia and the Mediterranean; on the east by Persia and Russian Armenia; and on the west by the Archipelago, the Dardanelles, the Sea of Marmora, and the Channel of Constantinople. There are at least three portions into which this extensive region may be divided, and which are distinct the one from the other—Asia Minor and Armenia; Mesopotamia, and the countries watered by the Euphrates and the Tigris; and Syria, including Palestine, or the Holy Land. The greatest extent of the Turkish territory in Asia is, from north to south, about 850 miles, and from east to west, about 1,200; but measured from Constantinople, diagonally to the mouth of the Euphrates, it is 1,400 miles; and from the southern border of Palestine to the north-eastern extremity of

Turkish Armenia, it is about 1,100. But the area does not correspond with a square of these dimensions, the outline being so much indented by seas on the one side, and by the sandy deserts of Arabia on the other, that the superficial extent hardly exceeds the half of that square, or about 500,000 English square miles.

Armenia consists of a series of plains and valleys, some of which rise to 5,500 feet above the level of the sea. Overlooking these there are ranges of mountains, several thousand feet higher. But elevated as it is, it is a fertile corn country, and abounds in pastures, though the climate is cold, and in winter is covered with deep snow. It is separated from the low country on the Black Sea, in the eyalet of Trebisond, by a triple range of mountains, which attain their extreme elevation of 6,000 or 7,000 feet, at the distance of twenty-four miles from the sea, and which are covered with forests to the height of about 4,500 feet; but in higher elevations the country is generally bare of trees, except in some recesses of the mountains, in which forests exist even in the more elevated central parts. There are many passes from the coast, but, with the exception of such as follow the courses of the larger rivers, most of them are difficult, and some are open only in the summer. There are two ranges of mountains, which proceed from Armenia westward into the peninsula of Asia Minor; the one the ancient *Taurus*, which lies parallel with the shore of the Mediterranean Sea, and is then divided into a number of branches, which intersect the western part of the peninsula, and form as many fertile valleys, watered by fine rivers terminating on the shore, or in the islands of the Archipelago. The other mountain chain, the *Anti-Taurus*, extends into the interior of the peninsula in a south-westerly direction, and is probably connected with Taurus, in the neighbourhood of Kaisariyah, and also with the lofty mountains which, under various names, occupy the country between the Kizil-Irmak and the Sea of Marmora. The central part, supported on all sides by these mountains, forms a series of table-lands, nearly destitute of trees, but abounding with pasturage, which affords a plentiful subsistence to the flocks of the wandering Turcomans. The plain of Kutahya is 6,000 feet above the level of the sea, and that of Sivas, 350 miles farther east, about 3,900. Some of the valleys are so completely surrounded by mountains that they have no outlet for their waters, which, in consequence, not only overflow large tracts of country in the rainy season, but also form permanent lakes. The south coast presents an irregular outline, with a bold front towards the sea. An almost continuous mass of lofty mountains presses close upon the shore, and at some points forms the coast, terminating in bold promontories. But near the eastern end the mountains are distant from the sea, and leave room for the wide plains of the ancient Cilicia. The outline of the west coast is very irregular, and consists of deep bays, with long peninsulas, promontories, and islands. Along the Black Sea the northern coast is also lofty and rocky, with deep water close to the shore. It is lined with mountains no great distance inland, these being covered with trees—the forests at one place being so extensive that the Turks have given them the designation of *Agatch-dengis*, the sea of trees. These mountains seem to be based on granite and other primary rocks; but in various places these are associated with beds of marble and quartz, hippurite, limestone, and schists, tertiary and lacustrine marine deposits, ancient and modern igneous rocks, and recent aqueous accumulations. The micaceous schist and associated rocks occupy, however, a very important place in the geology of Asia Minor, and form nearly all the mountain chains which intersect the western portion of the peninsula. The hippurite limestone, the only representative of that vast system of rocks which occupies a large portion of Europe, and is usually termed secondary, is not found in any abundance in the north-western part of Asia Minor. Tertiary lacustrine formations occur in almost every valley, and marine deposits are found in several places. Volcanic rocks occur frequently; trachyte is abundantly scattered over the western part of Asia Minor. The whole country between Is Nik and Katahya appears to consist of agate or chalcedony, the strata being beautifully varied; and, in the centre of the peninsula, the lofty peak of *Arjish dagh* (anc. *Argaeus*), which rises to the height of 13,000 feet, consists entirely of volcanic rocks and scoriaceous cinders, having its sloping sides studded all round with numerous cones and craters. *Hassan dagh,* to the south-west of Arjish, is also volcanic, and attains an elevation of 8,000 feet; and 90 miles east of Smyrna, *Kulah,* a volcanic peak, rises to 2,780. But the most singular portion of Asia Minor is the volcanic district of *Katakecaumené,* or the burned-up region, about 90 miles eastward of Smyrna. This region bears a striking resemblance to the volcanic district of Auvergne. It extends about 90 miles east and west, and about eight from north to south, and consists of volcanic mounds, which rise partly amidst the lacustrine limestone of the valley of the Hermus, and partly on the slope of the schistose hills, which bound it on the south. The mounds consist of scoriæ and lava, and are referable to two epochs, indicated by the difference in their state of preservation, and the appearance of the lava-streams. The older cones are low and flat; their craters have disappeared, or are marked by a slight depression, and all their prominences seem to have been smoothed by time. They are also covered with vineyards, which produce the Katakecaumené wine, celebrated from the time of Strabo to the present day; and the streams of basalt, or lava, which have flowed from them are level on the surface, and covered with turf. The newer volcanoes are only three in number. They have been extinct for many years—for more than 3,000—and yet they preserve all their characteristics unaltered; the craters are perfectly defined, and their lava streams are black, rugged, and barren.

If a line were drawn which would include the elevated table-land of the interior, and the field of burnt or volcanic matter, it would precisely trace the boundaries of the ancient Phrygia on the north, west, and south; following even the singular forms which it projects into Caria, Lycia, and Pamphylia. From the great elevation of the country, the cold is so severe that no plants are to be seen but such as are found in the highlands of Scotland, where they suffer less from severity of climate than here. The summer is of very short duration. Descending from this elevated country, every diversity of climate is met with till one reaches the productive valleys of the rivers and the warmer lands on the coast. In summer the heat becomes so intense as the day advances that it could not be endured if it were not for a cool breeze which sets in before noon, accompanied by a shade of clouds, and sometimes by flying showers. The heat again becomes oppressive in the early part of the evening, and the dews are very heavy. The cold of the winter is intense, so that neither the aloe, nor the cactus, nor any other succulent plant is to be seen in the country. It is with difficulty that orange and lemon trees are preserved in the sheltered valleys. The olive seldom flourishes even in such a situation, and any that live are inferior. The extremes of the seasons are shown by the migrations of animals, which are very extensive. In Lydia and Mysia the scenery is varied and beautiful, the hills being covered with splendid forest trees. The mountains are not so grand in their forms as they are beautiful. The valleys are so flat that they look as if they had been formed by lakes. The scenery is bolder in Bithynia. Its fine mountain of Olympus gives it a resemblance to Switzerland; its valleys are covered with luxuriant woods. The flat-topped hills and immense table-lands of Phrygia, which are often swampy, and which seldom produce a tree, present more of the wild and the dreary than of the picturesque. Pisidia, including the Taurus, partakes of the Alpine character; the woods, however, not being so fine as those of Bithynia. The extreme beauty of Pamphylia is derived more from distant views than from nearer objects. The marble mountains, which form the distant horizon, shoot their jagged peaks of silvery rock, sometimes capped with snow, against the clear sky, while their bases are washed by the blue sea, which they enclose in their wide-stretched arms. Lydia is more mountainous, and resembles, in the boldness of its cliffs, and the richness of its vegetation, the scenery of Parnassus. Its valleys, and particularly that of the Xanthus, are of peculiar beauty. Caria abounds in scenery of the most picturesque description; its coasts being broken into bold headlands, whose ranges, continued into the sea, rise into rocky islands. The south-east of Lydia is less beautiful, and much resembles Sicily or Calabria; but, on approaching Smyrna, this district contains valleys equal to those near Salerno or Naples. See Fellows's "Excursion in Asia Minor," pp. 300-303.

The country watered by the Euphrates and the Tigris is bounded on the north by the table-land of Armenia and by the Taurus; on the east by the long line of mountains (anc. *Zagros*), which, under the names of the mountains of Kurdistan, Louristan, Buklitiari, &c., divide it from the table-land of Iran ; on the west and south-west by Syria and the deserts of Arabia; and on the south-east it barely touches the Persian Gulf. Assyria, including Taurus, is distinguished by its structure, its configuration, and its natural productions into three zones, or districts : by structure into a district of metamorphic and plutonic rocks, a district of sedimentary formations, and a district of alluvial deposits ; by configuration, into a district of mountains, of stony or sandy plains, and of low, watery plains ; by natural productions, into a country of forest and fruit trees, of olives, wine, corn, and pasturage, or of barren rocks ; a country of mulberry trees, cotton, maize, sesame, tobacco, or of hardy labiate and composite plants, or barren clay, sand, pebbly or rocky plains ; and a country of date trees, rice, and pasturage, or a land of saline plants, liquorice, reeds, sedges, and rushes. The first of these districts comprises the hilly and mountainous country of Taurus, there being many different chains. The Taurus consists of a nucleus of granite, gneiss, and mica schist, with limestone, diorites, and diallage rocks; also of lateral formations of diallage rocks, serpentines, actquolite rocks, steaschists, slate-clays, and outlying sandstones and limestones. The Taurus varies in different places from 2,900 feet to 5,650. To the south of the main chain lies the plain of Diarbekr, 2,500 feet above the level of the sea, and separated from the mountainous district of Arghana by ranges of indurated chalk. The climate of Taurus has cold winters and much snow. In March, the almond-tree, the pear, the medlar, and the laburnum are in blossom in the valleys. The most remarkable feature is the abundance of trees, shrubs, and plants in the northern district, while they are comparatively scanty in the south. Among the more useful and cultivated plants may be named the vine, fig-tree, almond, olive, wheat, tricicum spelta, hordeum hexastichon, and hexastichon distichon. Gall-nuts, pears, apples, and apricots, are abundant. The second district, comprising the plains of *Syria*, *Mesopotamia*, and *the country to the east of the Tigris*, to the mountains of Kurdistan, consists of cretaceous and supracretaceous deposits, interrupted here and there by plutonic rocks. These plains vary in their character by means of the presence or absence of moisture. The upland field of rocks, which extends from Jezirah to Tel Sakhan, near Nisibin, and which has a mean elevation of 1,500 feet, is a stony wilderness, in which there is little or no cultivation; but where numerous flocks of sheep and herds of cattle obtain a scanty subsistence during a great part of the year. The great plains of Northern Syria, with a mean elevation of 1,300 feet, of Northern Mesopotamia, from Urfa to Rakkah, and from Nisibin to El Hathar, and the Chaldæan plain east of Nineveh, that of Arbil and of Altun-Kupri, are all very like each other—a level, almost uniform, with a soil possessing good agricultural qualities, but destitute of irrigation. There are exceptions to this where the plains are intersected by hills, or in spots at the head and on the banks of rivers or rivulets, which, in consequence, become the homes of agricultural tribes, the seats of cultivation and prosperity, or the temporary resort of wandering Arabs and Turcomans. There are many fertile districts. The plains of Urfa and Harran are watered by numerous streams. The climate is dry, and there are very great variations of temperature. Fahrenheit's thermometer has been seen at 115° in the shade in the month of August, while, in winter, it has fallen as low as 12°. From the Mediterranean to the Tigris, there is an increase of cold in the same parallels from east to west; but this is not the case in the plains of the Tigris, which, being sheltered by the mountains of Kurdistan, have a more temperate winter. Taurus being clothed with snow for many months in the year, has much influence in reducing the winter temperature, and from the absence of sheltering hills, the plains of Northern Syria and Mesopotamia have a vegetation really less southern than that of Sicily and Andalusia. The long extent of littoral mountains—Amanus, Cassius, and Lebanon—adds to these unfavourable circumstances by impeding the mild breezes from the Mediterranean Sea. The direct heat of the sun, increased by radiation and the equality of level, is almost without a moderating influence. There is scarcely any evaporation, and, therefore, where the winter temperature is low, the summer heat is intense. On this account there are few annual and tender plants; woody and tough stems resist better such opposite influences. For two months in the year, October and November, vegetation is dormant—everything is burnt up, and no new forms present themselves. But, after this period, clouds from Lebanon, and changes of temperature from the north and the east, bring down over Mesopotamia and Adiabne moderate and refreshing rains. The brown colour of the ground changes, grasses begin to increase and spread, and the succession of vegetation is maintained by those families of plants which have succulent roots, nodes, or bulbs, which preserve moisture, so as to maintain life even in the driest soil. Dormant during the summer heats, they are quickened into activity by the first rains. But they are soon covered with snow, and blasted by the wintry winds, till early in spring, when the same precocious plants again present themselves, with all that vivid beauty of colour and variety of form which have lent to the poet and the painter their not always fabulous pictures of the glory of the east. The absence of trees on these great plains is a phenomenon not easily accounted for. The vegetation is ephemeral, or it consists of succulent and herbaceous biennials. Willows grow on the banks of the Euphrates, and the Oriental plane, near springs and tombs, rises to an enormous size. The desert described by Xenophon, extending from Kabour to Rehoboth, has still the same characteristics:—" It is full of wormwood, and if any other kinds of plants grow there, they have, for the most part, an aromatic smell."

The alluvial plains of Babylonia, Chaldæa, and Susiana, form the third district, and have their northern limit a few miles above Felujah. On the west they are bounded by a line of rock and sand not far from the Euphrates; and on the east by the Hamrun Hills, a long range composed of tertiary sandstone, with salt, gypsum, and limestone, which crosses the Tigris above the 35° N. lat. In the upper, or north-western portion, the plain has a slight but well-defined southerly inclination, with local depressions above Felujah, undulating in the central part, and then subsiding into marshes and lakes. In the northern part the soil is pebbly, and lower down there are deposits of clay covered with mould, dust, or sand, or the more tenacious clay of recent and frequent inundations. The modern accumulations continue to be very great. There are many canals, extending from the one river to the other, which at certain seasons inundate the country, and in some places leave permanent marshes. But the natural level is everywhere altered by artificial works, such as mounds, walls, mud ramparts, and dykes. Elevated masses of friable pottery are succeeded by low plains inundated during the greater part of the year, and the old beds of canals are visible in every direction. There is still some amount of cultivation and irrigation; flocks pasture in meadows of coarse grass, and the dusky encampments of the Arabs are occasionally met with; but, except on the banks of the Euphrates, there are few remains of the date-groves, vineyards, and gardens which once adorned the country; and still less are to be seen the other results of the labour and skill of the population which must have made a garden of such a soil in ancient times. The greater part of the basin, which stretches forty miles along the Euphrates, and extends many miles on each side, is occupied by water or vegetation, with large herds of buffaloes. In some places, during the summer, the mud is covered with luxuriant crops of rice. The vegetation is characterised by saline plants, the river banks being fringed with shrubberies of tamarisk and acacia, and occasionally with groves of poplar. Below Lemlun there is little indication of change from any previous condition within the compass of ordinary history. Below Suk-el-Sheikh the country is occupied by an almost perpetual inundation, and at Omu-el-bak the waters spread out like a great lake, extending to the verge of the horizon, and only here and there interrupted with groves of date-trees and huts. There is a gradual and almost imperceptible elevation of the soil beginning near Lemlun, and leading on to plains of vast extent, only a few feet higher than the marshes and lakes, and which formed the ancient territory of Chaldæa. To the south of these great inundations of which we have spoken, as far as the confluence of the Euphrates and the Tigris, the land is covered by an aquatic vegetation, chiefly by a kind of agrostis which, like the cane-brake of North America, has the appearance of the true reed of Northern Europe. These tracts present everywhere great uniformity of feature—a boundless growth of plants, of the same kind, interrupted by lakes and ponds, or intersected by artificial canals. The character of the country below Korneh is very similar; the banks, however, are lined with date-trees, and at times afford a rich pasturage for buffaloes. Villages are numerous, but the population is scanty.

BABYLONIA, as distinct from the monarchy, comprised a narrow tract of country between the Lower Euphrates and the Tigris. It also included tracts, more or less extensive, to the east and west of those rivers, and on both sides of their united waters, corresponding to the present Irak Arabi, embraced in the pashalic of Bagdad. This district was the seat of the first independent kingdom of the earth, and within its bounds lie "the land of Shinar," or the country around Babylon, and "the land of the Chaldæans,"—a portion of it which extends towards Arabia. Upper Mesopotamia was the original country of the Chaldæans, and it was from it that Abraham came when he was divinely commanded to go to a land that he "would be told of."

The site on which the great city of BABYLON, the queen of nations, once stood, is now occupied, in part by the modern town of *Hillah*, and by enormous mounds of ruins, with low-lying tracts of desert or hollows intervening—the Euphrates spreading its inundations over them. Hillah is built chiefly of materials obtained from the ruins of the ancient capital, and is situated in latitude 32° 31′ north, longitude 44° 20′ east, about forty miles from Bagdad, to the south, and nearly three hundred miles up the river, following its windings. It lies on both banks, which are connected by a bridge of thirty-four boats, constructed of pontoons—the width at this point being about four hundred and fifty feet. The bed of the stream is here considerably contracted, and the current flows rapidly. Hillah was founded in the year A.D. 1117, and has an Arab population, with some Jews and a few Turkish officials, the total number of the inhabitants being about ten thousand. The place looks attractive as seen from a distance, surrounded as it is by date-groves and gardens. Near one of the gates is the Mesjid-el-Shems, or Mosque of the Sun, which is much reverenced by the Mohammedan population. The town has little about it to excite interest, except its site, which is within the bounds of ancient Babylon, and about mid-way between two of the most remarkable masses of ruins,—the Mujellibe on the north, and the more celebrated Birs Nimroud on the south.

Strabo, who died about A.D. 25, writing in the Augustine age, says that time and neglect had nearly completed the destruction of Babylon. Pliny, who died A.D. 116, who wrote in the time of the Flavian emperors, describes it as unpeopled and lying waste. And, not long afterwards, Pausanias says, "Of Babylon, a greater city than which the sun did not formerly behold, all that now remains is the temple of Belus, and the walls of the city." In the twelfth century, Benjamin of Tudela, a traveller in the east, tells us: "The ruins of the palace of Nebuchadnezzar are still to be seen, but people are afraid to venture among them, on account of the serpents and scorpions with which they are infested. Twenty thousand Jews live within about twenty miles of this place, and perform their worship in the synagogue of Daniel, who rests in peace. Four miles from hence (Hillah) is the tower built by the dispersed generation. It is constructed of bricks, called *al-ajurr;* the base measures two miles, the breadth two hundred and forty yards, and the height about one hundred *canna.* A spiral passage, built into the tower (in stages of ten yards each), leads up to the summit, from which we have a prospect of twenty miles, the country being one wide plain, and quite level. The heavenly fire which struck the tower split it to its very foundation." Abulfeda, the Arabian geographer, at the beginning of the fourteenth century, after giving the latitude and longitude, refers thus to the site: "Here Abraham, the friend of God, upon whom be peace, was thrown into the fire. At the present day, the city lies waste, and on its site there is a small village. Ibn-Haukal says, Babel is a small village, yet it is the oldest place of Irak; and after it, in ancient times, the whole province was named. Here the Canaanitish and other kings used to dwell. There are here the remains of buildings, which, as I conjecture, formed at a remote period a great metropolis." The tradition is commonly held by the Orientals, that the patriarch, refusing to worship idols, was cast into the fire by order of Nimrod, but came out uninjured. The probability is that this is a confused account of the real event recorded of the three Hebrew captives by the prophet Daniel. Sir John Maundeville gives similar testimony. Eldred, an English merchant on a journey to Bagdad, at the close of the sixteenth century, speaks of passing the "mighty old city of Babylon, many ruins of which are easily to be seen by daylight, which I, John Eldred, have often beheld." In the following century several Europeans visited the locality. Niebuhr, at a less remote period, surveyed these ruins.

But Mr. Rich, for many years the English resident at Bagdad, was the first to draw up a memoir upon the remains of the city. Mr. Rich says: "I had expected to have found on the site of Babylon more or less than I actually did. Less, because I could have formed no conception of the prodigious extent of the whole ruins, or of the size, solidity, and perfect state of some parts of them; and more, because I thought that I should have distinguished some traces, however imperfect, of many of the principal structures of Babylon. I imagined I should have said, 'Here were the walls, and such must have been the extent of the area; there stood the palace, and this most assuredly was the tower of Belus.' I was completely deceived; instead of a few insulated mounds, I found the whole face of the country covered with vestiges of building, in some cases consisting of brick walls, surprisingly fresh, in others, merely of a vast succession of mounds of rubbish, of such indeterminate figures, variety, and extent, as to involve the person who should have formed any theory in inextricable confusion. The whole country between Bagdad and Hillah is perfectly flat, and (with the exception of a few spots as you approach the latter place) an uncultivated waste. That it was at some former period in a far different state is evident from the number of canals by which it is traversed, now dry and neglected, and the quantity of heaps of earth, covered with fragments of brick and broken tiles, which are seen in every direction, the indisputable traces of former population." Subsequent investigations have been made by Sir Robert Ker Porter, Mr. Buckingham, Captain Mignan, and others—all of which have confirmed Mr. Rich's general accuracy.

That this is the actual site of ancient Babylon is confirmed by the latitude of the place, compared with the situation of that city as described by the classical writers; by its vicinity to the bituminous fountains of Is or Hit, mentioned by Herodotus as being eight days' journey from the city; by the magnitude, extent, and remarkable character of the ruins; and by the fact of the district's having been locally distinguished by the name of Babel from the earliest historical times.

There is no portion of any building in an entire state.

The ruins consist of great masses of brickwork, some of them more or less vitrified; of mounds of earth, formed by the decomposition of the buildings, channelled and furrowed by the weather, the wind and the rain; and of fragments of brick, bitumen, and pottery, strewed upon the surface. The bricks are of two kinds, one burnt, and the other simply dried in the sun. The burnt bricks are usually more than a foot square, and three inches thick. The shapes and sizes vary, however, according to the places which they were intended to occupy. They are of various colours. The finest are of a white yellow hue, the coarsest are red, and others are remarkable for their hardness, and, in colour, are dark, approaching to black. The sun-dried bricks are considerably larger, some of them weighing as much as thirty-six pounds. They are like clods of earth with which have been mixed reeds and chopped straw, for the purpose of giving consistency to the mass. The same materials are sometimes found in the kiln-burnt bricks. There is reason to believe that the common bricks formed the inner part of thick walls, while the finer kinds were used for an external casing. Three kinds of cement are observable in these remains—bitumen, common clay, and lime mortar.

On the fine Babylonian bricks there are frequently to be found inscriptions in the kind of writing which is called cuneiform, arrow-headed, wedge-shaped, and *tête-à-clou*, nail-headed; descriptions which refer to the resemblance which is borne by its parts to the barb of an arrow, a wedge, or a nail. One face only is occupied by the inscription. It varies from three to ten lines, and is generally enclosed in a small square. These inscriptions seem to have been stamped by a block while the bricks were in a soft state, so exactly do the same characters resemble each other. When flaws or blemishes occur they are found on many. This near approach to the art of printing was known to the ancient Egyptians, and is of great antiquity in China. The meaning of these records is uncertain. Ezekiel, an inhabitant of the district, was commanded—" Thou also, son of man, take thee a tile, and lay it before thee, and portray upon it the city, even Jerusalem," Ezek. iv. 1. In Babylonian inscriptions the name of Nebuchadnezzar, king of the land of the Chaldees, has been traced; and a cylinder in the British Museum has the legend, " Darius, the great King."

It is on the east side of the river that the greatest amount of remains is found, and the commencement of these is about two miles to the north of Hillah. There are three great masses of them, locally called the *Mujellibe*, lying detached; the *Kasr*, connected with the Amran Hill; and a long circular mound, like a boundary wall, extending from the south-east corner of the northern mass to the south-east corner of the southern, but making a wide *détour* towards the desert, the river forming the enclosure on the west. The area included by the rampart and the river measures two miles six hundred yards from east to west, and two miles one thousand yards from north to south. Besides these great mounds there are many others which are smaller, with various lines of embankment and dykes.

On approaching the site of Babylon from the north, or by the road from Bagdad, the first object of interest which presents itself is the grandest and most gigantic of the ruined masses east of the river. The Arabic name, *Mukallibe* or *Mujellibe*, signifies "overturned," and suggests the idea of a confused heap. The summit of the Mujellibe is an uneven flat, strewed with bricks, broken and whole, many of them with inscriptions in the arrow-headed character which are remarkably fresh. Pottery, bitumen, vitrified and petrified brick, shells, and glass, are also equally abundant. Regular brickwork may be traced along each front, particularly at the south-west angle, which is faced by a wall, apparently the fragment of a watch-tower or small turret. The Mujellibe stands alone, at the distance of rather more than half a mile from the Euphrates. It is an utterly forsaken site, not marked even by the habitation of a solitary goatherd. The isolation and the abandonment combine to impress the mind with awe and reverence. The summit commands an extensive view of the surrounding country. Buckingham says: "On gaining it we had the first sight of the Euphrates, flowing majestically along through verdant banks, and its serpentine course apparently losing itself in the palm-groves of Hillah, whose mosques and minarets we could just perceive, about five miles to the southward of us."

About a mile to the south of this mass of ruins is another called by the natives *Al Kasr*, or the palace. It is seventy feet high, very irregular in its shape, and furrowed by deep and broad ravines crossing each other. It forms nearly a square of two thousand one hundred feet on each side, and is composed of the finest furnace-baked brick. The walls are eight feet thick, and face the cardinal points. From the superior character of the remains at this spot, it is evident that here was the site of some important and magnificent edifice. The Kasr is in all probability the ruins of the new royal palace, with which the hanging gardens were connected. There seems to be a trace of these last still extant. These gardens were, in all likelihood stocked with exotics, and not with plants natural to the region. There is still here, then, an ancient tree of a kind quite unknown to the country—an evergreen, a kind of tamarisk, common in the land of the queen, a Median princess, for whose pleasure the hanging gardens are said to have been formed.

The *Amran Hill* is the third mass of ruins, and lies to the south of the Kasr, occupying more ground, and connected with it on the western side by a long mound. The remainder of the intermediate space, rather more than a quarter of a mile broad, is covered with reeds and tufts of rank grass. The soil is very damp, as if it had been submerged. Mignan believes this space to be a deserted channel of the Euphrates; and if this be admitted, the Amran Hill might represent the site of the old royal palace, as the Kasr does that of the new, the two, as we are expressly informed, being placed on opposite sides of the river. But Porter disbelieves this, and considers that the two masses conjointly form the remains of the great imperial dwelling of Nebuchadnezzar. In itself the Hill of Amran has no great amount of interest,—having been completely ransacked by excavators, for the purpose of obtaining the building materials. The name is derived from a small tomb on the highest part of it, which is traditionally reported to contain the body of a son of Ali, called Amran, who, with seven of his companions, was slain at the battle of Hillah.

These are the principal remains on the eastern side of the river, where the most recently built, and the most magnificent, part of the city was no doubt situated, the city of Nebuchadnezzar, Nitocris, and Belshazzar. On the western bank, the adjacent country presents, in various places, abundant evidence of ancient occupation. But there is only one object to which it is necessary to call special attention,—the tower of Nimrod,—the most remarkable feature of the whole plain of Babylon.

The *Birs Nimroud* is a long and venerable pile of ruins, and stands at a distance from those which have been named, being about six miles to the south-west of Hillah. Niebuhr was the first European who visited these remains, and he says, "Other ruins of Babylon are to be seen, a German mile and a quarter south-west of Hillah, on the west bank of the Euphrates. Here is an entire hill composed of the beautiful bricks formerly mentioned, and on the top stands a tower, the interior of which seems to have been built of these burned bricks. The outer walls are decayed through time. It is perforated with a number of holes, which had probably been opened for the free circulation of air and the prevention of damp. At the period when Babylon was in its glory, and the surrounding country in a state of high cultivation, this tower must have afforded an excellent prospect on all sides; for Meshed Ali seems to lie at its foot, though it may be at least six leagues distant. After I had read what Herodotus says of the temple of Belus, and its strong tower, I thought it highly probable that this might be the remains of it, and am, therefore, anxious that some succeeding traveller should accurately examine and describe it. I made the journey thither, accompanied only by a single guide, and I had seen but little of the monument, when I perceived some Arabs reconnoitring us, and deemed it safest to ride back to the tower. Had I supposed I was so near to the tower of Babylon, I should certainly have risked more for a closer survey."

The hill of the Birs is of oblong form, 2,286 feet in circuit, rising in a conical figure to the height of 198 feet, and surrounded by a distinct quadrangular enclosure. In itself it is a ruin, composed of sun-dried bricks, with others of the finer kind, the surface being deeply furrowed by the violence of the wind and rain, to which, for thousands of years, it has been exposed. The tower surmounting the summit is 37 feet high, by 28 feet in breadth, and diminishes in thickness towards the top, where it assumes a pyramidal form. It is a solid mass of beautiful masonry, built of fine kiln-baked bricks, so firmly cemented as to be inseparable without damaging them. It has been rifted or split from the top nearly half way down. At the base of the tower there are several immense masses of brown and black brickwork of irregular shape, changed into a vitrified state, and, at a distance, looking like so many edifices torn up from their foundations. The change exhibited by these vitrified masses shows that they have undergone the action of the fiercest fire, or that they may have been scathed by lightning. It has been contended, and not without apparent reason, that the intense heat manifested in these vitrified remains could only have proceeded from lightning.

It is now generally believed that the Birs Nimroud represents the temple of Belus, with its high spiral tower, the greatest ornament and the most extraordinary erection of ancient Babylon. This ruined memorial corresponds, as Heeren observes, with that celebrated idol shrine and astrological sanctuary,—first, in form, for of the eight stories which it had originally, three are still discernible; secondly, in dimensions, for its length and breadth agree with what is stated by Herodotus, so far as they can be determined from a mountain-heap of ruins; and, finally, it agrees with the statement of the same historian, that this pyramidal sanctuary stood within a square enclosure, for the remains of such an enclosure are still very distinctly to be traced. It has been objected to this conclusion that the historian represents the temple of Bel as being in the middle of the two divisions of the city, formed by the intersecting stream of the Euphrates, while the Birs is too far removed from the river to answer to such a description. But in countries with such a soil, rivers frequently change their course, and we know that great changes have actually occurred in the channel of the Euphrates.

But another and still more remote origin is claimed for the Birs, in accordance with its name, the tower of Nimrod. It has been alleged that we have here the remains of that elevated structure, commonly called the *Tower of Babel*, which the postdiluvians commenced and partly erected, certainly in this locality, and which was arrested in its progress by the special intervention of the Most High. As Heeren remarks, the site of that edifice may be assumed to have been westward of the river, inasmuch as it was built by the descendants of Noah, when they were journeying from west to east. "And it came to pass, as they journeyed eastward, that they found a plain in the land of Shinar; and they dwelt there." Gen. xi. 2. It was built of the same material as that of which the ruin consists,—" And they said one to another, Go to, let us make bricks, and burn them thoroughly. And they had brick for stone, and slime (bitumen) had they for mortar." Gen. xi. 3. In the sacred narrative there is no intimation that the building was destroyed, or even damaged, at the time of the confusion of tongues. The work was simply brought to an end. It was evidently of vast dimensions,—" Let us build us a tower . . . . whose top may reach unto Heaven"—a hyperbolical mode of describing a very elevated and conspicuous object, common to all languages. Hence, as ancient Babylon was renowned for a stupendous tower, comparable to the loftiest of the Egyptian pyramids, rising up from the enclosure of the temple of Belus, it has been believed by many high authorities that the primeval building erected by the assembly of nations formed at least its nucleus, which, after various vicissitudes, at last assumed the appearance which the ancient writers describe. Of course there can be no certainty on such a point, but the conjecture may be regarded as plausible. It is worthy of remark that though the Scriptures are silent as to any injuries having been inflicted upon the primitive structure, yet tradition says that the original Tower of Babel was rent and devastated by fire from heaven, while, as already mentioned, appearances at the Birs indicate the action of intense vitrifying heat.

On the western side of the site of Babylon, the general appearance of the country answers to the description given of it by ancient authors. The quarter of the capital in that direction is said to have been surrounded by lakes or swamps, which formed a natural barrier, and rendered the erection of walls and barriers unnecessary in that direction,—the city not being open to invasion on that side.

No certain remains of the walls of Babylon have been identified, so as to indicate its precise limits; but there is no difficulty in accounting for the deficiency. When we consider the perishable character of the materials of which these structures were composed,—sun-dried bricks generally; the many cities that owe their origin to its ruins; the ordinary operation of the weather, with the periodical overflow of the Euphrates left to inundate its site,—there is no ground for any surprise, unless it be that such a combination of destructive agencies has not made greater havoc.

We have here, then, the ruins of the first-built city of the world,—the most magnificent metropolis in the history of the ancient nations. We may say of them, "Come, behold the works of the Lord, what desolations He hath made in the earth." Connecting the past with the present, the ruin is most complete and striking. "Babylon is fallen, is fallen."

Ancient Babylon presents many points of interesting remark. Nimrod was its founder, and made it the capital of his kingdom. At such a period we must remember that at this date was the origin of permanent dwellings, political institutions, and civil society. The metropolis could, therefore, have been only an insignificant town, and the kingdom of its founder only a small extent of territory. The occurrence of the confusion of tongues, and the dispersion of the builders of the city, arrested its progress, and possibly induced a temporary decay; for, with the record of its first appearance, it vanished from the page of history, and did not become a place of importance until many ages had rolled away. Cities in general are of slow growth, and reach their greatness from very humble beginnings. We must not do violence to nature and ordinary fact in the case of Babylon. The germ of London was a stationary camp of Britons on the north bank of the Thames, nineteen centuries ago. Paris has resulted from a few fishermen's huts, the men being of the tribe of the Parisii, and who were found on one of the islets of the Seine. A band of Phocians voluntarily expatriating themselves to preserve their independence, reached the mouth of the Rhone, before the close of Hebrew prophecy, and laid the foundations of Marseilles. "Rome was not built in a day." A village on the Palatine Mount, inhabited by a handful of men, antedated the sevenhilled city. Bringing, then, the natural course of events to bear upon the interpretation of the record respecting Babylon, we can only gather from it that an enterprising chieftain formed a settlement, which gradually expanded into a place of importance, became the capital of a mighty empire, and the mistress of Western Asia. There are three other cities mentioned as having been nearly contemporaneous with Babylon,— "Erech, Accad, and Calneh," founded by the same chieftain, and also in the land of Shinar. They were probably in the vicinity of the principal settlement. Erech is supposed to be represented by the imposing mounds of El Assayah, "the place of pebbles," and is situated on the Euphrates, eighty-two miles south from the bridge of Hillah. Accad is identified with the great mound of Akarkuf, about seven miles from Bagdad, and fifty-five from the site of Babylon. The great resemblance of this ruin to the Birs is very striking. Calneh is not well identified, but is commonly believed to have occupied the site of Ctesiphon.

The growth and embellishment of Babylon are generally referred to Semiramis, the Assyrian queen. There is probably much that is fabulous mixed with the history; but she undoubtedly made Babylon the seat of her government, and adorned and improved the city with numerous great public works. The Chaldæans as a conquering people effected a complete revolution in the political condition of Western Asia, and founded the Chaldæo-Babylonian empire in the latter part of the seventh century before our era, or it may be about B.C. 630. The second sovereign of this dynasty, Nebuchadnezzar, began his reign in B.C. 604. In his time, the metropolis reached its highest distinction. In his pride, the arrogant monarch said, as he probably surveyed the city, "Is not this great Babylon that I have built for the house of the kingdom, by the might of my power, and for the honour of my majesty." References are frequently made to the magnificence of the capital, to its broad walls, its stately palaces, its splendid temples, and its golden idols. Babylon is represented as having been in the form of a square. Each side is said to have extended about one hundred and twenty stadia, or fifteen miles, giving sixty miles for the entire circuit. We must not form our ideas of the eastern and ancient from the western and modern—looking at our closely packed towns and condensed population as samples of the arrangements which obtained three thousand years ago in Central Asia. Not London or Paris, but Ispahan and Pekin will help us to right conclusions. The dwellings were usually detached. There were large open spaces for pleasure, and for cultivation—there being a sufficient quantity of land for the sustenance of the inhabitants in case of siege. With all this space, Babylon, in its most flourishing condition, did not, therefore, probably contain more than 1,200,000, or slightly more than one-third of the present population of London. A broad deep ditch, full of water, surrounded the city, and a high wall of bricks adjoined it, it being formed of the soil taken from the moat, and of such dimensions that the top of it was like a roadway. There were watch-towers upon the wall at intervals; and portals, furnished with gates of brass of immense strength and richness. The Euphrates flowed through the city, lined by a wall on each bank, with smaller brazen gates, from which steps conducted down to the stream. The streets ran in straight lines. The river was crossed by a bridge, and there seems to have been a tunnel under its bed. Two royal palaces occupied the opposite sides of the river, near the bridge. On the eastern bank stood the new palace of Nebuchadnezzar, erected on the site of a former royal residence, and to this were attached the hanging gardens. This construction rose to a great height, and rested on immense buttresses. Each terrace had mould of sufficient depth for the largest trees, and was supplied with water from the river by hydraulic machines. This remarkable work is said to have been undertaken for the gratification of the queen, a Median lady, who longed to look upon the vegetation of her own land. The imperial residence was defended by triple walls; and, with its appurtenances, gardens, and pleasure-grounds, included a circuit of little less than eight miles.

The Kasr being probably a remnant of the *new eastern palace*, is no doubt the one so frequently mentioned in the Book of Daniel. It was here that the king was smitten with his peculiar madness. The same structure we may reasonably suppose to have been the scene of Belshazzar's impious festivity, and of the miraculous hand and handwriting on the wall which declared his delinquency. It was in this palace that Alexander the Great died.

Whatever may be the mound which covers and includes its remains, the *Temple of Belus* was one of the great wonders of ancient Babylon. It was a quadrangle, two stadia in circumference. In the middle of it there was a great tower, eight stories high, these decreasing in size, and the whole presenting the appearance of a pyramid. A spiral staircase led up to the summit. The topmost tower was the sanctuary or temple, the residence of the god, in which there stood a table, and a couch of gold, but no statue. It was never penetrated by the public eye, but was used for vicious purposes by the priesthood. There was a golden image in a lower building, and to that the populace were admitted. Alexander desired to restore this erection, but the ruins were so immense that although he employed his army in an attempt to clear them away, he was obliged to abandon his purpose. The great decree could not be reversed—"Bel boweth down, Nebo stoopeth." Such was Babylon in the time of its greatest monarch, when Jewish captives trod its streets, or mourned their exile by its waters, and a prophet of that race interpreted the dreams of its ambitious sovereign. Probably no people were ever more luxurious. Every description of excess marked their lives. The Chaldæo-Babylonian empire suddenly appeared like a meteor, to glare transiently, and suddenly expire. In little more than twenty years after the death of Nebuchadnezzar, the confederate armies of the Medes and Persians, with many auxiliaries, were thundering at the gates of the capital, under the command of Cyrus, a new competitor for predominant authority over the western Asiatic nations.

The city sustained but little damage from the conquest; but a rebellion in the time of Darius Hystaspes, brought down upon it the vengeance of that monarch, who considered it necessary to dismantle the formidable stronghold. Three thousand of the principal citizens were cruelly impaled, the walls were demolished, and all the gates were removed. After the time of Alexander, the new capital of Seleucia, not far distant, was largely built of the materials of Babylon, and multitudes of the population were drained off to the new site. Ctesiphon, the capital of the Parthians, and other cities, in the same way contributed to its degradation. Thus it gradually verged for centuries towards poverty and desolation, till ultimately the site of the emporium of the ancient world, the great centre of attraction to the Oriental nations, became the solitude it now is, where the stillness is seldom interrupted by any sounds of life, besides the occasional visit of the Bedouin, the cry of the bittern, or the hooting of the owl.

The *Euphrates* bears through its entire course the name of *Forat* or *Frat* (the same word as the Hebrew *Phrat*, which means to fructify or fertilise), which is its denomination in the Old Testament. Including its windings it has a course of upwards of seventeen hundred miles. The distance in a straight line, from the source of the river to the Shat-el-Arab, is about five hundred and sixty miles. It proceeds in a direction from west to south, and then from north to south. Long before joining the Tigris, it comes within a very short distance of that river, and afterwards recedes from it. The breadth of the river is very variable. Xenophon makes it four stadia, or two thousand four hundred feet, in the central part, at the foot of ancient Thapsacus, where he crossed it with the Greeks: but at the bridge of ancient Babylon it was but one stadium, or six hundred feet. The fall from source to mouth is very considerable. The great eastern branch, or the Murad, at the distance of a hundred and twenty miles from its source, is four thousand one hundred and thirty-eight feet above the Black Sea; at Paloo, it is two thousand eight hundred and nineteen, flowing with a rapid current; and at Bir, the bed of the Euphrates is only six hundred and twenty-eight feet above the level of the Mediterranean. From this point it has still a distance of one thousand and fifty-five miles to run, which gives it a fall of only about seven inches per mile. Still, the stream is not sluggish till it has fully entered the flats of Babylonia.

There is a periodical rise occurring twice in the year. The first is slight and temporary, occasioned by the rains which begin to fall towards the end of October. The other, which is the greater and more permanent flood, commences about the beginning of March, at which time the snows in the highlands of Armenia are melting. It attains its greatest height about the close of May, the waters at Anah averaging from ten to twelve feet of increase. The country is then overflowed, and the ruins of Babylon are flooded so that many parts of them are inaccessible. The Lemlun marshes have the appearance of a vast sea. The river continues high for about a month, and its course is very rapid—no boats attempting to ascend it. "O thou that dwellest upon many waters," Jer. li. 13, is a description peculiarly applicable to Babylon at this season. A vast amount of sedimentary matter is brought down by the current, forming those great tracts of deep alluvial soil which are to be found in many parts. In ancient times much attention was paid by the inhabitants to the protection of their lands from the flood. This was accomplished by means of artificial embankments, which were remarkable constructions of baked and unbaked bricks; and by an extensive system of canals, which spread like network over the country, and which have excited the wonder and admiration of the world. The most celebrated of these was the Nahr Malikah, the royal ditch of Polybius, and the *flumen regium*, or royal river of other authors. There seems little reason to doubt the common tradition which attributes this great work to Nimrod. Undoubtedly it dates from the remotest periods of Babylonian antiquity. It had its outlet in the Tigris at Seleucia, and was sufficient for the navigation of merchant vessels. From Sumeiset downwards, through a distance of more than eleven hundred miles, the navigation of the Euphrates is unimpeded, except at a few points where ledges of rocks stretch across, and which at the low season are forded by camels. When the water rises these obstacles disappear, and the ordinary boats of the country can pass at all times, on lightening their burden. The fleet of Alexander ascended the river from the Indian Ocean to Babylon, and it was descended by the flotillas of Severus and Julian, from the Khabour, both proceeding through the Nahr Malikah to the Tigris. Round coracles, or basket-boats covered with leather or skins, still float upon the stream as in ancient times.

The Euphrates yields in the interest and importance of its associations only to the Jordan. It was connected with the paradise of unfallen man. After the flood, it was by its banks that the presumption of man dared to defy the Almighty by the attempted erection of the Tower of Babel. The native land of the father of the faithful lay upon its eastern border. Beside it rose the great Babylon. The Jews in their captivity sat upon its brink, and wept as they remembered their own Jerusalem. In this vicinity Daniel's wondrous life was lived; Shadrach, Meshach, and Abednego here underwent their fiery ordeal; Ezekiel saw his visions on one of its affluents; the battle-field of Cunaxa, in which the younger Cyrus fell, stretched along its banks; Alexander sailed upon its surface, and died upon its margin; Crassus perished near its waters; Marc Antony ingloriously retreated across this stream; and Trajan, Severus, Gordian, Julian, Jovian, and Heraclius, successively appeared at the head of the Roman legions on its channel.

The sources of the Murad Chai, the eastern and principal head of the Euphrates, are on the southern slope of the Ala Tagh, or beautiful mount, which rises to the height of about nine thousand feet, nearly midway between Lake Van and Ararat. The western source of the Euphrates is in the mountains on the north-east of Erzeroum, from which it descends to water the elevated plain of the city, but not approaching nearer than seven or eight miles.

Erzeroum is the capital of Armenia, and is important from its position as commanding the high road from Constantinople to Persia and Georgia. It is the thoroughfare of those countries, whether carried on by the Black Sea or the overland route through Asia Minor, and contains as many as thirty-six khans, and one of the largest custom-houses of the Ottoman Empire. But it has fallen from its former importance, and possesses scarcely the fourth part of the population which it contained in 1827, owing to the great emigration of Armenian families in the train of the Russian army. There are consequently many villages only half inhabited. Below Erzigan the river enters a long and narrow defile, and still further down passes through a vast rent in the mountains. Rocks, rapids, and shallows encumber its bed till it reaches its junction with the Murad. The Euphrates proper, now formed by the confluence of the two currents, is here about three hundred and sixty feet wide, and is very deep and rapid at the ferry of Keban Maden, five miles below. At Thapsacus, once a large and flourishing city, nothing remains but a long line of mounds above Racca. The river was here usually crossed by the merchants of Egypt and Syria, and by the Persian, Greek, and Roman armies, as in modern times by the Arabs, Tartars, and Turks, either by being forded, which is possible at low water, or by a bridge of boats. The ten thousand waded through it, the water coming up to their breasts. Xerxes here constructed a bridge of boats, one being tied to another; but it was destroyed by the Persian general on the approach of Cyrus. It was re-established, and again broken down by Darius on his retreat before the troops of Alexander.

A few miles below Racca the Euphrates is entered by the Belik, a stream flowing from the north. The course of the Belik is not much known, but within its basin is the City of Orfah, or Urfah, considered by the Jews and all the Orientals as identical with "Ur of the Chaldees," the birth-place of Terah, Abraham, Sarah, and Lot. There is a pool within the walls of the city called *Birket ul Ibrahim ul Khaleel*, "Lake of Abraham the Beloved, or Friend of God." A mosque attached to it is similarly designated. The population is estimated at about forty thousand, of which number one half are Christians. Few places have undergone so many changes of name and of masters. This is the Edessa of ecclesiastical history, and here the Christian Church effected one of its very earliest foundations. Here it was that Abgarus ruled, of whom it is alleged, though fabulously, that he had a written correspondence with the Saviour Himself. A tributary of the Belik is the

Khabour, or the Chetar, which is of interest in connection with the Jewish exile and the prophecies of Ezekiel. Returning to the main channel of the Euphrates, the river flows from the point we have reached through a woody, hilly, and thinly populated country, with an average width of 1,200 feet, and an ordinary depth of 18 feet, there being numerous islands in its bed. The castle of Rahaba, or Rehoboth, stands on the left bank—" Rehoboth by the river "— and is of great antiquity. There is also the town of Anah, presenting a pleasing appearance with its date-trees, pomegranates, and shrubs intermingled with its clay buildings. It is inhabited chiefly by Arabs. Eight islands occupy the channel of the swift-flowing waters. They are covered with a luxuriant vegetation, and ornamented with the remains of a castle, which was built by the Greeks, destroyed by Julian, reconstructed by the Saracens, and reduced to its present state by the Bedouins. The remains of the ancient City of Anatho lie on the opposite bank of the river, and occupy a considerable space. Arab villages, surrounded with cultivated lands, appear at intervals on either bank, on proceeding to Hadishah, the next place of importance, occupying an island, and representing the ancient Hadith. There are here most elaborate works in the form of aqueducts for purposes of irrigation. They are beautiful specimens of art and durability. These monuments of other times distinctly prove that the borders of the Euphrates were once densely populated by persons far advanced in the application of hydraulics to agricultural and domestic purposes. During the lapse of ages they have suffered, as may be supposed, from partial or entire neglect; but some have been repaired and used for the grinding of corn or the irrigation of the land. Approaching Hit the country along the river presents lower hilly ranges, with slopes less abrupt, which occur at a greater distance from each other, and which finally decline into monotonous levels. Hit is the Is of antiquity, and is now an unimportant place. It is one of the border towns of Irak, at which vessels usually touch. There are near it springs of bitumen and naphtha which have remained unchanged for many ages. The remains of aqueducts shortly disappear, and are succeeded at a lower point by rocky formations. The high minaret of Mesjid Sandabiyah stands upon almost the last promontory of rocky land that flanks the Euphrates on the western side; and on the eastern and hilly district there are the Pylæ, or Gates of Xenophon, marking the boundary of the diversified country, and indicating the commencement of the low level plains of Babylonia. Throughout this tract, and down to the plains of Babylon, the river flows over a bed of sand or mud, with much less winding. The stream is deep, and in its ordinary state the current is dull. Villages of mud houses, reed huts or tents, closely crowded together, are frequent, and there are flocks of goats, sheep, and cattle feeding near them—the inhabitants being busily employed in raising water for irrigating purposes by rude yet efficient machines. The black tent of the Bedouin is the commonest kind of habitation. It is formed of strong cloth made of goats' hair mixed with wool, supported on low poles, and always open on one side, that of shade or shelter. Such dwellings have descended from the most primitive times without any alteration in their general arrangement. On the left of the river at this part many important events have occurred. It was in this locality that the career of the younger Cyrus was arrested, his death utterly extinguishing the hopes of the ten thousand at the moment when their accomplishment seemed certain. This event took place on the field of Cunaxa, but the site cannot with preciseness be identified. It was probably near the present mounds of Mohammed, about half way between the Median wall and Babylon.

We have thus sought to indicate the course of the Euphrates from its remotest sources to its broad and placid basin in the plains. Under the sway of the Turks a great diminution has taken place in regard to the numbers of the people. Cities and towns, once flourishing, have gone to decay, and the traveller comes upon ruined villages in every direction, while a large extent of land has gone out of cultivation. The Turk is fully conscious of his impotence in competition with the European. While the nations of Christendom are rapidly growing in vigour, the Ottoman line is fast verging to complete decrepitude. Even the religious faith of the people shares the decay of their political power. Mohammedanism is maintained, and its ritual followed, but more from habit and ancestral pride than from any conviction of its truth. Mosques of former ages are to be seen in every part in ruins, but the sight of one undergoing repair is seldom witnessed. Nearly all the costly monuments of Moslem pride are the work of bygone days, and nothing new is rising to be to a future generation what the remains of the old are to the present.

The TIGRIS, if inferior to the Euphrates, is still a noble stream. It claims the same connection with the Eden of human innocence, and is closely associated with the names of the mighty kings and kingdoms of the ancient world. The second great city of history rose upon its banks, and became the Nineveh of sacred and secular annals.

NINEVEH.—Both Babylon and Nineveh come first into prominence in their greatness, not in their origin, and, consequently, it is difficult to say which had precedence of the other in respect to time. But Babylon seems to have been the earlier of these great cities. We read, Gen. xx. 8-13—and this is the oldest historical record—" And Cush begat Nimrod. He began to be a mighty one in the earth. He was a mighty hunter before the Lord; wherefore it is said, even as Nimrod the mighty hunter before the Lord. And the beginning of his kingdom was Babel, and Erech, and Accad, and Calneh, in the land of Shinar. Out of that land went forth Asshur—or 'he,' Nimrod, 'went forth into Assyria' [*marginal reading*]—and builded Nineveh, and the City Rehoboth, and Calah, and Resen, between Nineveh and Calah; the same is a great city." It may be assumed, then, that Nimrod, a bold and energetic chieftain of the Hametic race, having encroached upon the territory allotted to the Shemites, and founded Babylon, commencing there the first recorded instance of independent sovereign rule, extended his sway over a further portion of the country allotted to the other branch of the Noachic family, and originated the four primeval cities of Assyria. It was probably not until several centuries had elapsed that Nineveh exhibited any signs of its subsequent greatness. The monuments of Nineveh would appear to countenance the supposition that a race of powerful monarchs, who were for a lengthened interval the lords paramount of Western Asia, and who founded the magnificent buildings at Nineveh, Kouyunjik, and Khorsabad, antedated that line of Assyrian kings which the sacred writers had occasion to refer to. The most ancient sculptures are ascribed to a period as early as the thirteenth century before Christ, a date which coincides with the Israelitish conquest of Canaan. This ancient dynasty would seem to have been overthrown, Nineveh captured, and the then existing Assyrian Empire dissolved at the date mentioned, when the Medes commenced their struggle for independence.

A new line of kings restored political importance for

a season. In the time of the prophet Jonah, about B.C. 800, Nineveh had evidently recovered from the blow inflicted by its misfortunes, and was under regular regal government and in a flourishing condition. "That great city" is the emphatic indication of its general pre-eminence. "An exceeding great city of three days' journey" more particularly defines its extent.

There were 1,500 towers, each 200 feet high, crowning the walls of Nineveh, rendering its defences so strong that they were deemed impregnable. The walls themselves were 100 feet high, and so broad that three chariots might be driven abreast upon them. In this respect, as well as in others, they resembled the walls of Babylon. The population at the time of the prophet Jonah was "six-score thousand persons that could not discern between their right hand and their left hand." Adding helpless children, we may thus take the inhabitants to have numbered 700,000. In this population there must have been but few who differed from the multitude in the possession of qualities of moral goodness. It presented an unmitigated scene of guilty greatness and splendid atrocity, and this was the cause of Jonah's mission to its gates. "Arise, go to Nineveh, that great city, and cry against it; for their wickedness is come up before me," Jonah i. 2. The message portended a sudden and speedy destruction—"Yet forty days, and Nineveh shall be overthrown!" The precise nature of the judgment which impended over Nineveh has not been recorded; but some tremendous visitation is implied in the warning. The mission of the prophet opens a chapter of human history without a parallel in the chronicle of nations,—a city summoned to hear of a righteous judgment pronounced upon its evil works; an alarmed and penitent people reforming their ways, and pleading for a respite from the stroke. The successful divine ambassador fails to see his own success in the people's repentance, and, irritated and moody, clings to the hope that the great city would yet and speedily sink under the infliction of a just retribution. He waits and watches for such event; but the divine compassion reproves him—" Should not I spare Nineveh, that great city?" There may have been some sincerely sorrowful, but we are not warranted to believe that there were many who renounced their wickedness. But there was an extension of forbearance. The unnamed king who heard the voice of the rod was probably the last of the sovereigns who preceded those who are mentioned in the sacred record as having threatened and oppressed the chosen people. Pul appeared upon the frontiers of Israel, and compelled the king to purchase peace by an annual tribute. Tiglathpileser (Diglath-pul-Assur, Great Lord of the Tigris) made Judah also a stipendiary, carrying into captivity the Trans-Jordanic tribes; and Shalmaneser, provoked by a breach of faith, terminated the independent existence of Israel, transferring the people to his own territories and putting his native subjects in their place. Inquiry has interested itself in the fate of the ten tribes in consequence of their deportation, and many have refused to admit that they have been fused in the mass of mankind, but have been perpetuated as a distinct body in some remote region of Central Asia. The Affghans and the Nestorian Christians have been considered by different parties to be the descendants of the lost tribes of Israel; but the objections to such conclusions are strong and manifold.

When the next monarch, the bold and impious Sennacherib, came to the throne, the empire of Nineveh was at the height of its prosperity and power. Following the example of his predecessors, he suddenly appeared in the territories of Hezekiah at the head of an immense army, threatening Judah with the terrible fate of Israel.

> "The Assyrian came down like a wolf on the fold,
> And his cohorts were gleaming with purple and gold."

Pacified by a present of the gold of the temple, the invaders passed on to the conquest of Egypt, but subsequently deeming the possession of Jerusalem an important stronghold, the army returned upon the apparently doomed city, insolently defying the God that had spared Nineveh to save it from their power. The first great blow at the Assyrian power now fell upon it, and it shook the empire to its foundations. No spectacle more melancholy ever presented itself to the eye of man. The dead corpses of a hundred and four-score and five thousand of Sennacherib's army slain in the night; the dispersion of the survivors when the morning revealed the fate of their companions; the flight of their leader to his own capital; these are parts of the sad picture.

> "Like the leaves of the forest when summer is green,
> That host with their banners at sunset were seen;
> Like the leaves of the forest when autumn hath blown,
> That host on the morrow lay withered and strown."

"Who hath hardened himself against Him, and hath prospered?" From the date of the haughty defiance thrown at the God of Jerusalem, the doom of the Assyrian Empire seems to have been sealed. Misfortune followed the baffled king in his retreat to Nineveh, where he was slain in the house of his god, B.C. 711, and calamity ensued in the form of revolt. Esarhaddon, probably the Sargon of the prophet, succeeded to the government, but Media became an independent kingdom. Nabuchudonosor raised the empire for a brief period to a pitch of greatness; but his reign ended disastrously. Sardanapalus II. was the last sovereign; he was one of the most abandoned of voluptuaries, thoroughly effeminated by his vices, and yet he struggled gallantly for his throne when the crisis of the kingdom came. For a few years the bursting of the storm was delayed; but at length the confederate forces of Media and Babylon beleaguered Nineveh, which made vigorous but vain efforts at defence. An ancient tradition that the city could never be taken till the river became its enemy, encouraged the hopes of the people, such an event being deemed most improbable. But on the morning of the 30th of September, B.C. 610, the Tigris rose in inundation, and swept away twenty furlongs of the city wall, thus effectually aiding the besiegers. The king, in despair, perished in the voluntary conflagration of the imperial palace. Much of the city besides was consumed by fire. The Assyrian territory and the treasures of the kingdom were divided between the conquerors, and the city was razed to the ground, 771. Botta found at Khorsabad a great quantity of charcoal, portions of burned beams, remains of some half-burned thread; while in many instances the sculptured slabs of gypsum had been converted into lime, and were quite friable; plainly declaring that fire had been the agent of the wide-spread destruction. The same appearances presented themselves at Kouyunjik and Nimroud.

The past and the present are in striking contrast. Instead of embattled walls, palace-temples, and other stately monuments of architecture, uncouth piles of dust and fragments meet the eye, mixed up with groups of miserable huts belonging to the present occupants of the soil; terraced gardens, artificial streams, and bands of revellers listening to the voice of music, have given place to a large untenanted plain, with scarce a tree or bush upon its surface, the wild winds sweeping over the barren waste which they bury more deeply in sand.

The city of Mosul occupies the west bank of the

river opposite the ruins of Nineveh. Crossing to the eastern side by a bridge of boats, there are before us two great mounds, nearly due north and south of each other, Kouyunjik and Nebbi Yunus, separated by level ground and the small rivulet Khauser. They are both cultivated, and occupied by the dwellings of some villagers. The northern mound, Kouyunjik, is also called the Kalaa, or Castle of Ninawe, and is 43 feet in perpendicular height, and 7,691 feet in circumference. It is of an irregular form, with steep sides and a flat summit. There are traces of building about it; stones have everywhere been ploughed up, and, when openings have been made, sections of sun-dried brickwork have been found, mixed up with the remains of floorings or pavements, with portions of carved columns and other masonry. Fragments of pottery of the finest kinds have also been found, covered with beautiful cuneiform writing, similar to large cylinders common among the remains of Babylon. Mr. Rich brought away several specimens, with a seal of agate found by his servant, on which was represented a priest worshipping the sun, with other symbols. Some years previously, when search was being made for stones to repair the bridge over the flood-ground of the Tigris, the workmen came upon a chamber which they explored. Here were found, besides the inscriptions of the place, among bones and rubbish, a woman's *khoolkhal*, or bracelet for the ankle, of silver, covered with turquoise-coloured rust; another, differently formed, of gold, called a *hejil*, being without bells; and a perfect bracelet of gold beads, with pieces of engraved agate. The southern mound, Nebbi Yunus, or the prophet Jonah, was once the site of a church named after the divine messenger, from a tradition that he preached upon the spot. The church is preserved entire, but converted into a Mohammedan mosque. The hill itself is about 50 feet in perpendicular height, and extends 431 feet from east to west, by 355 feet from north to south. There is no doubt in respect to its antiquity. Many attesting proofs are found on digging into it, in the form of bricks and pottery, with cuneiform inscriptions. These two eminences are connected on the western side by a rampart and fosse, which run beyond them, turn towards the east, and circumscribe an area having the form of an oblong square. The rampart is composed of sun-dried bricks and earth, and is covered with grass. It varies in height from ten to twenty feet, has in several places been broken through, while traces of continuity still remain; the whole bearing a striking resemblance to some of the Roman entrenchments which are extant in our own country. The enclosed area is about four miles. In this ready-made entrenchment Nadir Shah encamped his army when he besieged Mosul, pitching his own tent on the mound of Kouyunjik.

Mr. Rich, who four times visited the spot during his stay at Bagdad as the English resident, finally left it in 1820, not much suspecting the treasures which were concealed beneath, and which have been discovered by subsequent research, copiously illustrating the history of Assyria, with the forms, religion, manners and customs of the people. Mr. Ainsworth, succeeding Mr. Rich in his explorations, has done much to identify the site of ancient Nineveh. Every traveller has remarked numerous lonely mounds, with traces of buildings and fragments of pottery, scattered over the country, on the east of the Tigris, extending to some distance beyond Mosul. It now appears that those sites are the ruins of palaces, halls, and temples, containing works of art in remarkable preservation. Through twenty-five centuries, Greek and Roman, Parthian and Persian, Arab and Tartar, have successively trodden them under foot with ignorant indifference, not dreaming of any memorials of powerful kings and a mighty empire below them.

It is easy to explain the origin of these shapeless masses. In a country unprovided with commanding sites, the founders of a palace, citadel, temple, or other public edifice, first laid down a solid compact platform, elevated somewhat to make the structure imposing and strong. The building was erected on this foundation, and consisted of thick walls of sun-dried bricks, lined in the interior with slabs of alabaster, upon which the sculptor exercised his skill. When war or fire desolated the building, the ruins of it remained upon the platform; and the lower parts of the walls, with their sculptures, were buried by the falling in of the upper, and these, with the roof, would be more or less preserved. Under the action of heavy rains, the sun-dried bricks would become a plastic yet compact mass, and would, from age to age, be increased by the dust and sand carried by the winds from the plains, as well as by the decomposition of the thickly growing herbage which covered the site. In this way, doubtless, have arisen the huge mounds of the Assyrian plain.

In addition to those which have been already named, they occur at various and distant points—at Khorsabad, Nimroud, Karamles, Baashićkha, Husseini, Yarumjeh, Karakush, and other places. The two former, with Kouyunjik, have already been explored; and the results have been most remarkable. In the summer of 1843, the French journals announced the success with which some excavations, conducted by M. Botta, had been crowned. To M. Botta belongs the honour of having found the first Assyrian monument. His letters, detailing a series of discoveries, were originally published in *Le Journal Asiatique*, a Paris periodical, exclusively devoted to oriental literature and art. Khorsabad, the scene of his operations, stands on the left bank of the Khauser brook, five caravan hours, or about fourteen miles, north-north-east of Mosul. The name of the village is supposed to be a corrupted form of Khosrauabad, the abode of Khosroes, many villages of the neighbourhood having Persian names from having been formerly under the sway of that power. It occupied a mound, for subsequently the site was purchased, and the dwellings removed to the plain. Beginning at the top of the hill, and sinking a shaft, the workmen at length reached a chamber, the sculptures of which at once declared to the explorer that the history of the ancient empire was beginning to be unfolded. The French government supplied funds, and a succession of chambers was opened, connected by passages, evidently the remains of a building constructed during the time of a rich and powerful monarchy. Slabs of gypsum marble covered the walls, bearing sculptured representations of battles and sieges, victors and vanquished, richly caparisoned war-horses and chariots, with lines of cuneiform inscriptions, so placed as to show that they explained the events depicted. There were many remains of articles in copper, but no trace of iron. The Louvre now contains a large collection of these antiquities; and a magnificent work, "Monumens de Ninève," has been published, which is devoted to their illustration.

The success of the Khorsabad excavations strengthened a desire which had long been entertained by Mr. Layard to open the great mound of Nimroud, situated in a direction opposite to Mosul, or south-south-east, at about eighteen miles distance, and near the Tigris. Embarking in a *kelek* to descend the river, from Mosul, one soon reaches the mound of Yarumjeh, on the left bank, the village, inhabited by Turkomans, occupying its south side. The flood-current of the stream has cut down this mass of mound, leaving it like a precipice, and exposing its artificial construction. Where the soil has been removed by the waters, remains of buildings are exhibited—layers of large stones, with burnt bricks and tiles. The villagers told Mr. Rich, when he was on the spot, that this was the "Pottery of Nineveh." There is near this point a dam of solid masonry, over which the water of the river flows with great impetuosity. At a short distance below this, on the east bank, rises the pyramidal tower of Nimroud, so called after the name of the adjoining village. It occupies the north-west angle of an elongated platform, traces of ruins being observable in various directions. It is 144 feet high, and 127 feet in circumference. The sides are steep, and the top narrow. The platform connected with the pyramid is 1,000 feet in length by 514 feet in breadth.

Mr. Layard commenced his excavations in the autumn of the year 1845. He has since published deeply interesting accounts of the results of his labours, entitled "Nineveh and its Remains." The chambers of vast buildings were successively opened and explored. The walls were of sun-dried brick, encrusted with slabs of gypsum marble, firmly united by plugs of brass or wood, as well as wedge-shaped cramps, like those common in the buildings of ancient Egypt. These were decorated with elaborate sculptures, and inscriptions in the cuneiform character. The bas-reliefs at the south-west palace were in the style of Khorsabad, while particular forms in the characters, observed on the monuments there, occurred here also. War and the chase were portrayed, while winged human-headed bulls and lions and colossal human figures occupied these sculptures. There were many ornaments in copper, ivories carved with various designs and bearing traces of gilding, white alabaster and glass vases, with portions of iron armour, or of iron inlaid with copper. There is a large collection of these interesting remains, with sculptures obtained from Khorsabad, in the British Museum.

On opening the mounds at another point, towards the centre, it was found that that part of the structure was composed of materials which had been removed from some older edifice—many of the slabs had been reduced in size, to make them fit into their new position. Here the excavators came upon more than twenty tombs, containing human remains, as well as vases, beads of glass, agates, and amethysts, with other ornaments in the Egyptian style. Carefully removing these relics, at the depth of five feet below them were the remains of a building with bare walls, the slabs with which it had been decorated having been removed. Many were found lying scattered about without any order,—at one point there were more than a hundred slabs packed in rows as in a stone-cutter's yard. Every slab was sculptured, and the whole were arranged in a regular series, according to the subjects, each of which was continued through several of them. These had been removed from the positions which they had originally occupied, preparatory to their being used in some other place.

At Kouyunjik, where subsequent explorations were conducted, edifices have been found of similar architecture to those at Khorsabad and Nimroud, with the bas-reliefs of warlike and other scenes, but no tombs or sarcophagi. The king whose name has been found here on bricks and slabs, has been ascertained to be a son of the builder of Khorsabad, which throws light upon the relative age of the two places. This same name occurring on tables near Beyrout, at the mouth of the Nahr-el-Kelb, proves that the Assyrian empire extended to the shores of the Mediterranean at the time of the building of the Kouyunjik palaces. Various facts lead to the belief that the edifices at Khorsabad, Kouyunjik, and the south-west palace of Nimroud, belong to the same general epoch; and that the north-west palace at the latter site was founded by an earlier dynasty of kings, itself being posterior to the central building buried beneath sepulchral soil. Moreover, these earlier edifices betray no evidence of having been destroyed by fire, while the plainest signs of conflagration are observable in the south-west palace of Nimroud, at Kouyunjik, and Khorsabad. Thus there have been recovered the remains of imperial structures at three different sites; and the inquiry is natural whether these sites can be supposed to have been included within the limits of one and the same city. It is quite possible to say that they were, without affirming that they were integral parts of ancient Nineveh; for though it undoubtedly occupied the locality of these ruins, and is certainly represented by some of them, we cannot dogmatically define its range with any great amount of preciseness. Yet the evidence favours this special conclusion. Diodorus Siculus says that Nineveh was an immense parallelogram, 150 stadia in length, 90 in breadth, and 480 in circumference—about 60 miles. The prophet Jonah mentions it as a city "of three days' journey"—the day's journey being certainly not less than twenty miles. A line drawn between the four points, Khorsabad, Kouyunjik, Nimroud, and Karamles, the latter a mound of Assyrian ruins, will define a parallelogram, such as corresponds with the form ascribed to Nineveh. The longer sides will measure between them about thirty-six miles, the shorter about twenty-four, the total strikingly according with the 480 stadia, or 60 miles of the historian, and the three days' journey of the prophet. The coincidence of the measurements is worthy of attention, even if it should not warrant confidently the conclusion that these wonderful remains define accurately the locality of the great city.

These sculptured marbles are in every way most remarkable, whether considered as works of art, engraved histories, or corroborations of the truth of Scripture. As embodying the peculiar characteristics of the Shemitic race they are especially valuable. That race delighted in personal ornaments, in wearing earrings and bracelets, in fringed and embroidered robes, long beards, and flowing hair,—a tendency to all this being discernible even now, wherever we have the opportunity of observing it. The Hametic race, on the contrary, as exhibited in the sculptures of Egypt, have short beards, no ear-rings, short robes, and, often, naked bodies. The Japhetic race, as exhibited in the Greek sculptures, show less abundance of ornament, the fringed and embroidered robe and elaborate beard being unknown in the monuments which have come down to us. These marbles are in a state of extraordinary preservation, many of them being as sharp and distinct as if they had just come from the studio of the sculptor. On several of the slabs the appearance of rich colours was distinctly visible when they were discovered; but, with slight exceptions, it perished when they were exposed to the light and air. The skill and the spirit with which the sculptures are executed, together with their anatomical fidelity, as displayed in the human form and in the groups of animals, arrest attention. They are vastly superior in such respects to the monuments of the Pharaohs. Sometimes, indeed, there is little regard paid to the relative proportions of the figures, there is carelessness of the laws of perspective, and other blemishes; but there is an energy in the forms, and a boldness and decision in the grouping, which impart a life-like aspect to the subjects, whether they be sieges, triumphal processions, or hunting scenes. It is a remarkable fact, that of these marbles those which are supposed to be the oldest, are equal in design and execution to such as are later. Ezekiel likened the chosen people in his day to a shameless woman. Speaking of their idolatrous tendencies, and of their admiration of the foreigner, and using that figure, he says:—

> "She doted upon the Assyrians her neighbours,
> Captains and rulers clothed most gorgeously,
> Horsemen riding upon horses,
> All of them desirable young men ——
> —— She saw men portrayed upon the wall,
> The images of the Chaldæans portrayed with vermilion,
> Girded with girdles upon their loins,
> Exceeding in dyed-attiro upon their heads,
> All of them princes to look to."—Ezek. xxiii. 12, 14, 15.

This quite accords with the sculptures of the palaces of Nineveh. The probability is, that the prophet had personal knowledge of what he describes, he being contemporary with the fall of the city, and a captive on the banks of the Khabour, which was not far from it. The images "portrayed with vermilion" are still extant in the sculptured slabs at Khorsabad, Kouyunjik, and Nimroud, on which a red colour was prevalent, sometimes a crimson of great brilliancy. The human figures usually represent a loaded adornment, and the horses exhibit the gay trappings which correspond with the attire of their masters.

Combinations of the human and the animal, as human-headed winged bulls and lions, eagle-headed winged human beings, colossal in their proportions, are among the subjects of these sculptures. There are specimens of all these forms in the Museum. In one there is the compound of a bull, a bird, and a man.

What was meant by such a figure we can only conjecture. The probability is, that such a conception was intended to symbolise certain ideas,—as intelligence by the human face, strength by the body of the bull or the lion, and swiftness by the wings of a bird. Among a superstitious people, such objects may have produced feelings of awe, and served to uphold the prevailing idolatry. One of the monuments from Nimroud is an obelisk, upwards of six feet in height, which was found in a recumbent position. It is composed of black basalt, which is abundant in the mountains of Kurdistan, in the neighbourhood of Jezirah. It bears twenty small bas-reliefs on its four sides, five on each, they being in very good preservation. A king is represented, followed by his attendants; a prisoner is at his feet; his vizier and eunuchs introduce men leading various animals, and bearing different kinds of tribute. The animals represented are the elephant, the rhinoceros, the Bactrian or double-humped camel, the wild bull, the lion, the stag, and different kinds of monkeys. The tribute-bearers carry elephants' tusks, shawls, vases of precious metals, fruit, bars of metal, and bundles of rare woods. Above, below, and between the sculptured figures is an inscription, consisting of two hundred and ten lines, the characters of which are as sharp and well-defined as if they had been but recently executed. This obelisk is evidently a memorial of conquest, and, according to Sir Henry Rawlinson, who has given a translation of the inscription, it commemorates the victories of Teman-bar II. The translation says,—being close to the original,—

"I took the city; I assembled my chiefs; I founded palaces, cities, and temples; I shut him up; I took eleven great cities; twenty thousand five hundred of their men I slew in battle, or carried into slavery; their leaders, their captains, and their men of war, I put into chains; Ahuni, with his gods, and his chief priests, his horses, his sons, and his daughters, and all his men-of-war, I brought away to my country of Assyria; I put Sut-bel-harel in chains; I condemned him and his chief followers to slavery; I took the city of Amia, the capital of the country; and I gave up to pillage a hundred of the dependent towns; I slew the wicked; I carried off the treasures."

Among the sculptures war-scenes are of the most frequent occurrence. The king and his army crossing a river, horses swimming, and men on inflated skins; the king followed by warriors, in battle with his enemies under the walls of a hostile castle; the siege of a castle, with a battering-ram and movable tower; charioteers returning in triumph from battle; enemies in flight along the banks of a lake or river. These are some of the subjects represented. The cavalry are shown armed with swords, spears, and other weapons. Upon the bas-reliefs from Kouyunjik, there are castles depicted with shields hung round the walls, in illustration of some of the allusions of the prophets. The ferocious character of the people is to be seen in these monuments. Butchery, preceded by torture or slavery, was the fate of prisoners of war. Soldiers are shown impaling captives, mangling the bodies of the slain, and bearing away heads that have been severed from their bodies. Eunuchs appear with scrolls, recording the number of heads that lie at their feet. The prophet Amos uses a most remarkable metaphor when he says,—

> "The Lord God hath sworn by his holiness,
> That, lo, the days shall come upon you,
> That he will take you away with hooks,
> And your posterity with fish-hooks."—Amos iv. 2.

On a bas-relief from Khorsabad, captives are represented as led by a rope fastened to rings passed through the lip and nose. There is by these means a new and valuable light thrown upon the sacred writings, illustrating their claims to reverence; while at the same time, extinct races are disentombed in their history and peculiarities, the past and the present generations of men being brought together in a manner which is most suggestive and impressive.

Before we leave this department of our subject, it may be proper to state a few particulars respecting the great river of Nineveh, to which as yet we have only incidentally alluded.

The *Tigris* rises in Central Armenia, on the southern slope of the Anti-Taurus, which forms the water-shed between its tributaries and those which ascend on the northern slope to the Murad branch of the Euphrates. The western and principal source is situated to the south of the Ghuiljik, or "little" lake, a beautiful fresh-water expanse, also, from its colour, bearing the name of Geukchch, or "sky-blue." The stream flows in a deep valley, through a region of grand and rugged highlands, to the mines of Arghana, a wild site to which the mineral wealth to be obtained from the mountains has drawn a population of Turks, Greeks, and Armenians. Arghana itself is a small dilapidated town, near the west bank of the Tigris, and at some distance from the mines, which, at Magharat, the principal one, carry numerous galleries into the rock. Great quantities of copper ore are produced, which is sent to Tokat to be smelted. Below Arghana the river, swollen by affluents from the mountains, finds its way across a table-land, 2,000 feet above the level of the sea, a space capable of high cultivation, but almost entirely uncared for. On passing across it in 1835 to Diarbekr, a route of nearly forty miles, Mr. Brant did not see a single village, and only some fields of wheat and millet belonging to an encampment of Kurds.

Diarbekr, "the tents or dwellings of Bekir," stands on the right bank of the river, at some little distance from it. Formerly it contained 40,000 houses or families, and had numerous cotton looms constantly at work; but the revolt and depredations of the Kurdish tribes in the vicinity, in the early part of the present century, put a stop to its prosperity. Since the re-establishment of the Ottoman authority, the condition of the city has not much improved. Turks and Armenians form the chief part of the population, which is supposed to be about forty thousand. Here are the ruins of a citadel, many baths and caravanseries, fifteen mosques with minarets, numerous mesjids with domes, and a few churches belonging to the various Christian sects. The Christians have been severely persecuted and oppressed. More recently, there has been some show of toleration towards them; but there is more pretence than reality. It is long before bigotry and superstition wear themselves out, and allow of a better state of things. When Mr. Fletcher visited those parts, in 1843, he was informed by the Jacobite bishop, Mar Athanasius, formerly known in London and Cambridge, that the Christians were required to wear dresses of a particular colour, and were forbidden to ride on horseback, and had to submit to many marks of indignity that they might so be known to the whole community, and treated accordingly. The finest remnant of antiquity in the place, the great mosque, was once a Christian church, probably the cathedral of ancient Amida,—the square tower being now used as a minaret. Relics of the distant past are few. Occasionally, the capital of a Doric column may be seen, or a tablet with an inscription half erased. A defaced inscription at one of the gates commemorates the emperors Valentinian, Valens, and Gratian, as benefactors to the town. As the Amida of the Romans, the history of the city is a most eventful one. It was strong by means of its natural position, and the Emperor Constantine had it further defended by the addition of walls and towers. It was besieged in the great invasion by Sapor, A.D. 359, and was captured after a prolonged and most heroic resistance, and those of the people—soldiers and citizens, with their wives and children—who failed to escape through the gates opposite to those by which the conqueror entered, were subjected to an indiscriminate slaughter. When Nisibin was ceded to the Persians a few years afterwards, many of its citizens, compelled to seek a new home, found shelter at Amida, and helped to restore it to its former importance. In the time of the younger Theodosius, the history of the city was signalised by a great and generous act performed by its bishop, Acacius. Vases of gold and silver, he said, were unmeaning as offerings to the Divine Being; he therefore sold the plate of his metropolitan church, and with the money redeemed seven thousand Persian captives, abundantly supplied their wants, and dismissed them to their native country to inform the king that this was the true spirit of that religion to which he was an enemy. By a variety of adverse circumstances, in the course of many years, it was captured by Selim, the first Sultan of the Osmanlee, A.D. 1515; and, considering all the vicissitudes from which it has suffered, no surprise need be felt that Amida the black, the modern Diarbekr, should exhibit few traces of its ancient greatness.

The Tigris at this point has a breadth of about 750 feet in the flood season, but it is not used for any other purpose than occasionally to bring down the floats of timber from the mountains. It flows in a direction nearly due east, sometimes having a rapid descent.

While maintaining this course it is joined by the eastern or second great branch of the river. Still lower it is further increased in volume by other two affluents. The Betlis-su, one of them, rises at a short distance from Lake Van, and descends to the town of Betlis, which is 5,156 feet above the sea. The population consists of 2,000 Mohammedan, and 1,000 Armenian families. There are three mosques with minarets, large and well-stocked bazaars, and khans for the accommodation of foreign traders, who bring British calicoes and woollens, East Indian indigo, and Mocha coffee, to this secluded spot. This celebrated country is covered in winter with immense quantities of snow, the melting of which swells the torrents, and contributes to the annual rise of the Tigris. Fenik, a small town still lower down, is surrounded with ruins, the remains of an ancient town. Near it are mines of copper and iron, and lead, in the mountains. Layard visited a disused copper mine, nearly blocked up with earth and rubbish, and known only to a few mountaineers. He found the metal occurring in veins, small crystals, compact masses and in powder, and recognised in the powder the material used to colour the bricks and ornaments in the Assyrian palaces. There are many Kurdish villages with rude forts on the cliffs behind them. There are large and luxuriant gardens, and the whole scenery is beautiful and picturesque. The next place of interest on the river is Jezireh-ibn-Omar, or the island of the sons of Omar, which is formed by the main stream and a small arm detached from it, which returns to a junction. The island, which is about two miles and a half in circumference, was formerly the site of the Roman municipality of Bezabde, surrendered to the Persians after the death of the Emperor Julian. It is now in utter ruin and desolation. Immense tracts of uncultivated meadow land, watered by many streams, and occupied only by migratory hordes, mark the course of the river from Jezireh to Mosul, between which places it receives on the left bank, the Khabour, a far inferior stream to the affluent of the same name belonging to the Euphrates.

Mosul is a walled city, with eight gates, and about forty thousand inhabitants. It is the centre of a considerable caravan trade, and the seat of a pasha, who, though of the second rank, receives investiture of office immediately from the Sultan, and is therefore independent of the great pashas of Bagdad and Erzeroum. It stands on the western side of the Tigris, but has no interest apart from its position, contiguous as it is to the site of the once mighty Nineveh, in the country on the opposite bank. In ancient times it was a celebrated commercial mart, and had some important manufactures. Those textile fabrics which first received the name of muslins, including gold tissues, silks, as well as fine cottons, were so called, either from their being made at Mosul in great perfection, or because they held a prominent place in its commerce. Marco Polo, who was there in the thirteenth century, says, that "all the cloths of silk and gold which are called *mosulin*," are the produce of Mosul; but he also denominates the great merchants of the city *Mosulin*, who imported Indian goods. Orientalists identify the name of the place with the Arabic *Mausel*, signifying "connection," an allusion to its bridge of boats. The present bridge consists of 21 rude boats, fastened together with iron chains, planks being laid from boat to boat, and the whole covered with earth. It crosses the river where the channel is narrow, but very deep, being as much as 50 feet at the middle of the stream. When the water is low the breadth is only about 300 feet, but during the flood in spring and early summer, it expands to 1,000 feet or more, and forms a noble current, flowing with great impetuosity.

Mr. George Smith, of the British Museum, who has profitably contributed to the explanation of ancient inscriptions, is at present making explorations among the Assyrian ruins, and he telegraphs from Mosul that he has had very gratifying success on the banks of the Tigris and the Euphrates. He has obtained a large number of inscriptions and tablets. One of them has reference to Merodach-Baladin, King of Babylon, and others are contemporaneous and historical memorials of Esarhaddon, Nebuchadnezzar, and Darius. At Nimroud he has explored the north-west palace of Esarhaddon, the temple of Nebo, and some portions of the south-east palace. He has also discovered a perfectly new text of the annals of Tiglath-pileser.

The origin of Mosul is involved in obscurity. It was known by its present name under the Caliphs; and was visited by Benjamin of Tudela in the twelfth century, who described it as of great extent and very ancient, "mentioned in Scripture as Ashur the Great," which it was supposed partly to represent. At that date it was an independent sovereignty. It fell into the hands of Ghengiz Khan, in 1256, the Tigris having been made red with the blood of the inhabitants, and at the close of the fourteenth century it was ravaged by Tamerlane.

The predominating formation in the neighbourhood is alabaster, commonly called Mosul marble. The remains of Nineveh show slabs of this material lining the interior walls, bearing the records of victories and triumphs in sculptures and inscriptions. Opposite the city, a small rivulet, called the Khauser, joins the river. It flows between the two mounds of Kouyunjik and Nebi Yunus, remarkable objects as seen from Mosul, and till lately deemed the only monuments of Nineveh. At a short distance from the springs of the Khauser, near Khorsabad, there are two remarkable localities, contiguous to each other, Rabban Hormuzd and Elkosh. Rabban Hormuzd was formerly an establishment of pure Chaldæans, but is now a Roman Catholic monastery. It is approached by a narrow opening or defile in the limestone mountains, which opening widens into a vast amphitheatre. The church is a heavy, square building, of a dusky red colour. The surrounding rocks are honey-combed with caves and grottoes of artificial construction, which, in ancient times, were probably the abodes of the dead. In these cells the few monks reside, but there are many more of them tenantless. The place is said to date from the fourth century. The market town of Elkosh, called the *Kabash*, is a little to the west, and is likewise under the dominion of the Roman Catholic faith. The prophet Nahum resided and was buried here. There are now no Jews in the place; but there are the remains of a synagogue, which contains the supposed tomb of the prophet, and many pilgrimages have been made to it by Jews from a remote period. The same connection with the prophet, however, is claimed for a place of a similar name in Palestine. But Nahum styles himself the "Elkoshite," in the introduction to his prophecies, which were written after the captivity of the ten tribes; and the fact that his predictions apply exclusively to the Assyrian capital, taken in connection with the tradition of the Assyrian Jews, may be regarded as of weight in favour of the Assyrian Elkosh.

Descending the river, the region between the point just mentioned and Bagdad, a distance of more than 200 miles, following the course of the stream, there are some ancient remains of interest on the right bank, with important tributaries entering on the left. The Greater Zab, which marks the southern extremity of the pashalic of Mosul on the eastern side, joins the river about twelve miles below the celebrated dyke of

Aawaze, and enters it by two mouths; its clear blue waters boiling up at the confluence, repulsing the muddy tide of the Tigris. This stream is the Zabetus of Xenophon, and the Lycus of ancient geography. The Zab flows through the heart of the Chaldæan territory. The Christians have, at different times, suffered much persecution in these parts. Mr. Ainsworth, in 1840, visited one of the villages, Lizan, and found it in itself beautiful and interesting, but with sad traces of the relentless cruelty of the Kurds towards the Christians. Layard visited the same spot in 1846, there having been much cruelty and bloodshed in the interval. He says, "We reached the village through scenery of extraordinary beauty and grandeur, but exhibiting on every hand memorials of dreadful outrage. I need not," he remarks, "weary or distress the reader with a description of desolation and misery hardly concealed by the most luxuriant vegetation. We rode to the graveyard of a roofless church, slowly rising from its ruins—the first edifice in the village to be rebuilt. We spread our carpets among the tombs, for as yet there were no habitable houses. The Melek, with the few who had survived the massacre, was living during the day under the trees, and sleeping at night on stages of grass and boughs, raised on high poles, fixed in the very bed of the Zab." Upon the approach of the Kurds the inhabitants of Lizan and of the adjoining villages, hastily collected a few movables, and fled to a rocky ledge in the mountains, almost inaccessible, hoping to escape observation, or, if not. to maintain the post. Men, women, and young children, were here crowded together, on ground which even the chamois could scarcely reach. But, their retreat being discovered, the Kurds resolved to blockade the place, and to wait the slow but sure working of the effects of famine. Reduced to extreme distress, the unfortunate people offered to capitulate and to surrender their arms and property on terms to which the enemy acceded, and even ratified the agreement with an oath on the Koran. The Kurds having been admitted to the stronghold, the Christians delivered up their weapons, upon which the treacherous Moslems began the work of massacre, until, weary of the toil, they hurled the survivors over the precipice into the Zab. When Layard visited the spot, many melancholy signs of the catastrophe were apparent. There were skeletons almost entire, and heaps of blanched bones intermingled with shreds of discoloured linen, and the long plaited tresses of women's hair. The bridge of Lizan was the scene of a most affecting part of the tragedy. Upon ten Chaldæan girls being led across it, doomed to slavery, they threw themselves into the river and perished in its waters.

There is a stronghold of the Kurds, Rowandiz, just before emerging from the mountain region. It contains about one thousand three hundred houses, and is defended by a wall with round towers. To the eastward of the town there is a mountain which rises to the height of 10,568 feet. The Zab is shortly after this increased by the Khazir, or ancient Bumadus, below which it joins the Tigris, which, at the low season, is here 400 feet wide at the narrowest point, and from 12 to 18 feet deep, with occasionally occurring shallows. The banks of the river in this vicinity have been the fields of ancient sanguinary battles, and have oftener than once witnessed the fall and rise of great empires. Wild animals are numerous in such a scene, which affords them all suitable shelter. Wild boars, wolves, jackals, hares, and foxes abound.

Enclosed by the jungle, but conspicuous from a distance, is one of the greatest monuments of ancient Assyria, on the right bank of the Tigris, directly washed by its waters. The Arabs call it Kalah Sherghat, which signifies the "castle of the earth." It has a circumference of more than 4,685 yards. Its height is about sixty feet. When Mr. Layard commenced excavations here, his workmen ere long uncovered a sitting figure in black basalt of the size of life, but much mutilated, with inscriptions on three sides. It is no doubt the monument of a sovereign, and here must certainly have stood a great Assyrian city. Westward, about twenty-eight miles from the Tigris, are the ruins of Al Hadhr, the Atra of the Roman campaigns. They form nearly a perfect circle, surrounded by a wall of great thickness, which is more than three miles in circumference, with many ruined bastions at irregular intervals. Outside the wall is a broad ditch, now dry, with a thick rampart. The space inside is everywhere covered with ruins of buildings, public edifices and tombs. Near the centre are the remains of what must have been a palace, a temple, or a citadel, of great extent, and, in the perfection of its style, of surpassing grandeur. Only the ground story remains perfect, and it consists of a series of vaulted chambers or halls, of different sizes, all of them opening to the rising sun, and regularly succeeding one another from north to south. There are many inscriptions, generally of one or two inches in size, either a Chaldaic letter, a numeral, or an astronomical sign. The mirror and handle, emblematic of the planet Venus, are very common. In the chambers there are various sculptures, as human busts carved in high relief, figures of females apparently in the air, having loose flying robes, griffins, serpents, and other animals—the style of the carving seeming to indicate the peculiarities of Greek or Roman art. Dr. Ross was the first of our countrymen to visit this spot, which he did in 1836. As he approached the ruins, a thick black cloud behind him was darting out vivid flashes of lightning, followed by peals of thunder. The Bedouin who attended him shook his head, saying: "I do not like this, sir; we should not have come here; this ground belongs to Iblis." Mr. Layard also visited these ruins in 1846, and was in like manner caught in a thunderstorm. He says: "It was a fit moment to enter ruins like these."

About sixty miles below the mouth of the Greater Zab, the Tigris is entered by the Lesser Zab, which follows a course somewhat parallel to that of its namesake. This stream is the Caprus of antiquity, and has its source on the south-west of the lake of Urumiah. Soon afterwards, the Hamran hills abut upon the Tigris. The river forces its way through them, by the pass of El Fatthha, which means "an opening." It is here four hundred and fifty feet broad. Sulphur and naphtha are found in this locality in large quantities. Having cleared the pass, the river again expands into a noble stream, and flows by Tekrit, an impoverished place, surrounded by extensive ruins, the remains of former greatness—the city having been laid waste by Tamerlane. Below it, on the opposite side is the town of Dur. This place is no doubt the Dura of ancient history. But the distance from Babylon is fatal to the supposition that it is the Dura on whose plain Nebuchadnezzar set up his great golden image. Before reaching Bagdad, a traveller must pass through a country covered with the ruins of forts, cities, deserted canals, and decayed villages. There is a town of considerable extent in the mountains, near which there are fountains of liquid naphtha. They are usually about three feet each in diameter, and some of them eight or ten feet deep. The naphtha is perfectly black, liquid, and in quantity inexhaustible.

BAGDAD stands on both banks of the Tigris, and is surrounded by a high wall of brick and earth, with round towers at intervals. The circuit of the walls, including both sides of the stream, is about five miles. There are six gates on the land side, three in each division; and in addition the Gate of Talisman, the largest and most imposing, through which the Sultan Amurath IV. entered when he captured the city, and which, according to an Oriental custom, was then built up, and has ever since remained closed. Seen from a distance, the appearance of the city is pleasing, surrounded as it is with groves of trees, with lofty minarets and beautifully shaped domes rising above them. In its interior the town is mean. It presents a series of narrow streets, a kind of necessity in Eastern cities, affording shade to the passenger from the sunbeams; but it is mainly a labyrinth of crooked lanes and alleys. The streets are unpaved, full of inequalities from accumulated rubbish, and rendered noxious by the filth and offal cast into them, which a tribe of half-savage dogs, without owners, alone clear away. The public buildings include a few imposing mosques, extensive khans and bazaars, the latter well stocked with merchandise, but frequently ruinous, and without any pretensions to architectural distinction. There are also open spaces, devoted to the sale of particular kinds of goods, and named after them, as the "thread market," the "muslin market," and the "corn market." The ancient glory of this renowned capital is gone. There are still traces of it, it is true, but one looks in vain for the realisation of his previous conceptions of the times of Haroun al Raschid. The palace of the Caliphs is no more—even the site of it is unknown. The proud temples of former days, with the far-famed seats of learning, have either entirely vanished or remain in great decay, and in some instances are devoted to other purposes. For example, even the celebrated *Medresseh*, or college, founded in the thirteenth century, by the Caliph Moostanser, although it still exists as a building at the eastern extremity of the bridge across the Tigris, is partly transformed into a khan, and partly into a customhouse.

The two divisions of the city are connected by a bridge of boats, which vary in number according to the state of the river. The surface of the water is covered with crowds of keleks, coracles, rafts, and various kinds of craft, engaged in passenger and goods traffic, which, with the constant throng upon the bridge in the day-time, give a very animated aspect to the stream. In the east, it is a favourite tradition that the spot selected for the building of the city formerly belonged to a celebrated Christian hermit, whose name is given to the place, Bag-Dad, "the garden of Dad." It was founded by Almansor, the second Caliph of the race of Abbas, in the year of the Hegira 140, or A.D. 763, the materials being obtained from the remains of Ctesiphon and Seleucia. At first it occupied only the western side of the river; but the renowned Haroun al Raschid adorned it with many noble and stately edifices, and built also on the eastern bank. Through five centuries the capital continued to flourish and increase, but was captured by Tamerlane in 1393. The city was afterwards the object of perpetual contest between the Turks and Persians, and was finally reduced by Amurath IV., at the head of an army of three hundred thousand men, in A.D. 1638. He signalised his conquest by causing the greater part of the population to be slain by torchlight on the night of the surrender, although they capitulated expressly on condition that life and property should be spared.

In later years the city has endured much adversity. In 1830, under the government of Daoud Pasha, the population is supposed to have numbered about 110,000; but, in the year following, the triple calamity of pestilence, flood, and famine swept off more than two-thirds of the inhabitants, and converted the place into a vast sepulchre. The city has not recovered from these terrible visitations, and even now it scarcely numbers half the population which it contained before their occurrence. In connection with the plague especially there were most harrowing scenes; but all three evils were most disastrous. In its best days the city had a population of 2,000,000. Its chief manufactures at present are red and yellow leather—much esteemed—and silk, cotton, and woollen cloths. It supplies Asia Minor, Syria, and a part of Europe with East Indian goods, which are carried to Bassora, and by the Tigris in boats, and by caravans to Tokat, Constantinople,

Aleppo, Damascus, and the western parts of Persia. There is also some trade in jewels.

Leaving Bagdad, a course of more than twenty miles brings the Tigris to the mouth of the Diyalah, one of its largest affluents. It is formed by the union of the Shirwan and Holwan rivers. On the lower part of the Shirwan there appears to have been formerly a city of the same name. The Holwan rises on the western slope of the Zagros mountains, about eight miles to the north of "the gates of Zagros," a pass so called, through which runs the great caravan road, which connects Bagdad with Hamadan and Central Persia, and anciently a line of communication between Assyria and Media. Holwan was a great city, which gave its name to the river. There are still sculptured remains of it. Jewish traditions abound in this part of the country, and David is still regarded by the tribes as their great tutelar prophet. They are now generally Mahometans however. A few miles further down the Holwan receives the Deira, which is crossed by several bridges, and spanned near the point of junction by a natural arch of rock, which bears the expressive name of Puli-Khuda, or "God's bridge."

Beyond the mouth of the Diyalah, the Tigris washes the sites of two renowned cities of the ancient world, opposite to each other, Seleucia on the right bank, and Ctesiphon on the left. Seleucia was founded by Seleucus Nicanor, who, on the partition of the empire of Alexander, succeeded to the sovereignty of the greater part of his Asiatic conquests. But the city, which was built principally from the ruins of Babylon, flourished long after the fall of the empire of the Seleucidæ. It became like Venice in the Middle Ages, the seat of a powerful independent republic. The citizens numbered 600,000, over whom presided a senate of 600 nobles, distinguished by their love of freedom. But internal division arose among the people, and involved them in destruction. The opposite bank of the Tigris had frequently been the camping ground of the warlike and nomadic Parthian kings, and it became the site of a permanent settlement. This advanced from a mere village to the rank of a capital. This was the origin of Ctesiphon, which, profiting by the party factions of its neighbour, became the superior of the two, and a bridge across the river connected the two quarters of one great city. There is nothing left on the site of the once populous Seleucia to indicate its former magnificence. On the opposite bank, the site of Ctesiphon, the wrecks of remote antiquity are prominent, the stupendous Tank e Kesra, or "Arch of Khoosroo," silently proclaiming the majesty of the edifices it has survived. This great fragment of the past is probably the façade of a large structure composed of two wings, with an immense arched hall in the centre. It is in a state of marvellous preservation, and is of these dimensions: Length of the front of the building, 284 feet; width of the arch at the base, 82 feet; height of the arch, 101 feet;

thickness of the wall at the base, 19 feet; and depth or length of the hall, 153 feet.

The Euphrates and Tigris now shortly merge their waters in the one tidal channel known by the name of the Shat-el-Arab, which generally follows a straight course from Kornah, the point of junction, to the Persian Gulf. It is increased by the Kerrah and the Karoon as affluents, and over the whole space which it traverses the ground is strewed with the remains of ancient times. At Bisitun there are some ruins, with inscriptions of a deeply interesting character. And not far from the Kerrah is the site of the ancient Susa, or Shushan of Scripture, represented by the vast and desolate mounds of Sus. It was here that the remarkable events recorded in the Book of Esther occurred. The mounds occupy an immense space, extending not less than twelve miles from one extremity to the other. The early course of the Karoon lies through a mountainous country. It is a noble stream, but there is not much matter of historical interest presented on its banks, except at Bassora, founded in the year A.D. 636, and which commands an extensive navigation. Thus augmented by large affluents the Shat-el-Arab finds its way to the ocean. No rivers in the world have gathered around them greater interest than these, and it is deeply saddening to find along their whole course principally the mementoes of a greatness which is past.

CHAPTER III.

TURKEY IN ASIA.—(Continued.)

KURDISTAN forms the north-eastern portion of ancient Assyria, and extends also into Persia. It is an immense succession of hill and valley, with dells and plains of exhaustless fertility, and having many towering mountains. The summits of the great range of Zagros rise to upwards of 14,000 feet. Their ridges are clothed with forests as far up as 6,000 feet; above that height the country is less covered, though in some of the recesses there are forests even in the more elevated parts. The climate is cold during the greater part of the year; and the hills are covered with snow for eight months.

Taurus, in its progress westward from the Euphrates, sends out several spurs into Syria, the principal and most westerly of which bears the names of Alma-dagh and Jawur-dagh, the ancient *Amanus* and *Pierius*, which terminate near the mouth of the Orontes, and form the boundary between Syria and Asia Minor. On the south side of the mouth of the Orontes, is Jebel el-Akral (Bald-hill), which rises abruptly to the height of 5,318 feet, and is continued to the east by Jebel Chaksinah, and the hills of Antioch, as far as to the southern valley of the Orontes. To the south the hills of Antioch are continued by the Jebel Kraad to the Nosairi mountains, which extend southwards in connection with Lebanon. About 34° N. lat. the chain divides into two parts, the eastern and the western; the former being the Libanus, and the latter the Anti-Libanus of the Greeks, which enclose between them the long narrow valley of *El Bakaa*, or Hollow Syria. The western branch terminates near the seacoast, to the southward of Sidon; while the eastern branch, in nearly the same parallel, divides again into two ridges, the one of which passes into Arabia, along the eastern side of the valley of the Jordan. The other extends along the western side of the Jordan, southwards, forming the water-shed between the basin of the Dead Sea, and the valleys which send their waters to the Mediterranean. Mount Carmel forms a bold promontory on the south-western side of the Bay of Acre, and has an extension south-eastwards till it joins the mountains of Judea. The diverging range of the Libanus, which forms the north-eastern part of the valley of the Upper Jordan, was the Hermon of Scripture; and farther south were the mountains of Gilead. These mountains form many valleys, most of which extend north and south; but in addition to these there are transverse valleys, the chief of which run parallel with the sea-coast and also into the interior. El Bekaa (the Κοιλα Συρια, *Koile Suria* of the Greeks, *Coclé Syria* of the Latins), is a beautiful valley between the two branches of Lebanon. It is about ninety miles in length by eleven of average breadth, and is remarkably rich and beautiful. The valley of the Jordan extends about a hundred and seventy-five miles from the sources of the river to the southern extremity of the Dead Sea. From the Lake of Tabariah to Aïn-el-Arus, twelve miles south of the Dead Sea, where it meets the Wadi-el-Arabah, it is called *El-Ghor*. On the east side of the valley, between the two lakes, the mountains rise almost precipitously from the river, but on the west there is a narrow strip of land of singular fertility. To the north of the Dead Sea, the country opens into the plain of Jericho, eighteen miles in length by seven in breadth, surrounded by an amphitheatre of hills, which concentrate the rays of the sun, making it very hot and parched. Still it produces good crops of wheat, barley, and balm. The valley of the Jordan is considerably below the level of the Mediterranean—how far has not been ascertained. The valleys of Galilee are usually small, but beautiful, with an abundance of wooding. Between Galilee and Mount Carmel is the great plain of Esdraelon, which extends from the Bay of Acre to the south-east. It is watered by the river Kishon. In Scripture it is called the valley of Jezreel or Megiddo. It is very fertile, well adapted for corn, but is uncultivated, and merely affords pasture for a few scattered herds. The plain of Haouran lies to the south of Damascus, between Hermon and Gilead and the Jebel Haouran. It is famous for wheat, and contains many scattered hummocks, which are the sites of villages. The whole of these hummocks, as well as the round stones found in the fields, and also the mountain of Haouran, consist of black basalt. All the houses are built of this stone, and present rather a sombre appearance. The inhabitants are Turks, Druses, and Arabs. Sometimes in spring and summer the locality is visited by parties of Bedouins. The whole of the rocky wilderness, comprehending the uneven country which extends along the eastern side of the plain of Haouran, from near Damascus to Bozra, is called El Ludja, and the Jebel Haouran, and is supposed to be the ancient *Trachonitis*. The plain of Haouran itself is the ancient *Auranitis*.

It would be wrong to conceive of the Great Syrian desert as a bare waste of sand. Generally it has a fine black soil, which is covered in winter with long grass and herbs, and peopled with antelopes, wild asses, and boars. In summer the grass is burnt up, and the animals which had occupied it are compelled to take refuge on the borders of the cultivated country. It is true there are sandy tracts in the interior, but even in the midst of them, at various points, there is a scanty herbage. There are numerous hills all along Syria, which divide the country into small plains. Eastward of Palmyra, the desert presents a surface of unbounded level as far as the eye can reach. In summer the soil is parched, and the vegetation is destroyed; but when the winter rains commence the herbage shoots up with amazing rapidity and luxuriance. The herds and flocks feed on the dry herbage in summer, and have to be congregated near pools and wells; but in winter the Bedouins make long journeys with their flocks, there being abundance of food for them everywhere. The Arabs of the desert belong to the great Aenezé tribe. During the former Turkish dominion in Syria they were quite independent; but under the later rule they have been obliged to acknowledge the supremacy of the Pasha, and even to pay him tribute.

There are three climates in Syria. The summits of Lebanon are generally covered with snow, which diffuses coolness over the interior, while the low-lying sea-coasts are subject to heat and moisture, and the eastern lowland adjoining Arabia is exposed to a dry and scorching heat. The seasons and the productions consequently vary. In the mountains, the winter lasts from November to March, and is sharp and rigorous. No year passes without falls of snow, which, for months together, often cover the ground to the depth of several feet. The spring and autumn are agreeable, and the summer is not oppressive. But in the plains, when the sun has passed to the north of the equator, a sudden change takes place which lasts till October. The heat is overpowering. But the winter is so temperate that orange trees, dates, bananas, and other delicate fruits grow in the open field. Sometimes it seems as if a few hours were sufficient to produce the change from spring to winter. If art were called in to give its help to nature, there might be brought together, within the space of fifty miles, in Syria, the vegetable treasures of the most distant countries. Wheat, rye, barley, beans, and cotton are cultivated everywhere. The hills of Latakia, and indeed all the mountains, produce tobacco. The white mulberry thrives on Lebanon and along the coast, and forms the wealth of the Druses on account of the beautiful silk produced by its worms; and the vine, raised on poles or creeping, furnishes red and white wines equal to those of Bordeaux. The clusters are remarkably large, and the grapes are often the size of plums. The mountains which diverge from Taurus, in Northern Syria, are richly wooded. There are all the kinds of domestic animals possessed in Europe, with the buffalo and camel in addition. The gazelle takes the place of our deer; and instead of wolves there are jackals, hyænas, and ounces. The locust is the great scourge of these countries. They come in clouds which darken the sky, and when they descend every particle of vegetation is consumed. The evil is mitigated only by means of a bird called samarmar, which devours them, and by the south-east winds, which drive them into the Mediterranean.

Palestine is well known from its associations with

the chosen people and the history of the Divine revelations to men. The name is supposed to be derived from the ancient Philistine coast, and has been used from the most remote ages to the present time. The country is about 170 miles in length, north and south, and nearly as much in extreme breadth. It is bounded on the west by the Mediterranean. On the north it ranges along the southern skirts of Libanus; and on the east and south it passes into the Arabian desert, amid long ranges of rocky hills. Judea is a high country, rising from a shore that is in many places bold and lofty. The principal eminences—Carmel, Bashan, and Tabor—do not rise into bleak and rugged peaks, but are covered with villages, rich pastures, and luxuriant woods. On their slopes are vineyards, and in the clefts of the rocks numerous bees deposit their honey. There are still many traces of former occupation and cultivation, in the form of such artificial terraces as are yet to be found in the most advanced parts of the East. But there has been here a busy work of rapine and oppression, extending farther than in many other parts of the Turkish dominion. Acre, under the sway of Daher, of Omar, and of Djezzar, scarcely paid even a nominal submission to the mandates of the Porte. The first-mentioned of these had great qualities; but Djezzar converted all the countries over which he tyrannized into deserts. But a line drawn from north to south, through Judea, attaches a large portion of the territory to the pashalic of Damascus, which has long been perhaps the best-governed part of the Turkish empire. Within these limits, reaching from the Sea of Galilee through Napolose, to the vicinity of Jerusalem, the region displays much of its ancient fertility. Even the declivities of the mountains are forced into terraces, that they may retain the moisture, and be fit for bearing ample crops. But the country is infested by bands of Arabs. Similar to this is the condition of the whole territory. Judea in its largest sense was divided into maritime and inland, and again subdivided into Judea on this side, and Judea beyond Jordan. The most notable division is that which was made among the twelve tribes, by lot, under the Divine superintendence. Of these two and a half were allotted their portion beyond Jordan, and the rest on this side. Solomon divided the kingdom into twelve provinces or districts, each of which was to supply his household for a month, in turn, *i.e.*, each for one month in the year. But another and most fatal division was occasioned by Rehoboam, the son of Solomon, when ten of the twelve tribes revolted, and formed the kingdom of Israel in opposition to that of Judea. The kingdom of Israel took also the name of Samaria from its capital. Under the Romans it began to be divided into tetrarchies and toparchies. The larger were those of Judea, Samaria, and Galilee, Upper and Lower; the lesser were those of Gilead, Peraea, Gaulonitis, Auranitis, Batanæa, and Decapolis.

The extent of this country is variously stated. It

may be taken as 170 or 180 miles from north to south, and 140 in breadth where broadest, though not much more than half of that measurement where it is narrowest. It is partly in the pashalic of Acre and partly in that of Damascus, as we have just observed; but, although the ancient pashalic boundaries are respected, there is one ruler, one pasha, at present in charge of the three divisions of Damascus, Aleppo, and Acre.

Reaching this country by sea, the usual port is Jaffa, the ancient *Joppa*, the only point of communication which David and Solomon had with the Mediterranean. At present this is a bad haven, being so encumbered with rocks and shoals that vessels can anchor only at the distance of a mile from the shore. But there is an ancient harbour, now choked up, which might be made to contain ships of 300 tons. Great antiquity is ascribed to this port, which gives access to the Holy Land. In the middle ages it rose into fame as the landing-place of the great crusade under Richard Cœur de Lion and Philip of France. Jaffa continued to be the head-quarters of the Christians in that celebrated campaign; and to the south extends the wide field of Ascalon, where the arms of the Crescent sustained so signal an overthrow. Bonaparte captured the place, and there was afterwards a cruel massacre of the prisoners found there. The traveller from Europe, arriving at Jaffa, with the design of exploring Palestine, hastens on his way. He passes by the vale of Sharon, still beautiful, and at the foot of the dark hills which form the centre of the country, he reaches Rama or Ramla, the ancient Arimathea. He then arrives at Lydda, and onwards, till the exclamation is made, "El Kods!" (the holy city). But we must enter into details, and speaking generally of the territory of Turkey in Asia, refer to this as a part.

In Asiatic Turkey there are various *Gulfs*, inlets and natural harbours, which, from the ocean indent themselves into the land, and furnish the means of intercourse and trade. In the Black Sea, the Gulfs of Samsoun and Sinub or Sinope; in the Sea of Marmora, the Gulfs of Is-mid and Mondania; in the Archipelago, the Gulfs of Besiche or Besika, near the entrance of the Dardanelles,—Adramyti, Sandarli, Smyrna, Vourla, Scala-nova, Asyn-Kalesi, Cos, Symi; in the Mediterranean, the Gulfs of Marmorici, Macri, Satalia or Sadalia, Iskenderoon or Scanderoon, and the Bay of Acre. On the other hand there are many *Capes* or *headlands*, projecting themselves into the sea; Batoun, Kourchlih, Zephira, Aio-Vasisli, Poslepei, Voua, Jasoun, Thermeh, Tcherchenbeh, Judjeh, Kerempe (anc. *Caramtis*), Baba, Kirpeh, and Kara Bournon, all on the north coast of Asia Minor. Cape Janisary, at the entrance of the Dardanelles; Baba Burun, Kara Burun, and Krio on the west coast; Khelidonia, Anamour, and Karadash on the south coast of the peninsula; and Khyn Zir, Bosyt, Ras-el, Shakaa, and *Mount Carmel* on the coast of Syria. The *Islands* are — Cyprus (the *Kupros* of the ancient

Greeks), near the north-east corner of the Mediterranean. Its length is 140 miles, and its breadth 63. The population is supposed to amount to about 60,000, of whom two-thirds are Greeks. The towns are Nicosia in the centre of the island, situated in a fine plain, bounded by lofty mountains. It contains about 4,000 families. Larnakia, on the south coast, is the chief seat of commerce, and the residence of the European consuls. Famagosta (the ancient *Arsinoë*), the capital of the island when it was in possession of the Venetians, stands on the east coast, and still has traces of its former grandeur. Baffo (anc. *Paphos*) is on the south-east coast, but is now a mere village, although it contained in former times the temples and groves of Aphrodité-Kupris (the Cyprian Venus), the goddess of love and beauty. Rhodos (*Rhodes*) is near the south-west coast of Asia Minor, forty-six miles by twelve. It contains 460 square miles, enjoys a delightful climate, and has the heats of summer cooled by the lofty hills which occupy its centre. Rhodes was renowned in ancient times for its wealth and civilisation, and for the wisdom of its laws—to all of which it owed its prolonged independence. It acquired a new distinction in the middle ages, when it became the home of the Knights of St. John of Jerusalem. It is now almost deserted. Its chief town in the north-east of the island, and it bears the same name, is, however, of some importance, and is fortified and used as a place for ship-building. It occupies very nearly the site of the ancient *Rhodus*, which was one of the most splendid of the commercial cities of Greece. There are no traces of the former splendour of the city. The only public buildings are two Gothic castles, and several massive Gothic churches, which have been converted into mosques. The population consists of about 5,000 Turks and 1,000 Jews. No Christian is allowed to reside within its walls. The rest of the island is inhabited by Greeks, to the number of about 14,000. Samos lies about fifty miles to the south of Smyrna, and is separated from the promontory of Mycalé by a channel of only about a quarter of a mile in width. It is about sixty miles in circuit. It was famous for the worship and temple of Juno, who was said to have been born on the island. It is very fertile. But the people have suffered much from the desolating influences of war, and the island is now well-nigh deserted. Scio (anc. Greek *Chios*, mod. *Khio*) is a beautiful and fruitful island west of Smyrna, celebrated in latter times for its college, rich library, printing-press, and numerous and industrious population (formerly for its wine, the *Chian*). It is now deserted and covered with ruins. It was invaded by the Turks in 1822, the whole Greek population being murdered or carried into slavery, and their property plundered or destroyed. Mytilini (*Lesbos*) is north-west of the Gulf of Smyrna, containing 435 square miles, and a population of 40,000, who are principally maintained by a trade in oil. Taushan and Tenedos are small rocky islands near the entrance to the Dardanelles. Marmora is famous for its marble quarries. Kalolimno, Rabi, and the Prince's Islands are in the Sea of Marmora. Kos (*Istankhio* of the Turks), Astropalaia, Nisyro, Piscopi, Symi, Khalkhi, St. John, Eskriti, Plaka, Adelphi, Stazida, Cairo, Scarpanto, Kalimno, Levita, Zenari, Lero, Patmo, Gaitharo, Furni, Nikaria, are all on the south-west coast. The Grambousa and Khelidonia Isles are off Cape Khelidonia, Provençal is south-west of Selefkeh. Kefkem is a small island to the east of Cape Kirpee, in the Black Sea.

The *rivers* which drain and irrigate this part of Asia are:—

The Jorukh, which rises in Armenia, and flows into the Black Sea at Batum. The Jekil-Irmak (green river) rises to the south-west of Tokat, flows through the province of Sivas, passes Tokat (where it is called Tokat-Su), Amasia, and Charsambeh, below which it falls into the Dead Sea. The Kizil-Irmak (red river), formed of two branches, the one rising on the frontier of Sivas, the other in the Hassan-dagh, and falling into the Black Sea, between Sinub and Samsoun, after a course of 570 miles. It is the ancient *Halys*, the largest river in Asia Minor. The Sakaria, rising in the neighbourhood of Angora, and joined by the Pursak from Kutaya, has a course of 250 miles, and falls into the Black Sea. The Kodos rises in Murad-tagh, and falls into the Gulf of Smyrna, after a course of 190 miles. The Mendere has a course westwards of

180 miles into the Archipelago, south of Samos. It is celebrated for its windings, from which all similar windings in rivers have been called meanders. The Sihoon rises near Bostan, and flows south-west past Adana into the Mediterranean. The Jihoon has a nearly parallel course, a little to the eastward, and falls into the Gulf of Scanderoon. The Aazi or El-Asi (the rebel), the ancient *Orontes*, rises on the east side of Anti-Libanus, north of Damascus, flows north and north-west through a long valley to Antakia, where it turns south and south-west, and falls into the Mediterranean, after a course of 225 miles. To the north-east of Antakia the streams which descend the valley of Taurus form a great lake, Aggi, or Oloja-denghis (White Sea), which empties itself by one stream, called the Kara-su, into the Orontes. The Leitani (*Leontes*) rises at the northern end of the valley El Bakaa, and flows south by west into the Mediterranean, a little to the north of Tyre. The Jordan, Orden, or Sherya, as has already been noticed, rises in a small lake, called anciently Phiela, in Mount Hermon, flows south into the lake Hoolya (the Waters of Merom), and passes onward through the lake of Tabariah (*Sea of Galilee*), and then flows with a winding course through a spacious valley called El Ghor, and falls into the Dead Sea. In the higher part of its course, the Jordan, after it leaves Lake Tabariah, flows between banks which are often picturesque; and in spring it fills its deep channel, passing onwards with great rapidity. The Zerka

(*Jabbok*) flows from Jebel Haouran westward into the Jordan, nearly midway between the two lakes. The Mandhour flows also from Jebel Haouran to the Jordan, a few miles south of Lake Tabariah. The Kison passes through the plain of Esdraelon into the south side of the Bay of Acre. The Koje, Kasab, Arsouf, Petras, Roubin, Sorek, and Besor, or river of Gaza, all flow into the Mediterranean Sea.

We have already referred at large to the Euphrates and the Tigris, and therefore need only observe here that, after those rivers have come together, the united stream, as we have observed, is called *Shat-el-Arab* (river of the Arabs), and flows with a somewhat winding course in a direction nearly south-east from Kornah; entering the sea by a single channel called the Khoré-el-Bussrah, over an extensive bar, which has only a depth of three fathoms at high-water, and a bottom of soft oozy mud. It is described as being everywhere broader than the Nile, and its waters much deeper, while the banks are more thickly covered with groves of date trees, and more nearly approaching the surface of the water, so being more favourable to the purposes of irrigation than the Egyptian river. Ships which can pass the bar may be easily navigated up to Bussrah. The tide ascends the Euphrates 60 miles, and the Tigris 35 miles above Kornah. Not far below Kornah the Shat-el-Arab is joined by the Haweeza or Kerkah, a large river from Louristan; and below Bussrah it communicates, by the Hafar canal, with the Karoon or Kûran, and as was supposed, till Chesney's expedition proved the contrary, by the Jerahi also—the three rivers together forming seven mouths. The four eastern mouths belong to the Karoon and the Jerahi; the fifth, named Khoré-omeyah, leads directly into the Shat-el-Arab, and is believed to be navigable by ships drawing ten feet of water; but being so close to the main body of the river its passage is never attempted. We have already referred to the Khoré-el-Bussrah as the principal entrance into the river, and the only stream now navigated by ships; and the seventh, Khoré-Abdallah, is supposed to have once been a mouth of the Euphrates, when that river reached the sea by a channel of its own, before it was united with the Tigris at Kornah. At present it is rather a creek, or inlet of the sea, than the mouth of a river. It is said to be four times as broad from land to land at its entrance as the Shat-el-Arab is at the same point, and it continues to be twice as broad throughout its whole length; the depth of water in mid-channel, decreasing from ten fathoms at the entrance to five fathoms at the head.

There are several great *Lakes* in this country.

The great Lake of *Van*, in Armenia, is situated between 38° and 39° N. lat. and 42° and 43° E. long., extending nearly 80 miles in length from S.W. to N.E. The eastern half has a breadth of only from five to nine or ten miles. In the middle it is 37 miles; but it contracts again at the west end to fifteen or sixteen. It lies at the bottom of a valley, surrounded with lofty mountains. Its waters are bitter, except at the mouths of the rivers which flow into it. There is a species of herring or sardine caught in it at certain seasons, which is salted and exported to all parts of Asia Minor. This lake is very beautiful. It includes two islands of considerable size, with Armenian convents, one of them being called Akhtamar, which is also the Armenian name of the lake itself. The Turks call it Arjish. There are a few small vessels plying upon this lake at most seasons. A singular substance is found floating on the water, which the surrounding population gather, and use for washing purposes. It is an alkaline salt, composed chiefly of carbonate of soda and chloride of sodium, or sea salt.* The lake is 5,467 feet above the level of the sea.

The great *Tuzla*, or Salt Lake of Koch-Hisar, is near the centre of Asia Minor. It is 30 leagues in circumference. It is narrow, but it is nearly 50 miles long. So extremely salt is the water that no fish or other aquatic animal can live in it. Even birds are not disposed to touch it, as their wings soon become stiff with a thick coating of salt; and anything thrown into the water is quickly covered with that substance. There are the remains of a causeway across the lake, which is covered with salt, and the bottom is covered with a thick layer of the same material. The salt is a government monopoly, and is collected for mercantile

* Southgate, ii. 306.

purposes at only four places.* The surface of the water is 25,000 feet above the level of the sea. It is called by the neighbouring population Tuz-choli ("salt desert"), sometimes Tuz-goli ("salt lake"), Agi-gol ("bitter lake"), or Kock-hisar-goli ("Lake of Kerk-hisar").†

The *Dead Sea* is situated in the northern part of Palestine, between 31° and 32° N. lat. and 36° E. long. It is called Bahr Lout ("Lot's Sea"), and Bahr Mutneh ("stinking sea"), by the Arabs, and by the Latins, *Lacus Asphaltitas*, or *Mare Mortuum*. It is about fifty miles in length, from north to south, and from seven to twenty in breadth. Mr. Costigan, with a Maltese sailor as his servant, made an excursion on this lake in a boat, in 1835. It took him eight days, and he was so completely exhausted by his exertions that he died without having been able to give an account of his voyage. Mr. Stephens found the servant at Beyrout. As a sailor he had carefully observed the coast and the soundings. His information was to the effect that his master and he had moved in zigzag directions, crossing the lake several times; that every day they sounded, frequently with a line of 175 brachia (each about six feet); that they found the bottom rocky and of very unequal depth, sometimes ranging 30, 40, 80, 20, all within a few boats' length; that sometimes the lead brought up sand, like that of the neighbouring mountains; that they failed but once to

---

* Hamilton, Jour. of Royal Geog. Soc., viii. 147.
† Jour. of Royal Geog. Soc., x. 298.

find the bottom, and in that place they were surrounded by large bubbles for about 30 paces—these they supposed to rise from a spring; that, in one place, they found on the bank a hot sulphureous spring; that in four different places they found ruins, and could distinguish large hewn stones which had evidently been used for buildings; that at the south end of the lake a long tongue of highland projects into the water, and is composed of solid salt, which has at a distance the appearance of an island, the extremity being higher than the isthmus. Messrs. Moore and Beke again surveyed the lake in 1837, and found its depth in certain places to exceed 300 fathoms; and, from several observations on the temperature of boiling water, and by the barometer, they estimated the level of its surface to be 500 feet below the level of the sea. Professor Schubert has supposed the depression to be 598 or 600 feet by the barometer. M. Russegger, also by barometer, has concluded that it is 1,400 feet—so wide sometimes is the difference of calculations. The waters are intensely salt, and most nauseous,—salt, bitter, and sulphureous, and so pungent that the eyes smart severely for some time after having been dipped in them. By analysis, it has been found that these waters contain, in 100 parts 0·920 of muriate of lime; 10·246 of magnesia; 13·360 of soda; and 0·054 of sulphate of lime. The south-western side of the lake is skirted by a long, low ridge of about 150 feet high, the whole mass of which consists of solid rock salt, covered with layers of soft limestone, marl, and other substances, through which the salt breaks out, and appears on the sides, in precipices 40 or 50 feet high, and several hundred feet long. The salt is often broken off in pieces, which are strewed along the shore like stones, or accumulated at the foot of the precipices. The extreme saltness of the lake is thus easily accounted for. The Arabs carry salt from the Dead Sea to all parts of Palestine. The principal supply of water is from the river Jordan, which, even two or three miles from its junction with the lake, is impregnated with the salt and bituminous matter; but, in the rainy season the liquid contents of this inland sea are also augmented from the south; for not only the waters of the valley El Arabah, but those also of the western desert, far to the south of Akaba, flow north towards it. Nothing can be more dreary than the surrounding scenery, the soil is destitute of vegetation, and furnishes food for neither bird nor beast. The water is extremely buoyant, and the air above it has an oppressive weight. Asphaltum or bituminous matter is found floating on its surface.*

The Lake of *Tabariah*, or Sea of Galilee, is situated about 70 miles north from the Dead Sea, in a basin surrounded by lofty and naked hills, and is about 500 feet below the level of the Mediterranean Sea. In length it is about sixteen miles, and in breadth about nine. It is celebrated by all travellers for its pic-

* "Stephens' Incidents of Travel;" Jour. of Royal Geog. Soc. vol. ix.

turesque grandeur and beauty. The water is greenish in colour. It abounds with fish, some kinds of which are to be found only here and in the Nile. It is perfectly clear and sweet, although it receives several hot salt streams so impregnated with gases that they change the colour of the stones over which they pass. The Jordan flows through the middle of the lake with a strong current. Storms of long continuance are unknown, but the lake is occasionally subject to whirlwinds, squalls, and sudden gusts from the hollows of the mountains. There is not now any navigation upon it—not even a fishing boat.

The *Aggi*, or Owja-denghis ("White Sea"), is formed by the streams which descend from the valley of Taurus to the north-east of Antioch, and it empties itself by one stream, the Kara-su, into the Orontes. It is about ten miles long, by four or five broad, and affords a navigable passage along its west side, to Murad-pasha, on the Upper Kara-su, and through the Lower Kara-su and the Orontes to the sea.

Besides these, there are in Syria the *Bahr-el-Margi*, or "Lake of the Meadow," which is the receptacle for the streams which water the plain of Damascus. In summer it is only a marsh; but in winter it contains a large body of water. The Lake of *Homs* is formed by the Orontes; and the *Sibkah*, or Salt Lake of Geboul, is to the south-east of Aleppo. In Asia Minor there are many other lakes, the principal of which are: the lakes of Is-nik, Abulliout, and Maniyas, on the south side of the Sea of Marmora; Egerdir, a beautiful sheet of water about thirty miles in length, surrounded by lofty mountains, which are clothed with wood, and emitting at its south end a copious stream, which is said to fall into another very large lake, 35 or 40 miles in circumference, at the distance of four hours' journey; Eber, Ak Shehr, Beg-shehr or Kereli, Seidi-Shehr, or Soghla, the Ak-Ghieul ("White lake"), Ochardak, a salt lake, from which great quantities of salt are collected; all to the north of the Gulf of Adalia; Gheuljik ("Little lake"), 50 miles north-west of Diarbekr, between Kharput and Arghana-Maden, twelve miles long by three or four broad, and 4,453 feet above the level of the sea. Some have affirmed of the water that it is salt, but it is not so.*

As to the PEOPLES of this great territory of Turkey in Asia, the Osmanlee are the dominant race. They are spread all over the empire, but are most numerous in Asia Minor, which they seem to consider their proper country. There are many other families of *Turks* besides the Osmanlee. Those who live in Armenia, and along the eastern frontier, take the name of Turks, which completely distinguishes them from their western brethren, who spurn it.

Next to the Turks in number are the *Arabs*, who form the principal part of the population between Bussrah and Bagdad. Their aggregate number is about two hundred thousand.

* Jour. of Royal Geog. Soc. vi. 208.

The *Annizah* and *Jerboa* are the other great Mesopotamian tribes. It has always been a part of the Turkish policy to foment jealousy among these tribes, and so to preserve a balance of power, as otherwise, by combining, they might drive the Turkish lordship out of the country.

The *Kurds* are the descendants of the ancient *Carduchii* or *Corducni*. They inhabit the region which lies to the south-east of Armenia, and give their name to it. It is about 300 miles in length, and half as much in breadth, and presents an endless succession of hills and valleys, with dells and plains of great fertility, under the shelter of towering mountains. Their language is essentially Persic, with a mixture of the Arabic and Chaldæan. They are generally Mahometans, but they incorporate with their religion many superstitions which seem to be the remains of the ancient Magian faith. About a tenth part of them are Nestorian Christians, or Chaldæans. These inhabit the wild mountainous districts to the south of the Lake of Van, round Jumalerk, their chief town. But they are a lawless and uncivilised race, whatever may be their religious profession. From time immemorial, their country has been the scene of turbulence, robbery, and warfare; and they have seldom, if ever, been more than nominally subject to any of the great empires which have had dominion in this part of Asia. At present, Kurdistan is nominally divided between Persia and Turkey, without being really subject to either.

The Kurds are divided into numerous tribes, and also into two social classes—the nobles and gentry, who spend their time in idleness or war, and the slaves, serfs, or peasants, who cultivate the fields, and seem to be of a different race from their haughty masters. There are many Kurds beyond the limit of Kurdistan, scattered through Armenia, Asia Minor, and Northern Syria, where they lead a wandering, pastoral life, like the Turcomans, and sometimes prove troublesome neighbours to the inhabitants of the plains. Everywhere the name Kurd seems to be considered as nearly synonymous with robber.

The *Turcomans* are, like the Osmanlee, a branch of the great Tûrkee family; and, like the Kurds, they lead a pastoral and unsettled life. They are by far the most numerous and most civilised of the nomadic tribes of Asia Minor. They live in tents during the summer, but have frequently settled villages for their winter quarters. They possess large herds of camels, buffaloes, goats, and sheep. They also breed horses, and sell them, with milk, butter, and meat, in the towns and villages, taking in return arms, clothes, and money. Their women spin wool and make carpets. Each camp is under a chief, whose power is regulated by customs and circumstances, the abuse of which is restrained by public opinion. They pay a certain price a tent to the pashas for the privilege of pasturing over the unenclosed and uncultivated parts of the provinces. A large portion also of the Moslem population between

Bagdad and Mosul call themselves Turcomans, and speak the Turkish language.

The *Yorukhs* are another nomadic people of Asia Minor, who live in tents all the year round, and almost exclusively in the mountains. When in the neighbourhood of towns they generally work as burners of charcoal, and supply the population with that article. They also cultivate small patches of ground.

The *Yezedees* are a singular race, who principally inhabit the mountain range of Sinjar in Mesopotamia, between the rivers Euphrates, Tigris, and Khabour; but they are found also in great numbers in Kurdistan, and near Mosul, and a good many in the province of Diarbekr. There seems to be no doubt that they derive their origin and name from Yezid, the son of the Caliph Moawiyah, who destroyed the race of Ali; although it is said by some that they are descended from a saint named Yezid, who lived about the same time (in the seventh century). Being detested by the Persians on account of the destruction of the house of Ali by Yezid, and by the Arabs, as worshippers of the devil, they have been driven into the strong and isolated hills of Sinjar, and the rugged mountains and defiles of Kurdistan. Their religion is a strange mixture of devil-worship with the doctrines of the Magians, Mahometans, and Christians. Religion and religious ceremony seem, however, to be merely nominal among the Yezedees of Sinjar. Those in Kurdistan, holding the same faith, such as it is, are more given to the practice of religious observances. They admit a good and an evil principle; and judging that the evil only is to be feared, it is its representative only that they seek to propitiate. They name him *Al-sheikh Almoazzem*, or the Great Sheikh. They would rather be put to death than curse him. They worship the sun at his rising; but they hold Christian priests in great veneration. Their lives are very simple. Their character is superior to that of their neighbours. They are brave, hospitable, and sober, faithful to their promises, much attached to their native soil, but cruel and vindictive, considering their proper means of support to be robbery and theft. They differ from the surrounding tribes in the fact that they are not polygamists. They used to keep the whole country between Mosul and Nisibin in a state of constant alarm; but in 1837 they were reduced to subjection by the Pasha of Diarbekr, and registered as tributaries of the Sultan.*

The *Armenians* constitute one of the most ancient nations of the world. They were the original possessors of Armenia, although now they form only about a seventh part of the population, the rest of the inhabitants being chiefly Turks and Kurds. They call themselves in their own language *Haji-Haji*. Being constantly exposed to the wars waged by the great neighbouring potentates, they have been forced in large numbers to leave their country; and though formerly

* "Forbes's Visit to the Sinjar Hills in 1838;" Jour. of Royal Geog. Soc. ix. 409.

a warlike and brave people, they are now distinguished for their love of peace, and their willing submission to the government of the countries in which they live. Devoted to commerce and manufactures, they have prospered wherever they have settled, finding their way to places not frequented by Europeans. Their scattered colonies are to be found in Hungary, Venice, Calcutta, and even in China. They are also to be met with in many parts between Russia and South Africa. In their own country, as well as elsewhere, they generally live in large families, in domestic peace, under the rule of their oldest member. But this family union and attachment is sometimes found to be quite compatible with perfidy, insensibility, and injustice towards persons of a different race. They form a kind of branch of the Oriental Christian Church. This Church is superintended, in Armenia, by four patriarchs, of whom the chief bears the title of *Catholicos of all the Armenians*. They acknowledge but few holy days, and condemn the worship of images. Some of them have acknowledged the Roman Church, and have an archbishop at Nashtshiran on the Don, and another in the Isle of St. Lazaro in the lagunes of Venice. There are, moreover, several thousands of them in other parts of the Ottoman empire, particularly at Constantinople, under the superintendence of an independent patriarch.

Besides these races there are many Greeks spread over the countries which have been named, but chiefly in the towns of Asia Minor in its western part. They are also found along the southern coasts, and in all centres of population in Syria and Palestine—everywhere preserving their nationality and their religion.

Syria having been successively invaded by the Persians, the Greeks, the Romans, the Saracens, the Latin Crusaders, and the Turks, has a very mixed population. The aboriginal Syrians form but a very small part of the community anywhere. The Turks are usually found in the towns, and formerly were the only civic functionaries. There are many Arabs throughout the country, chiefly engaged in agriculture. Bedouins are also frequently to be seen. The entire population of Syria is supposed to be 1,250,000, or ranging from that to 1,500,000. Two-thirds of them are Mahometans, and most of the remainder are Christians. In the northern provinces or eyalet of Aleppo, are hordes of Turcomans and Kurds; and the mountains between Aleppo and Damascus are occupied, in great part, by the single and separate tribes, *Ansarians*, *Druses*, *Maronites*, and *Motoualis*. The *Ansarians* (who are sometimes called Neceres, Ensyrians, and Ismailys) live in the mountains which lie between Antakia and the river Kebir. They are usually considered to be Mahometans, and are said to have been founded, by one Nassar, in the seventh century. But very little is in reality known about either themselves or their religion. They were established where they are now found long before the Ottoman conquest, and all that can be said of their religion is that it is a mixture of Mahometanism and idolatry. Their principal centre, and the residence of their emir is Masiat, or Maszyad, a castle forty miles north-east of Tripoli.

The *Druses* number about 150,000. They live among the valleys and in the hills of Western Lebanon. Their origin is uncertain. They are believed to be the descendants of the ancient Iturœi, who possessed the same territory in the times of the Romans. They are under the government of an emir, who resides at Deir-el-Kamar, "House of the Moon," a town which lies about mid-way between Lebanon and the sea, nearly twelve miles E.N.E. of Saide. As to their religion it is involved in mystery. They believe in one Supreme Being, who appeared last incarnate in the person of Hakem, Caliph of Egypt, about A.D. 1030. This pretender to divinity was supported by a prophet who came from Persia into Egypt. Both the caliph and his abettor perished by violence; but their doctrines survived them, and their persecuted followers took refuge in Lebanon. The Druses tolerate differences of opinion among themselves in reference to religion, and therefore, at various times, have united in a body to oppose Crusaders, the Sultans of Aleppo, the Mamelukes, and the Ottomans. After the Ottoman conquest of Syria, the Druses often descended from the mountains to harass the conquerors. But after the middle of the sixteenth century they became subject to the Porte, and were, by payment of a yearly tribute, permitted to maintain an almost undisturbed independence. In general, they are fierce, restless, and enterprising—their bravery even approaching to rashness. In extremity they could muster 20,000 men, horse and foot, with firelocks—the larger portion being cavalry. Of their religion we have said that it is a mystery. Many of them have most peculiar notions, but as a body they are indifferent to everything which bears the name—following the Maronites or the Turks just as they find it convenient. On the mountain, their emir is a Christian; when he visits the towns on the coast, he is a believer in the prophet. He resides in a large and costly palace called Beteddin, near Deir-el-Kamar. Unfortunately this latitude is extended also to essential points of moral duty. The Druse women wear tantaroos, or horns, on the head, which gives them a singular appearance. From these they suspend their veils. The Fellahs, south of Damascus, are also Druses; and to the east of Sanamein is a ridge of hills called Jebel-ul-Droos, "the Mountain of the Druses," the inhabitants of which are governed by a tributary prince of their own.

The hill country between Beyrout and Tripoli is occupied by the *Maronites*. They live in villages round the convent of Kannobin, the residence of their patriarch. They are divided into various tribes, each cultivating its own small territory. They live frugally and peaceably, and beneath their humble roof the Christian traveller is sure to find a welcome. The sound of bells and the pomp of processions attest the full liberty of conscience here enjoyed by the Christians. Two hundred monasteries rigorously adhere to the rule of St. Anthony, and many hermits have taken up their abodes in the grottoes and caverns of Lebanon. The Maronites derive their name from Maron, a saint of the fifth century, whose proselytes, having been stigmatized as heretics, sought refuge here. After long braving the Saracen and the Turkish power, they were reduced by Sultan Murad III., in 1558. They were compelled to acknowledge his supremacy, and to pay a yearly tribute; but in every other respect they were uncontrolled. They have connected themselves with the Church of Rome, which connives at their retaining some of their former opinions and practices, and particularly at the marriage of their priests. Full of superstition as it is, their devotion is fervent and steady, and throws an agreeable interest over their territory, which is surrounded by the darkness of Islam. They number about 150,000. They recognise no distinctions of rank, and have, among themselves, scarcely any form of government. The villages form so many small communities, and settle peacefully among themselves the disputes which elsewhere would furnish a pretext to governors to plunder and oppress the people. But in personal quarrels they exercise the barbaric right of vengeance. They are all armed, and can muster 35,000 men. Their monks cultivate the ground, and practise all the usual handicraft trades. The priests are supported by their people; but the maintenance being insufficient, they are obliged to supplement it by secular engagements. Even the bishops have revenues amounting to not more than £60 sterling a-year.

The *Moutoualis* or *Metwalis*, are Sheahs, or heterodox Mussulmen, who worship the Caliph Ali and his descendants, while they curse Abubekr, Omar, and Othman. They formerly occupied the valley of El Bakaa, and sometimes rendered themselves very formidable to the Turks. They are supposed to be ancient Syrians, though as a distinct sect their name does not occur before the eighteenth century. Their name signifies "Sectaries of Ali." The Moutoualis are now very much reduced in numbers, and are chiefly to be found in Eastern Lebanon, and among the Maronites. Their emir resides at Baalbec; but the lower part of the valley is not under his rule, being occupied by Turks.

The *Arabic language* is spoken over the whole country, the old Syrian tongue being used in a few districts only, and those are chiefly in the neighbourhood of Damascus and Lebanon.

The Arab and Turkish part of the people are Mussulmen. Of the Christian sects the most numerous are those of the Greek Church; the Jacobites have also many adherents; and there are besides some European and American Christians, Armenians, Nestorians, and Jews. No country presents a greater diversity of creeds.

The Supreme Government of Turkey, which has

dominion in all these parts, is an absolute monarchy, vested in a *Padishah* or Emperor, of the race of Othman, who, by means of a compact made with the last descendant of the Fatemite Caliphs of Egypt is also *Khalif*, or Vicar of the Prophet, and, as such, Head of the Mahometan religion. His official duties in that capacity are, however, delegated to the Grand Mufti, or Sheikh-ul-Islam. Both in spiritual and temporal affairs his authority is absolute, and his imperial prerogative admits of his putting to death fourteen persons a day, without sin. Hence he is called *Unkiar* (or Hunkiar or Khunkiar), *i.e.*, "the Manslayer." He is also called the Sultan; and in Europe was accustomed to be designated by the Italian title of Grand Seignior. His authority in civil and military matters is usually delegated to the Grand Vizier, as his absolute lieutenant, who is his Prime Minister, charged with all the affairs of the empire, domestic and foreign. The principal Ministers of State, according to their rank, are—1. The Sheikh-ul-Islam; 2. The Grand Vizier; 3. The two Kadi-asters of Roumili and Anadoli; 4. The Ministers of the first class, the Minister of War and Commander-in-Chief of all the regular troops; the Seraskier, or Commander-in-Chief of the troops of Anadoli; the Capudan Pasha, or High Admiral; the Minister of Commerce; the Captain of the Guard; the Minister of Finance; the Minister of Foreign Affairs; an office formerly held by the Reis Effendi, or Chief Secretary; the Chaoushbashi, or executor of the judgments of the Divan; the Hakimbashi, or Chief Physician, and President of the Board of Health; 5. Ministers of the second class; namely, the Reis Effendi, or Secretary of State; the Treasurer of the Sultan's income; the Beilikshi Effendi, assistant to the Reis Effendi in the executive department of his office; the Master of the Ceremonies: the Director of the Wakuffs, or charitable institutions; the Interpreter of the Porte; and the Director of the Customs. The Council of Ministers is called the *Divan*, from the circumstance of their having formerly met in a certain room in the palace, which had no other furniture than a divan, or wooden bench placed along the wall, about three feet high, and covered with cushions. It is in this apartment, or rather its successor, that laws are made, suits decided, firmans issued, troops paid, and the representatives of foreign sovereigns prepared for their introduction to the august presence of the Sultan. The Imperial Court itself is usually called by Europeans by the French designation of the *Sublime Porte*, a name derived from the *Bab-Humayon*, the principal port or gate of the outer wall of the palace, from which the Imperial edicts are issued. But the principal officers of the household frequently possess great power and influence, and exercise more control over public affairs than the ostensible Ministers, who are sometimes only their instruments or tools. The Sultan has no legal wives, but he chooses several of the *odalisques*, or women of the palace, generally three or four, never exceeding seven, who bear the title of *Kadine* or lady, and have each a separate establishment. She who first bears a son is called *Chakessi Sultana*; the mothers of the other princes have the name of *Sultana Chassecki*. The daughters of the Sultan have the title of *Sultana*; and, while yet in the cradle, are married to viziers, pashas, and other great officers. Including the eunuchs, women, guards, and others, the court establishment includes 10,000 persons it is believed. At the death of a Sultan his wives are removed to the old palace; but the *Sultana Validé*, or Sultan's mother—*i.e.*, the mother of the succeeding Sultan—remains in his palace, and is sometimes allowed to interfere and use influence in respect to public business.

For the purposes of administration, the empire is divided into provinces, which are called *eyalets*, the larger of which are governed by Pashas of three tails, with the official title of *Vizier*; and the smaller by Pashas of two tails, with the title of *Merimiran*. The eyalets are subdivided into districts called *liras* or *sandjaks*, each of which is under the charge of a Pasha of one tail, with the title of Mira-lira, or *Sandjak bey*; the cities and towns are governed by *Mutselims*. These provinces are usually called pashalics by Europeans. Pasha is not, however, an official title, but is merely a personal honour, like knighthood in Europe, conferred by the Sultan. There are three ranks of pashas: the first, or highest class, have the privilege of bearing a standard of three horse-tails; the second of two, and the third of one. The pasha is invested with all the powers of absolute government within his province, is the chief of both the military and financial departments and of police and criminal justice, with the power of life and death, of making peace and war; in short, of doing what he pleases, so long as he can procure or purchase the favour of the Sultan and his ministers, or set them at defiance. The provinces have almost invariably been sold to the highest bidder, and the successful pasha of course makes it his business to reimburse himself for his outlay by means of every possible extortion, and uses his power in the most tyrannical and reckless manner. Nor is this system of venality confined to the sale of provinces; corruption seems to pervade every department of the State, civil, legal, and ecclesiastical; and under its baneful influence the provinces have been made little better than deserts, and the empire again and again brought to the verge of ruin. In later years there have been various attempts at reform; but the progress has been slow.

The GOVERNMENT and the RELIGION of Turkey are inseparable. The law and the religion of the Moslem being both founded on the Koran, the clergy and the lawyers form but one order, named the *Chain of the Ulema* (*i.e.* of the learned), at the head of which is the Grand Mufti, or Sheikh-ul-Islam, who alone holds his office for life. He is the fountain of law, and the representative of the Khalif or Sultan, in his spiritual capacity; and as all new laws, and even the question of peace or war, must have his sanction, he thus participates in the legislative powers of the Sovereign, and bears a share in all the movements of the Government. The chain of the Ulema consists of various ranks, and admission into it and promotion to its highest dignities are nominally open to all; but here, as everywhere else, birth, wealth, and official influence, are of more value than the qualifications of the candidates. There are schools or colleges, called *medreses*, for the instruction of its members, at all the imperial mosques. The first step of promotion obtained by the student is when, after completing the required term of study, his name is inscribed in the list of those who aspire to legal offices. If he then acquit himself well in the prescribed trials, he obtains a *medrese*, or professorship, of the lowest income; and afterwards advances by regular steps to the highest rank of the medreses, that of the Suleiman-yeh, out of which the senior muderis are promoted to the rank of Mahrej-Molla, or superior judges, a body numbering eight, and holding office only for a single lunar year. The next step of promotion by seniority is to one of the four superior mollaships of Adrianople, Brusa, Damascus, and Cairo; the next to the two titular mollaships of Mecca and Medina; one of whom is further promoted in turn to the rank of Istamboul-effendi, or Master of the Police of Constantinople. From this office, the next step is to that of Kadi-aster of Anadoli; then to that of Kadi-aster of Roumili; and, last of all, to the supreme rank of Grand Mufti. Of course very few can reach these high offices; and the greater part of the students are content with the rank of simple cadis or judges of Naib, or sub-delegates of the judges in the towns and villages throughout the empire. All these officers, except the Grand Mufti, hold their offices only for a lunar year; and the price which they pay for them is a principal source of the Grand Mufti's revenues.

Besides the chain of the Ulema there is the *Chain of the Sheikhs*. The title of Sheikh is borne by the superiors of monasteries, and the preachers at the imperial mosques. The ministers of religion are a distinct class from the lawyers, and, having assumed sacred functions, can obtain no further advancement. The privileges common to all the members of the clerical body are exemptions from taxes and arbitrary imposts, and from the punishment of death and confiscation. Their systematic organization gives them a firm coherence, and makes the ecclesiasticism of the Ottoman Empire the strongest part of it. This class naturally supports the present state of things, and forms an almost inseparable bulwark in opposition to all change. The Ulemas have invariably been concerned in every political revolution in the empire, and have uniformly shown themselves the enemies of every reforming Sultan. It is difficult to reform law and religion, even when they are taken separately; but, when united, they offer an inert, or even an active resistance, sufficient to baffle the strongest efforts of the best-intentioned despot.

The religion of Islam, or Mahometanism, professed by so many of the peoples to whom we have had occasion to refer, and by so many others who shall yet come under our notice—the religion of Turkey in all its provinces—is a pure theism. Its creed may be summed up in the brief formula—" There is no God but Allah, and Mohammed is his prophet." It was founded by Mohammed of Mecca, about the year 611 of the Christian era. Its adherents acknowledge the divine authority of Judaism and Christianity; but contend that Mohammed was the last and greatest of the prophets, and that his doctrine has accordingly superseded that of his predecessors. *Islam* is the name of the religion itself, and signifies submission to God. Those who profess it are called Moslem, Moslemann, Mossolman, or Mussoulmann (*i.e.*, true believers); but among Europeans, they are generally called Mahometans, from the name of their prophet, which in Roman characters is variously expressed: Mohammed, Muhammed, Mahomet, Mahmoud, Mechemet. The principal precepts of Islam are —1. Purification; 2. Prayer; 3. Fasting in the month *Ramazan*; during which every kind of food must be abstained from between sunrise and sunset. This abstinence is amply compensated for by the licence which is given to the faithful during the succeeding festival of *Bairam*; 4. Almsgiving, the legal amount of which, without regard to casual charity, consists in giving every year to the poor the fourth part of all movable property; 5. Pilgrimage to Mecca. Every

Mussulman in good health is required to undertake this at least once in his life. Prayer five times a day at set hours is enjoined, but it may be performed at home, or wherever else the individual may happen to be. The solemn prayer on Friday is the only one that must be made at the mosque and along with the congregation. Friday is the holy day of the Mahometans, and is called *gemaat* (assembly). On this day all believers must repair to the mosque at the hour of prayer; but, during the rest of the day, they are at liberty to work, or do whatever they please. They have two festivals that require absolute rest, one of which is the feast that succeeds the fast of Ramazan. The Mahometans practise the rite of circumcision. They have also adopted the Mosaic distinction of clean and unclean animals. They believe in good and bad angels, and are persuaded that while evil spirits pursue men incessantly to draw them into evil, good angels are charged by God to support and guide them in the present state of trial. They believe in the immortality of the soul, or rather, to speak correctly, in a future state. They expect a future and final judgment, in which every man will be rewarded according to his works. Mahometanism forbids the use of wine and intoxicating liquors. It permits believers to marry four wives, and, moreover, leaves their female slaves at their disposal. Mahometans are devoted in this world to the gratification of their animal propensities, and in the world to come they expect to lead a life of voluptuous enjoyment, amidst cool groves, upon the banks of clear streams, or beside sparkling fountains, in the company of the Houris, who, always young and ever-blooming, will be constantly ministering to the pleasures of the blessed. The Mussulman is persuaded that whatever befals him is predestinated, whether it be good or evil. Their doctrines and precepts are all contained in the Koran (*i.e.* reading or lesson), of which Mahomet pretended that it was gradually and successively revealed to him by the angel Gabriel. It contains the religious, civil, and military code of Mahometan law. It is written in Arabic, and that, therefore, is the sacred language of the Turks, the Persians, and other Mussulman nations. These nations also agree in adopting as their common era the flight of Mahomet from Mecca, which they call *Hegira*, or *Hejirah* (hedgerah, *i.e.* the flight). In all their arrangements their years are lunar, and the first of them commences with the 16th of July, A.D. 622. In the early periods of Mahometanism, those princes who succeeded its founder as the chiefs of his new religion were called *Khalifs*, or *Vicars* of the Prophet, and also *Emir-el-moumanin*, Commander of the Faithful. There have naturally been conflicting claims in respect to the right to the Khalifat. The Sultan at Constantinople is only invested with temporal authority, although he considers himself the chief of the Moslems; the Mufti, in concert with the Ulemas, judges of all questions of doctrine. The King of Persia stands also in the same relation to this religious system. The Emperor of Morocco is the only prince who pretends to unite in his own person the spiritual and the temporal functions, but his political influence is small. In addition to the ordinary and working clergy, if so we may call them, there are in Mahometan countries persons who pretend to lead pious and retired lives, who bear the appellations of *fakirs* and *dervishes*, names derived from the Arabic, and signifying a state of poverty. Of these there are several orders.

The adherents of Islamism have always been divided into a number of sects, and their schisms have sometimes occasioned destructive wars. So small an amount of union obtains among the Mahometans that some of the Mussulman doctors say that "the Magian religion is divided into 70 sects, Judaism into 71, Christianity into 72, and Islam into 73; only one of the latter of which can lead to salvation." These divisions began immediately after the death of Mahomet, who left no son, and having neglected to nominate his son-in-law Ali, to be his successor as the head of the new religion, his companions-in-arms successively elected Abubekr, Omar, and Osman to the khalifat. The principal sects are the *Sonnites* and the *Sheahs*. Their differences have respect chiefly to the true succession of the head of their religion after the decease of the prophet.

In all parts of Turkey in Asia, the *productive industry* of the people is in a most backward and unpromising condition. Agriculture is much neglected. Manufactures are slightly better in the larger towns. In dyeing cotton, silk, wool, and skins, the Turks have excelled. But, generally speaking, there is a complete stagnation of industry, enterprise, and energy. The principal arts and manufactures of Asiatic Turkey are the silk stuffs of Aleppo, Damascus, Mardin, Bagdad, and Brusa; the cotton stuffs of Mosul, Damascus, Aleppo, Guzel-hisar, Diarbekr, Smyrna, and Manissa; the cloth of Brusa, Tokat, Amasia, Trebizond, Rizah, Mardin, Bagdad, and Diarbekr; the ordinary cloth of Khanak-kalesi, Guzel-hisar, and Hillah; the camlets and shawls of Angora; the carpets of Brusa, Kara-hisar, Pergamo, Aleppo, Damascus; the leather of Konieh, Kaisariyah, Kuskin, Diarbekr, Orfa; the saddles of Aintab; the bridles of Hillah; the tobacco of Latakia; the opium of Kara-hisar; the stone-ware of Khanak-kalesi and Hillah; the soaps of Damascus, Bagdad, and Aleppo; the cutlery of Damascus; the copper utensils of Tokat and Erzeroum, and the glass of Mardin and Hebron.

Few countries in the world are better adapted than Ottoman Asia for being the centre of an immense commerce. Therefore, from the highest antiquity, and throughout the course of the middle ages, this country was the seat of the greatest commerce in the world; but from want of safety to traders, the absence of great roads and navigable canals, as well as encouragement on the part of the Government, its present trade is scarcely the shadow of what it was in former times. Still, the central position of these fine provinces, the rich productions of their soil, the results of the industry of some of the great towns, and the convenience of the caravans of Damascus and Bagdad, which are used by the pilgrims to Mecca, contribute to the production of commercial enterprise. The business of the interior is the most considerable, and it is carried on by caravans as in other parts of Asia. The maritime trade is conducted almost entirely by Europeans, except at Bussrah —the English, the French, the Dutch, the Russians, and the Austrians sharing it among them.

Of the CITIES AND SEATS OF POPULATION in Asiatic Turkey we can notice only the principal, in addition to those which have already come under observation. We shall first regard those of Asia Minor and Armenia.

Smyrna (*Ismir* of the Turks) is in lat. 38° 29′ N., long. 27° 11′ E. It is situated at the bottom of the gulf of the same name, and is built in the form of an amphitheatre, on the slope of a hill, the top of which is crowned with the ruins of a castle. It has a population of 130,000, 10,000 of whom are Spanish Jews. It is governed by a pasha of three tails. The extent and safety of its road for shipping have made it the general emporium of the Levant. The French quarter is inhabited principally by the English, French, Dutch, and Italian merchants, whose persons and property, with those of their families and European servants, are exempt from Turkish rule; and who in civil, commercial and criminal matters recognise no other judges than their own consuls. The Casino was built by subscription. It is a magnificent structure, and there are in it all the principal periodical publications of Europe. There is also a Greek college; and a gazette is published in French. The summer heat is very great; the thermometer in July, in a cool room with the shutters closed, varying from 78° to 83°, and in the shade, out of doors, from 84° to 94°; but the heat is generally tempered by a westerly breeze called the *inbat*, which continues from mid-day till sunset. Hot winds blow occasionally from the south and burn up the country. *Manissa* (Magnesia) is a large town 25 miles north-east of Smyrna, which has a flourishing trade and extensive plantations of saffron. The population is 100,000. *Fokia* is 25 miles north-west of Smyrna, and is built on the site of the ancient Phocæa, renowned for its colonies in Spain and Gaul, one of the most distinguished being Marsilia (Marseilles). *Sart* (Sardis) is 50 miles to the east, and is a miserable village, inhabited by a few Turks; but it is the site of the splendid capital of the Lydian kings. The principal ruins are those of the great church, the temple of Cybele, and the tomb of Alyattes, the father of Crœsus, which consist of a conical hill of earth 200 feet high, and 4,000 round the base. There are similar monuments of smaller size around it. *Ak-hisar* (anc. Thyatira) is 60 miles east of Smyrna. Allah-Shehr (anc. Philadelphia), is 85 miles, and is said to contain more than a dozen Christian churches, and the bulk of the population is nominally Christian. *Pergamo* is 48 miles to the north, and is a large and still flourishing town. There is a magnificent temple to the honour of Æsculapius, and a great library, inferior only to that of Alexandria, and to this place is due the invention of parchment (*charta pergamena*).

Brusa, or Prusa, is about 63 miles south-by-east in a straight line from Constantinople. The most remarkable buildings are the Oulou-jami, or chief mosque, which dates from the Ottoman conquest of the city. This was formerly the capital of the kings of Bithynia, and was afterwards the seat of the Ottoman empire till the taking of Adrianople. The population is 100,000. *Mondania* is the port of Brusa. *Kutahya* is 180 miles east-north-east of Smyrna, and has a population of 50,000. *Konieh* is a large town 300 miles east-by-south of Smyrna. It has a population of 30,000, and has a mosque built on the model of St. Sophia at Constantinople. *Tokat* is a large town of about 30,000 people. *Trebizond*, on the coast of the Black Sea, has, since its foundation, been a place of importance. There are in it about 30,000 people, Greeks, Armenians and Mahometans. *Amasia* is the ancient metropolis of Pontus, and the birth-place of Mithridates, and of Strabo the geographer. *Sinub* (Sinope) still contains about 5,000 inhabitants. It was anciently the capital of Pontus, to which the rule was transferred from Amasia.

Erzeroum is the chief town of Armenia. It is situated in a fertile plain, lat. 39° 55′ 12″ N., long. 41° 17′ E. The plain is 30 or 40 miles in length, and from 15 to 20 in breadth. The pashalic yields in rank and extent only to that of Bagdad. The population is

130,000, but it fluctuates so much by the arrival and departure of strangers that it is sometimes as low as 25,000.

Kars, celebrated in recent years for a noble defence against war and siege, is now little better than a heap of ruins. Such is war. It is governed by a pasha of two tails. Formerly it contained about 2,000 families. Only time can restore it to its former condition. *Van* is a town on the great lake to which it gives its name, and is one of the bulwarks of the Ottoman Empire in its contests with Persia. It is a business place, and has about 12,000 inhabitants. It has always been called the town of Semiramis, and the people of the neighbourhood still venerate the memory of the Assyrian kings.

In Syria and Palestine we have many towns, mostly in ruins, but well worthy of remark.

Haleb (Khelbon of Ezekiel), Chalybon and Berœa of the Greeks, Aleppo of the Franks, is situated on the banks of the Koikh, and of all the Ottoman cities was inferior only to Constantinople and Cairo in extent, population and wealth. It used to have a population of 250,000, but by two successive earthquakes in 1822 more than half the city was destroyed, and its finest buildings ruined or injured. But still there are in Aleppo 4,000 looms employed. The beauty of Aleppo is in its gardens. The town is about 60 miles from the sea on the one side, and about the same distance from the Euphrates on the other.

Scanderoon, Iskenderún, or *Alexandretta*, is 60 miles

west-north-west of Halet. *Latakia* is 90 miles south-west-by-west of Halet. *Antakia* (anc. Antiochia, or Antioch the Great) is 60 miles west of Aleppo, on the banks of the Orontes. It was once the proud capital of Syria, with 700,000 inhabitants, but is now a town in ruins, with not more than 20,000 people. The ancient *Seleucia*, the port of Antioch, still retains some stupendous relics of its former greatness. *Palmyra*, the Tadmor of Scripture, is a mass of impressive ruins. It is the residue of a vast commercial city, which was at its greatest in the third century. The present inhabitants are a few Arabs, who occupy about 30 mud huts among the ruins. *Aintab*, 65 miles north-by-east of the great pass leading between Mount Rhosus and Amanus from Aleppo to Scanderoon, is a town of 20,000 inhabitants. At *Manbej*, 56 miles east-by-north, there are still standing walls which attest the ancient greatness of Mabog or Hierapolis (Holytown), sacred to the worship of the Syrian goddess Astarte, called in Scripture the Queen of Heaven.

Tripoli, lat. 34° 26', long. 35°, 52', is surrounded by luxuriant gardens, and is one of the finest towns in Syria. The population is about 15,000. *Acre* or *Akka*, or St. John d'Acre, was a place of great importance in the time of the Crusades, and sustained many sieges alternately from the Saracens and the Christians. The harbour is the best on the coast. Acre is the great mart for the cotton of Syria, and the principal commercial nations of Europe have consuls here. *Mount*

Carmel forms the south-west side of the Bay of Acre. It terminates in a rocky promontory about 2,000 feet high, containing a number of grottoes once occupied as cells and chapels by the austere order of monks called Carmelites. There are still a few remaining, who lead a recluse life, and who have their wants supplied by the Mahometans, who venerate their character. *Nazra* (Nazareth) is 20 miles from Acre, and is only a village of 3,000 people. But there is a Latin convent, and the church of the Annunciation is the finest in Palestine after that of Bethlehem and the Church of the Holy Sepulchre at Jerusalem. *Sûr* or Tyre, 28 miles north-by-east of Acre, was once the queen of the sea, the cradle of commerce, and the chief city of Phœnicia, but it contains now only about a dozen miserable huts, which shelter a few fishermen. *Sidon* (Saide), the mother city of Tyre, is 23 miles farther north, and is still a considerable town, though somewhat decayed.

Beyrout is one of the ancient cities of Phœnicia, and has more commercial activity than any other Syrian port. *Baalbec*, about 50 miles distant, is now a mere village of 200 inhabitants.

Damascus (El Sham of the Arabs) is situated in a beautiful plain, on the east side of Eastern Lebanon, watered by numerous streams which flow from the mountains into the desert. The plain is so extensive that the hills which bound it to the north and south can barely be discerned from the opposite sides. The gardens are planted with a great variety of fruit-trees, which are kept fresh and green by the waters of the Barrada, and many of the streets have rivulets running along them from the same source. There are many mosques and minarets. The gardens which compass the city extend not less than 30 miles. The principal mosque was formerly a Christian church, and it is now held so sacred that Europeans are rarely permitted to enter it. This great building is one of the finest which the zeal of the early Christians produced. The architecture, which is Corinthian, is of superior beauty and variety. Next to it in architectural importance is the grand Khan, a large and splendid building, with a very lofty roof supported by granite pillars, and surmounted by a large dome in the centre. The population is about 100,000. The city has lost the manufacture of sword-blades, for which it was formerly famous; but it has still considerable manufactures in silk and cotton. Damascus is a place of the highest antiquity, and is the point of union for the caravans of pilgrims from the north and east of Asia. These caravans, with the pilgrims who travel in connection with them, greatly promote the trade of the city. The ancient *Boszrah* is 63 miles to the south of Damascus, still celebrated for its vineyards, but now inhabited by only about fifteen families.

Jerusalem, in many respects so important, has been so frequently and fully made the subject of description, that we need not occupy space in regard to it. It is called El Khoddes by the Arabs, is situated in lat.

30° 48', long. 35° 14', and stands on four small hills, nearly surrounded by deep ravines, and is enclosed with Gothic embattled walls, about two miles and a half in circumference. The houses are heavy, square masses. The streets are narrow and unpaved. The population is estimated at from 20,000 to 30,000. There are no manufactures except of objects accounted sacred. These holy toys are purchased in large numbers by pilgrims and travellers. The principal support of the city is derived from the numerous pilgrims who resort to it. The greatest and most conspicuous edifice is the mosque of Omar, built on the site of the Temple, and inferior in holiness only to the Beitullah (House of God) at Mecca. It is an octagon standing in the middle of an oblong square area, paved with white marble. The walls are externally covered with painted tiles, adorned with arabesques and verses from the Koran in gold letters, and, altogether, it is one of the finest buildings in the Mohammedan world. It stands on the east side of the city overlooking the deep valley of Jehoshaphat. There are still in its vicinity undoubted remains of the former really sacred edifice, whose position it has supplanted. The *Church of the Holy Sepulchre* was built by Helena, the mother of Constantine the Great, on a site which is supposed to include the scene of the greatest events of the Christian religion—the crucifixion, the entombment, and the resurrection of the Saviour. The original structure having been destroyed by fire, the present building was erected by the Greeks and Armenians, at an expense of £200,000. Not many Catholics visit it. Of the many thousands who visit Jerusalem in Lent, the most are of Greek, Armenian, and other Oriental churches. So has died out the spirit of the Crusades.

Bethlehem, where the Saviour was born, is seven miles distant from Jerusalem. It is still a considerable village of nearly 4,000 inhabitants. There is a fine church, built over the place of the nativity. *Jericho* is a miserable village, called Rayah, with about fifty huts. *Hebron* is a cheerful town. *Nablous* (Shechem) is one of the most prosperous places in the Holy Land; its inhabitants number about 10,000. *Jaffa* or Yaffa (formerly Joppa) is one of the most ancient seaports in Palestine. It is the port of Jerusalem.

Samaria retains its distinctiveness. It is a hilly country, with intervening valleys, productive of wheat, silk, and olives.

Contemplating Turkey in Asia, *Scutari* must of necessity be named. It is the ancient Chrysopolis, on the Bosphorus, opposite to Constantinople, and sometimes considered a suburb of that capital. It is built on several hills, has a palace and large gardens belonging to the Sultan, and about 60,000 people.

Constantinople, though not in Asia, is the capital of Turkey in Asia, as also in Europe, and, ruling so large a part of Asia, it naturally comes into consideration. The Turks call it *Stamboul*. It is almost surrounded by water, having the sea of Marmora and the Bosphorus on the south and east, and the Golden Horn, an inlet of the latter, on the north. On the opposite side of the Golden Horn are the suburbs of Galata, Pera, and Tophana. There are about 300 mosques in Constantinople, many of them distinguished by great grandeur and beauty. The largest is that of Suleimania, standing in the middle of a large square, and surrounded by an arcade resting on pillars of granite and marble. Next to it in extent, and of much older date, is the mosque of St. Sophia, the pattern of almost every mosque in the land. It was originally a Christian church. It was afterwards burnt; but restored by Theodosius the younger in 415. The present building was erected by Justinian. It was less than seven years in building. Ten thousand workmen were employed. The materials were procured from every part of the empire, and comprised the remains of many celebrated pagan temples. It is rich in its furniture as well as in its structure, there being many vessels of gold employed in the service. It cost £13,000,000. The bazaars and squares of Constantinople are numerous, but in no way very remarkable. The population has been variously estimated at the wide range of from 400,000 to 700,000, and is composed of Turks, Arabians, Greeks, Armenians, Jews, and Europeans. The streets are dull and ill-paved. The throng in the evenings is in the coffee-houses. Dogs, without owners, infest the whole place. The public is ill-supplied with the means of hired conveyance. There are "sedan-chairs," but the most ordinary means of transport are caïques, a kind of boat, of which there are about 80,000, and which may be hired like cabs in a European city.

Such is Turkey in Asia—a country or series of countries, many parts of which abound in natural resources, both above the ground and below it, but these almost universally fail to yield what they might because of the lack of spirit in the supreme government, the cupidity of local rulers, and the absence of industry and enterprise on the part of the people. These were once lands of light, but they are now shrouded in darkness, or in the haze of bewildering superstition

CHAPTER IV.

ARABIA.

THERE is no country whose characteristics are more marked than those of Arabia. Extending from the mouth of the Nile eastward to the Euphrates, a distance of a thousand miles, and from the Arabian Gulf northward to the region around Palmyra, a space of fourteen hundred miles, it may be regarded as one great sea of sand. Its mighty rocks seem like waves, whose tumultuous waters had been suddenly arrested in the midst of a storm, and congealed in all fantastic shapes into granite. "Araby the Blest" is the chief of its isles,—rich, fertile and luxuriant. Its islets are innumerable: oases are embosomed in every valley, and surround every fountain; one being startled to find them so green and beautiful in such a waste. But the general aspect is uninviting, uninteresting, and repulsive. The sun smites it by day, and the moon by night.

But, with one exception, there is no other land which may be compared with this in historic interest and

NATIVES OF ARABIA

moral power. From one of its desert parts, the region of Sinai, came forth that system of monotheism which shone as a light for ages amid the darkness of heathendom, and which involved in it, though obscurely revealed, all the peculiar and remedial elements of Christianity. And from another of its desert parts came forth, in a later age, that gigantic system, which, originating in imposture, yet recognising the unity of God and the exclusiveness of his worship as its first principle, at a time when Christianity itself was reduced by those who professed its name to a cunningly-devised idolatry, has been a scourge to many nations, and a blight on their hearts and minds for thirteen centuries.

We are indebted to this land for our science as well as for our religion. Many of our present names for the elementary sciences are derived from its primeval language. Alphabet and cipher, algebra, alchemy, and chemistry, almagest and almanack, are Syro-Arabian words. And though astronomy, and geography, and navigation, have acquired new names of European derivation, they, no less than astrology, and magic, and divination, were cultivated by the nations which spoke the various dialects of the Syro-Arabian, including the people of Arabia Proper, of which we speak, and prove the energy with which they sought, both to unravel the secrets of the material universe, and to solve those dark and mysterious problems which have perplexed the thinking mind of every age.

Arabia is divided into two unequal parts by a valley,

which extends from the Dead Sea to the Eastern or Elanitic Gulf of the Red Sea. On the west this valley is bounded by a lofty line of cliffs, forming an abutment of the Desert of Sinai, which has a general elevation of twelve or fifteen hundred feet above its bed. On the east the mountains of Edom rise a thousand feet above the opposite bluffs on the west, and raise the plateau of the great eastern desert to a similar elevation above that of the western. Both the eastern and western mountain boundaries are intersected by innumerable wadys (valleys), but there are none of them made glad by a perennial stream. The occasional torrents which flow down through them are partly lost in the sands of "The Plain," and partly find their way to the Red Sea on the south, and to the Dead Sea on the north.

The existence of the great valley of the Arabah between the two seas was unknown until the present century.

The Arabs derive their name from Yarab, said to be one of the sons of Joktan, and the founder of the kingdom of Yemen. The popular opinion has long been that the inhabitants of Arabia are the descendants of Ishmael. This is likewise their own opinion. The earliest inhabitants of Arabia seem to have been the posterity of Cush, who sent colonies across the Red Sea to the opposite coast of Africa, and hence Cush became a general name for both Arabian and African Ethiopia. Dr. Kitto says, "There can be no doubt that the descendants of Ishmael form so large and absorbing a part of the Arabian population as to allow us, in a general sense, to consider him as the progenitor of that great and extraordinary nation." Of Ishmael it was predicted, "He will be a wild man; his hand will be against every man, and every man's hand against him." This means, in short, that he and his descendants should lead the life of the Bedouins of the Arabian deserts. The designation *wild* is precisely the term by which we should choose to characterize Arabs. The hand of the Arab is now as ever against every man. Aggression on all the world has become a condition of the existence of these people.

The scene of the giving of the Law is still a question with travellers and geographers, but the preponderance of evidence seems to be in favour of the present Horeb, and the plain of Er-Rahah. The highest summit, on the ridge of which Horeb is the extremity, is called Jebel Mûsa, and is regarded by tradition as the spot on which God appeared to Moses, and where the Ten Commandments were proclaimed in such circumstances of grandeur and awe. In the middle of the third century of the Christian era these mountains were the refuge of Egyptian Christians in times of persecution, where they were sometimes seized as slaves by the Saracens or Arabs. The whole region is most desolate. There is a monastery, and there are the remains of many convents, chapels, and hermitages, with perhaps six or seven thousand monks and hermits dispersed over the mountains. The convent of St. Catherine was founded by the Emperor Justinian, A.D. 527. The monks are ignorant and credulous. Their library contains 1,500 Greek volumes and 700 Arabic manuscripts, but is entirely neglected. Bibles, presented to them by the Rev. Joseph Wolff, for their own perusal, have been thrown carelessly aside and forgotten. But not so is it with the vain dreams of their superstition. The holy place of the Church of St. Catherine is the "Chapel of the burning bush" behind the altar. It is customary for all who enter to put their shoes from off their feet; and all respect is shown to the edifice.

The rock-inscriptions of the peninsula of Sinai are involved in mystery. They extend along the route from the Gulf of Suez to the very base of Sinai, but are found neither on Jebel Mûsa, nor on the present Horeb, nor on St. Catherine, nor in the Valley of the Convent. Not one has yet been found to the eastward of Sinai. The place where they exist in the greatest number is the Wady Mukatteb, the "Written Valley," through which the usual road passes to Sinai. They here occur in thousands. In the immediate vicinity of the Wady Mukatteb is another valley, famous for inscriptions of another order. It is the Wady Maghârah, or "The Valley of the Cave." The faces of the rocks are everywhere cut into tablets, and covered with hieroglyphics, many of them beautifully executed. These are the most ancient sculptures in the world; and yet it is evident that when they were executed the arts were by no means in their infancy, but that centuries must have elapsed since their unknown and remote origin.

On the east of the valley of the Arabah there is a country of vast extent, and of interest only inferior to that of the peninsula of Sinai. The first part of this great territory, if one travels from Sinai, is a border of mountains—the mountains of Edom. This part of Arabia is commonly called "Stony." The chief town is Petra, which name itself means a rock. Arabia Deserta lies eastward of Arabia Petræa, and extends on the north to Syria, on the north-east to the Euphrates, and on the south-east to the Indian Ocean. The third division of Arabia, Arabia Felix, feels the effects of its proximity to Arabia Deserta. It forms the coast of the Red Sea, which bounds it on the west, and of that part of the Indian Ocean which terminates Arabia on the south. This is called the Hedjaz, or "Land of Pilgrimage." It is the birth-place and cradle of the Mahometan imposture, containing both Mecca, where the prophet was born, and Medina, where he was buried. It is the holy land of the Moslems, whither they resort from all parts of the East. It is in this country that we must look for the Sheba, whose queen was attracted to Jerusalem by the fame of Solomon.

It is proper to remark here on the permanence of Arabian customs. The Arabians are now what they were at an early period of their history, and the lapse of time which has broken other nations to pieces, and scattered them from land to land, still finds these people the same. There have been changes. It is morally impossible for any people, even of one blood and of one land, to pass through a long series of ages without some change. Mahometanism itself was a great change, the effect of which, in modifying the habits of the people, has never yet, perhaps, been truly estimated by European writers. But in all the ordinary customs of life the people remain the same. The Arabs are physically a fine race of men. Mr. Layard says, " The Shemite possesses in the highest degree what we call imagination. The poor and ignorant Arab, whether of the desert or town, moulds with clay the jars for his daily wants in a form which may be traced in the most elegant vases of Greece or Rome; and, what is no less remarkable, identical with that represented on monuments raised by his ancestors three thousand years before. If he speaks, he shows a ready eloquence; his words are glowing and apposite; his descriptions true, yet brilliant; his similes just, yet most fanciful. These high qualities seem to be innate in him; he takes no pains to cultivate or improve them; he knows nothing of reducing them to any rule, or measuring them by any standard." But the moral condition of the Arabs is not good. The spirits that dwell in the well-formed bodies of the Arabs are godless and unholy.

This country was the scene of a very early civilisation. Of this we have abundant illustration in the recent discoveries which have been made on the plains of Assyria. The book of Job is probably the oldest in existence. The scene of its events was Arabia, and as illustrated by the remains of Nineveh we see a lifelike picture of the state of Arabia. The art of writing was known there, as we see, at a very early period. The allusions of the book exhibit a familiar acquaintance with metals, and their origin and uses. The history of the introduction of the Christian religion into Arabia Petræa is involved in obscurity. Paul "went into Arabia" from Damascus at a very early period after his conversion (Gal. i. 17). The invasion of the Crusaders shed a few faint rays of light on the darkness of this land; but it was short-lived. It melted away before the victorious arms of the Sultan Saladin, and in A.D. 1188 ceased to be. Burckhardt was the first European who, in modern times, penetrated into this region. He visited it in 1812. But the publication of the great work of Laborde and Linant, in 1830, forms quite an era in our knowledge of Arabia. Dr. Robinson and his fellow-travellers arrived in Wady Mûsa on the 30th of May, 1838, and they have made us familiar with the country as we previously were not. Dr. Wilson followed in the track of Dr. Robinson. Captains Irby and Mangles were the first Europeans of modern times to ascend to the top of Mount Hor. Here is the reputed tomb of Aaron, which is nothing more than a small Mahometan mosque.

The races which now possess this territory belong in general to that great family of tribes which are scattered over the entire region lying between Egypt and Assyria.

In the part called Jebel, which is the northern portion of Idumæa or Arabia, and in Esh-Sherah, the southern, are the Fellahin, or tillers of the ground, who are half Bedouin in their manners, inhabiting the few villages, but dwelling likewise partly in tents. The chief tribe of Bedouins in the district of Jebel are the Hejâya. Besides these there is also a branch of the Ka'âbiueh, who dwell in the region of Wady-el-Ashy, and sow near a well called El-Malih. In the district of Esh-Sherah, the Bedouins are all Haweitât, with a few allies. This is an extensive tribe, broken up into several subdivisions, and dwelling in various and distant parts of the country.

Like the patriarchs of old, these people live in tents. The wealthy among them have two sets of tent-coverings—one new and strong for winter, the other old and light for summer. They encamp in summer near wells, where they frequently remain for a whole month at a time, their flocks and herds pasturing all around, at a distance of several hours, under the care of slaves or shepherds, who bring them every second or third day to the well for water. It is on these occasions that one tribe of Arabs makes an attack upon another; for it becomes known that certain people are encamped near a particular well, and may be easily surprised. If anything of this kind be apprehended, the men of the encampment are in constant readiness for defence, and each keeps a saddled camel before his tent, so that all may hasten the more quickly to the assistance of their shepherds. Most wells in the interior of the desert are exclusive property, either of a whole tribe or of individuals whose ancestors dug the wells. If a well be the property of a tribe, the tents are pitched near it whenever rain water becomes scarce in the desert, and no others are then permitted to water their camels there. But if the well belongs to an individual, he repairs it in summer time, taking the assistance of his tribe, and receives presents from all strange tribes who pass by the well or encamp at it, and refresh their camels with its water; and these presents are particularly exacted if a party should pass on its return home after plundering an enemy. The property of such a well is never alienated; and the Arabs say that the possessor is sure to prosper, inasmuch as all who drink of the water bestow on him their benediction.

It is the practice, whatever may be the form of encampment, to place the chief's tent always outermost, on the side from which either friend or foe is expected. The Syrian Arabs expect their enemies and their guests from the west, and it is even disgraceful for a great man to pitch his tent on the eastern side. The custom must have been the same in the time of Abraham.

The law of blood-revenge is universal throughout the whole Arabian family. The Arab regards this blood-revenge, which extends to the fifth generation, as one of his most sacred rights as well as duties, and no consideration would induce him to relinquish it. The two tribes of Omran and Heywat act upon a rule which forms an exception to the general Bedouin system of blood-revenge. When one of their people is killed by an unknown hand of a known tribe, they think themselves justified in retaliating upon any individual of that tribe, either innocent or guilty; and if the affair be compromised, the whole tribe contribute to make up the fine in proportion to the respective property of each tent. For this reason, the Arabs say that "the Omran and Heywat strike sideways,"—a practice which is much dreaded by their neighbours.

The property of an Arab consists almost entirely of his horses and camels. The profits arising from his butter enables him to procure the necessary provisions of wheat and barley, and occasionally a new suit of clothes for his wife and daughters. His mare every spring produces a valuable colt, and by her means he may also expect to be able to enrich himself with booty. No Arab family can exist without one camel at least. A man who has but ten is reckoned poor. Thirty or forty place a man in easy circumstances; and he who possesses sixty is rich. There are tribes originally poor, among whom, from the possession of ten camels, a man is reckoned wealthy. There are other tribes the Sheikhs of which have as many as 300 camels. But wealth among the Arabs is extremely precarious, and the most rapid changes of fortune are daily experienced. The bold incursions of robbers, and sudden attacks of hostile parties, reduce the richest man to beggary in a few days.

The position of the women is very degraded. To them are assigned all the menial offices of the tents. They are regarded as much inferior to men, and, although seldom treated with neglect or indifference, they are always taught that their sole business is cooking and working. While a girl remains unmarried, she enjoys much more respect than a married woman; for the fathers think it an honour to possess an unmarried girl in the family, and expect to derive profit from the presents anticipated when she shall become a wife. Once married, a Bedouin woman becomes a mere servant, busily occupied the whole day, while her husband is stretched out in his own apartment, comfortably smoking his pipe. He says his wife ought to work at home, since he undergoes so much fatigue on journeys. The fetching of water is the most toilsome part of the work of the Bedouin women. The tents are not often pitched close to a well; if this should be but half an hour's distance from the camp it is not thought necessary that the water should be brought upon camels, and the women must carry it every evening on their backs in long water-skins.

The women do not eat with the men. They take what is left. There is thus a painful degradation of the one half of the human kind.

Those are the races which now possess the mountains and fastnesses of Arabia—ancient Edom. This land, naturally possessing "the fatness of the earth," in many parts of it, was the abode of civilisation from the very dawn of history, and rose to a high condition by cultivation and commerce; but it is now "a land of barrenness and of the shadow of death." Laborde says, "Every one that passeth by Edom is astonished at it." "Its present aspect would belie its ancient history," says Dr. Keith, "were not that history corroborated by the many vestiges of former cultivation, by the remains of walls and paved roads, and by the ruins of cities still existing in this desolated country."

The Arabs are of the Caucasian or white race of mankind, and they speak various dialects of the Semitic language, which are all classed under the general name of Arabic.

The character of the country keeps the Arabs divided into petty tribes, and nowhere admits of large bodies being consolidated into powerful states. The Arab governments are therefore of the simplest kind, and their princes have very limited powers.

Mecca is situated in the Holy Land of Arabia, in a barren valley, N. lat. 21° 36', E. long. 40° 20', and is two days' journey from Jiddah on the Red Sea. Ishmael and his mother took refuge here after having been driven from the house of Abraham. The Arabs say that Abraham visited Ishmael several times at Mecca, and built the Kaaba, which has ever since been an object of religious veneration. Mecca is a handsome town, built of stone. The population, probably, is about 30,000. The people are an idle and desolate race, depending upon the visits of the pilgrims, who number,

on the average, about 100,000 a year. It used to be an independent state, but is now under the dominion of Turkey.

Medina is about 250 miles N. by W. of Mecca. It is a small town. The great object of attraction is the mosque which contains the tomb of Mahomet, and of the first two caliphs, Abukehr and Omar. In Yemen, *Saana* is the capital of the Imamat of Saana, which is one of the most powerful states of Arabia. It occupies a beautiful valley about 4,000 feet above the level of the sea, and has 40,000 inhabitants. *Mocha* is 160 miles S.W. of Saana, and is a decayed town with 3,000 houses. This was formerly the port from which all the exports of Yemen were dispatched—coffee being among them. *Zebid* is 60 miles north of Mocha, a town of 8,000 inhabitants. *Aden*, on the coast of the Indian Ocean, was once a great emporium of commerce, and has still a good harbour; but its trade has been lost, and the town is in ruins. The English government has taken possession of Aden, and the population is rapidly increasing.

In Oman, *Muscat* is a large town in N. lat. 23° 38′, long. 58° 42′ E., in the gorge of an extensive pass. It is somewhat mean as a town; but it is the principal seaport of Oman. The common language is Hindostanee. The population, including the suburb of Matereah, is estimated at 60,000.

CHAPTER V.

PERSIA.

THIS was formerly a very extensive kingdom. But Russia has pressed it down, and its Turkish neighbour has also limited its sway. It still rules, however, over a territory of from about eight hundred to a thousand miles square. It lies between 26° and 40° north latitude, and 44° and 59° east longitude. The present population may be estimated at ten millions. The provinces of Persia are Fars, Irâk, Laristân, Kuristân, a portion of Kurdistân, Azerbijân, Ghilân, Mazanderân, and the western sections of Khorasân and Kermân. The capital at present is Teherân, in the province of Irâk, which is in the northern part of the kingdom. Elam is the ancient Scriptural name of Persia. Irân is the designation given by the people themselves to their country. The general aspect of the towns and villages of Persia is very uninviting. The houses are of three orders, corresponding in appearance and expense to the higher, the middle, and the lower classes of the people. The outsides are plastered with a mixture of mud and cut straw; but, in those of the better class, the rooms internally are tastefully covered with white gypsum much firmer, harder and more dazzlingly white than anything we possess, and the floors are covered with rich carpets. What may be called the middle-class houses are frequently plastered inside with a material which corresponds with that of the outside, and, of course, the decorations and furnishing are also inferior. The roofs are flat. The lowest class of dwellings is of a very inferior order.

As soon as it is light a Persian performs his morning devotions. After an early meal, which varies according to circumstances, but in which fruit and coffee always have their place, there comes the business of the day. In the evenings the people are given to visiting.

The Persians have but little sternness or firmness of character. They are supple and intriguing under the cover of great politeness. As to *Religion*, the ancient Persians were not worshippers of images. Their idols were the natural elements, and in particular fire, as the purest and most characteristic symbol of God. This superstition is not yet extinct. But the Moslem religion now prevails in Persia, and is there much like what it is in other countries. It must be understood that the law and doctrine of those who may be called the orthodox Moslems—as the Arabians, Turks, and others —are derived from the Koran, in the first instance, but are supplemented by traditional sayings, and the two became consolidated into one general belief. There came to be a schism; a section was called the Sunnee. The four sects or schools founded by them have been denominated the four pillars of the Sunnee faith, and each of them has a separate oratory in the temple of Mecca. The parties are, however, disposed to act in unison in defence of the common faith.

The Sheahs have for three centuries and a half been predominant in Persia. The name Sheah means heretic. But the heresy lay not in any essential difference of doctrine. The question was who should and who should not succeed to Mohammed. Into these controversies we need not enter. The Persians hold the unity of God in such a sense as precludes them from acknowledging a plurality of persons in the Godhead. In 1806, the Baptist missionaries at Serampore began a translation of the Scriptures into the Persian language, but only the Book of Psalms was ever published. Henry Martyn published two of the Gospels in Persic. In 1821, Meerza Jaffier, a native Persian, accomplished a translation of the Pentateuch. The Rev. Dr. Glen did work in the same direction, at Astrachan, where he was a missionary. There has, by such means, been much accomplished in favour of Persia, for these books have been widely circulated.

The Mohammedan law requires prayer at five times of the day; but, practically, the number has been reduced to three—" morning, noon, and night," according to the Jewish custom. The prayers, and the usages connected with them, are much the same as among other Moslems. The principal difference is in posture—the Sunnee spreads forth his hands, and the Sheah folds his. To us this seems to be making religion small. The Sunnee places before him as he prays a small bag containing a portion of the sacred soil from the Kaabah at Mecca; and the Sheah is usually content with a little mould from the tombs of the martyrs at Kerbelah. The prayers are in Arabic, learned by rote, and not understood by the body of the people. Like other Moslems a Persian will apply himself to his prayers, when the appointed time comes, wherever he may happen to be; but he generally shows by the movement of his eye or head that he is discharging a merely mechanical duty, while he is fully awake to all that is passing around him. Almsgiving is general and liberal—it is a means of salvation. But it is ostentatious. Ramazan, the ninth month of the year, is a time of fasting among the Persians as among all other Mahometans. The months being lunar, of course this occurs at different seasons in the course of the solar years. The fast is very strictly observed by the Persians. Judgment, mercy, and truth are not usually so much cared for as religious ceremony by such people.

The Mohammedans are all required to make a pilgrimage to the Kaabah at Mecca; but the Persians frequently do this by deputy, obtaining, by the hands of the persons who have gone the journey on their behalf, certificates from the Sheriff of Mecca, which are quite sufficient for every purpose. Personally, the great body of the Persians rather go to Bagdad, where Ali established his government, and where he lost his life. *Kufah*, in this region, is the sacred locality. It is about thirty miles from the ruins of Babylon. There are splendid mosques at Kerbelah, Meshid Ali, and Kathem, all in the same district, or not far removed, built and enriched by the gifts of pilgrims, and by costly presents from Persia and India.

Sooffeeism has taken a strong hold of the national mind. The term *Sooffee* means "wise" or "pious." It may have been originally adopted from the Greek Σοφοὶ, *sophoi*, or "wise men." It is the common belief of the Sooffee, that every man is an incarnation of the Deity—all, at least, are partakers of the Divine principle. And this idea may be traced in the whole literature of the people. The Sooffees pay but little respect to the outward forms of worship, and rigid Moslems accordingly despise them. These principles are on the increase in Persia.

In the tillage of the soil the means employed appear to be those which have been in use from the remotest ages. The Persians devote much attention to their gardens, and with successful result.

Many of the manufactures of the people of Persia are especially beautiful, particularly their gold and silver brocades, their silks, and their imitations of Cashmere shawls. They work skilfully in iron and steel, and are tasteful in enamelling upon gold and silver. Chemistry, as known in Europe, is not in possession of the Persians, alchemy being the favourite pursuit in that country. In medicine their practice is just as they derived it from the ancient Greeks. They are wholly unacquainted with the anatomical structure of the human form, the Mohammedan religion not permitting dissection. The Moslems forbid representations of animate objects, but the Persians so explain the interdiction as to admit of their having many paintings of human and animal figures in their houses. Many of the Persian painters excel in the accuracy of their likenesses, and in the truth of their colouring. Generally, the rules of perspective are disregarded. In the higher branches of science they have made but little progress, their mathematics, their astronomy, and their geography being very defective.

Kingly power and the usages of royal courts in the East are in all essential respects the same now as in ancient times. The people exult and glory in the power and splendour of their king. In the books of Ezra, Nehemiah, and Esther we have a picture of the Court of Persia as suitable as if these compositions had been written but yesterday. Whatever sentence is pronounced by the King of Persia, whether of the bastinado, of mutilation, or of death, is inflicted on the spot in his presence. And, indeed, as we have said, so it is in all respects as we find in the ancient records. Enlargement is therefore unnecessary.

The Iranee, or Persians, are divided into two great classes, the fixed and the erratic, called respectively the Eilauts and the Sheherees. Jews are met with in all the great towns, as are also Armenians and Nestorians, and a few Sabeans, or Star-worshippers. The Persians received their arts and sciences originally from the Arabs. A spirit of liberal inquiry begins to affect society, and the Shah even speaks of visiting Europe. The stolidity of the national character, however, is indicated in the fact that a whole year from the time of the resolution was intended to elapse before the visit should be performed. European patience could not last so long.

As these pages pass through the press, the Shah, the "King of kings," has left Teheran on the first stage of his journey westwards. The first stage of the royal progress was very short, and his Majesty was expected to remain at Kaad till the first of May, to make arrangements for the administration of affairs during his absence. Nasr-ed-Din is accompanied by his Prime Minister, and in a few weeks will be in this country. The present Shah is the fourth sovereign of the Kadjan dynasty, with whose accession to the throne, eighty years ago, the modern history of Persia may be said to have commenced. Born in 1820, Nasr-ed-Din is now in his fifty-third year, and during his reign has been known as one of the most progressive among Oriental sovereigns. It was during the first Napoleonic era that Persia may be said to have entered within the domain of European politics; and the Crimean war brought her more prominently forward. In 1855 the Shah concluded a treaty with the Czar, the object of which was supposed to be the abandonment of the neutral policy hitherto pursued by Persia. Misunderstandings between England and Persia in 1856 have never been fully explained; but the result was not hurtful, if it has not proved the opposite, to both parties. Since 1857 there has been no reason presented by Persia for any anxiety on the part of England in respect to her Indian territory. Within his own dominions the present ruler of Persia has maintained peace and order such as have not been usual in the annals of the State. He has encouraged the introduction of foreign capital and enterprise, and has reorganized his army upon an European model. But what effect this visit to Europe may produce, who can tell? As to Orientals "their ways are not our ways." Nasr-ed-Din will return to Persia, very probably, with the conviction that "there is no place like home."

With the introduction of railroads, telegraphs, and commercial enterprise, Persia is now entering on a new era, if she can avail herself of the opportunity. Even as it is, she is the chief Oriental State which could offer any serious resistance to the advance of Russia towards India; and ever since the Court of St. Petersburg entertained the idea of extending the Russian dominion to the Himalayas, the arts of corruption, intimidation, and cajolery have been employed to induce the government of Teheran to "make one purse" with that of its colossal neighbour. This policy has been favoured by the intense jealousy with which the Turks and Persians regard each other as rival sectaries, not less than as neighbours whose frontiers are disputed. Much depends upon the "moral" effect produced by the Shah's visit to England. Her greatness and her power must impress him one way or another; and will affect, favourably or otherwise, our security in the East.

Ispahan contains the largest and most important university. There is also a university at Shiraz, and a third at Meshid. Besides these there is a school which furnishes learning for a certain class of mollahs at Kerbelah, where there is also a seminary for the study of law and philosophy.

The government is an unmitigated military despotism. The nomadic tribes are ruled by their local chiefs.

For the purposes of justice *Iran* is divided into large provinces, under the surveillance of great lords, who are called *beghlerbeghs*, who, under them, have governors of districts, *hakim*, and *darogas*, or governors of towns. But the limits of these provinces do not always comprise the nomadic tribes.

Persian Kurdistan, or *Ardelan*, is situated to the north-west of Iran, and is about 160 miles in length by 100 in breadth. It is composed of hills and table-lands and narrow valleys, in which are many villages. The soil is good in many parts, but the Kurds content themselves with raising grain sufficient only for their own maintenance. The country is inhabited by various tribes of Kurds, the principal of which acknowledge the rule of a chief who is under the supremacy of the King of Persia. *Azerbijan* adjoins the north-western frontier, and is one of the most fertile and productive of the provinces, but is high, and rugged, and cold. *Ghilan, Mazanderan,* and *Astrabad* occupy a low tract which lies between the shores of the Caspian Sea and the table-land of Iran. *Khorasan* is a large province of uncertain limits, forming the north-eastern portion of Iran. *Irak Ajemi,* or Persian Irak, is one of the most valuable provinces of the kingdom. It is almost everywhere intersected with valleys of indefinite length, seldom exceeding ten or fifteen miles in width. *Khuzistan* is the ancient Susiana, and a large portion of it lies along the eastern or left bank of the Tigris and Shatt-el-Arab, at the head of the Persian Gulf. *Fars,* or Farsistan, is the original Persia, and lies along the north-eastern side of the gulf, extending towards Irak and Kerman. There is scarcely a human inhabitant. *Laristan* is a small province on the northern side of the gulf. *Kerman* lies to the east of Fars and Laristan. It is mountainous and barren, destitute of rivers, and dependent for water on springs in the hills. Kerman, the capital of the province, has a population of about 30,000. It is celebrated for its manufacture of shawls, felts, and match-locks. *Seistan* is a small province in the eastern border of the kingdom, and is a complete desert of sand and rocks, through which flows the River Helmund from Affghanistan.

The Persians are temperate in eating, and use little animal food, pilau, rice, and fruit being their favourite dishes. They luxuriate in baths. Almost the poorest among them endeavours to possess a horse. Women of rank never appear in public without long veils. Arts and sciences are professedly held in esteem, but are by no means in a flourishing condition. The study of the Koran, divination, astrology, a sort of ethics, medicine, and poetry, are the chief parts of education. The architecture is simple, sculpture being almost unknown. The music is very inferior. The last great Shah, or head of the nation, estimated his income at £2,250,000 a year. The nomadic tribes live in a kind of independence. So it is generally with tribes, or clans, all over Asia.

AFFGHANISTAN.—This is the north-eastern portion of Persia, and is bounded on the north by the ridges of the Himalayas and Hindoo-koh, and the Paropamisan mountains; on the south by Beloochistan; on the east by the river Indus; and on the west by Khorasan and Seistan. It measures from west to east about 630 miles, and from north to south, 450; and contains an area of 240,000 square miles.

This point is of great importance, politically. If ever it were to occur that Britain and Russia were again to go to war, it is here that Russia could most easily effect an entrance into our Indian possessions, and the entrance would by no means be difficult. Affghanistan is a congeries of high valleys and table lands, which are separated by lofty mountains. The Hindoo-koh and Himalayas, which bound it on the north, appear in some places to form four distinct ranges, the most northerly of which is always covered with snow. It is not of equal elevation throughout. In some places the range is surmounted by peaks of great height and size, rising at once from their bases with great boldness and grandeur. The height of some of these peaks is 20,493 feet. The secondary ranges decrease in their elevation very greatly; their sides being covered with wood of various kinds, with ferns and other varieties of plants, making them ever verdant, while there are also clear streams constantly flowing to refresh the herbage. The summits of these mountains are all bare. In the lower portions the summer heat is sometimes excessive.

The Affghans have all the appearance of Jews, and many believe them to be really the descendants of the captive tribes of Israel. They are divided into a number of sections, which have distinct territories. The chief of every tribe bears the title of Khan, and is generally elected by the people, who pay some small amount of respect to primogeniture, but more to age, experience, and character.

The ordinary government of the tribes is conducted by the Khans, who meet in assemblies called *jirgas*. Such an assemblage of many commonwealths is the Affghan nation.

After the death of Nadir Shah, in 1747, Ahmed

Abdallee fought his way to Candahar, where he established a kingdom, which subsequently included the whole of Affghanistan and Beloochistan. He was succeeded by his son Timûr Shah, and he, successively, by two sons. The latter of these, Shujah, was deposed, but recovered his rule by means of the British forces in India, in 1840, after which date Affghanistan was virtually annexed to the English dominion. So turbulent and independent a people as these tribes compose cannot well be left to the unaided command of their own prince. Foreign allies seem to have to keep their king on his throne.

Cabul is a chief city of Affghanistan. The population numbers about 60,000, of many races, but who all converse freely in Persian as their mother tongue. The Pushtoo, or Affghan, is spoken in the neighbouring villages. The gardens and the fruit are celebrated. *Candahar* is the western capital of Affghanistan. It also has a population of about 60,000. It is said to have been founded by Alexander the Great, but the present city is comparatively modern. *Ghuznee*, which was once a great town, is completely in ruins. *Peshawer* stands in a large plain, which is watered by the river Cabul, and which extends westward from the Indus. The town is five miles in circuit, but beyond this there are many gardens and orchards, more or less cultivated. There are about 105,000 inhabitants. The *Kyber Pass* is about 30 miles in length, lined with precipices, and completely commanded by those who have possession of the upper ground. This pass is of painful historical interest, as having, not many years ago, been the scene of a bold and defiant advance of the English troops against their enemies, and of their cold-blooded massacre in the helplessness of their position, those who opposed them being on the cliffs above.

The principal river of Affghanistan is the Indus, which forms its eastern boundary. The others are the Aboo-Seen, with its tributaries; the Lundye; and the Helmund. The Furrah-rûd, or river of Furrah, runs into the Lake of Zunah after a course of 200 miles. The Gomul is lost in the desert, after flowing a similar distance. The only lake is the Ab-i-Standeh (*i.e.* the still water), about 60 miles east of Ghiznee; about three or four miles diameter in dry weather, and twice as much after floods.

The importance of Affghanistan to England, in respect to the securing of an undisturbed possession of her Indian territory, cannot ·be over-estimated. If England keeps this country of passes and defiles well defended, she will secure the quiet which is necessary in order to the promotion of the welfare of the immense multitudes which have in India come under her sway; but if these are neglected, any great power which can command a large army of land soldiery, whatever may be its resources at sea, would be able, by entering through these great natural gateways, to embarrass, if not to overthrow, a rule which has already proved in many ways so beneficial.

BELOOCHISTAN, the remaining division of Persia, lies between Affghanistan on the north, and the Indian Ocean on the south, and has an area of about 150,000 square English miles. The greater part of the country is mountainous, or occupied with table-lands. A large portion of it is desert. Not a hundredth part of it is cultivated; but where it is so, all the grain products of India grow there.

The people, to speak generally, are divided into two nations, the *Beloochees* of the west, and the *Brahoes* of the east. The former profess to be Arabs by descent, but they do not, in physical conformation, resemble that race. They are a rude, nomadic, pastoral people, moving from place to place with their flocks and herds. Their language is a corrupt dialect of the Persian. The Brahoes are inferior in person to the Beloochees. Their habits are still more unsettled. Formerly these territories were under the rule of the Khan of Kelat. There is still a nominal lordship permitted to the more local authority; but the welfare of the whole country has been promoted by the influence of the British. Villages are numerous. Gundara is the capital.

CHAPTER VI.

RUSSIA IN ASIA.

THE next great power in Asia is Russia. There are other and independent kingdoms or tribes, lying close to the countries of which we have spoken; but to these we shall subsequently invite attention.

The Russian Empire in Asia comprehends several countries and provinces of vast extent, which may be arranged in two distinct portions,—the Caucasian Provinces and Siberia. It is to the former of these that we shall more particularly refer, inasmuch as the latter is in many respects more Polar than Asiatic, although it is included in the Asiatic boundary.

RUSSIA IN THE CAUCASUS.—This country has a very irregular outline, and forms a kind of isthmus between the Black Sea and the Caspian. Its northern boundaries are the rivers Kouma, Mantyoh, and Kougoi-Jeia; the western, the Sea of Azov, the Strait of Yenikaleh, and the Black Sea; the southern, Turkish Armenia, the river Aras, and Persian Azerbijan; the eastern, the Caspian Sea,—this space comprising an area of more than 200,000 square English miles. The most prominent feature is the mountain chain of the Caucasus, which reaches across from near Anapa on the Black Sea to the peninsula of Abcheron on the Caspian, a distance of more than 700 miles, with a breadth varying from about 60 miles to 120. The highest part of the chain is to the east of Mount Elbûrz, 43° E., and contains many summits, which rise above the snow-line; but in the peninsula of Abcheron the elevation sinks down to that of ordinary hills. The loftiest pinnacle is Elbûrz or Elborus, according to usual European nomenclature; but such a name is applied by Circassians to all snow-capped mountains, without being distinctive of any. The proper Circassian name is *Osha-makhua* (or "mountain of happiness"). The Arbassians call it the "heavenly mountain," or the "mountain of the Great Spirit," while the Tartars style it the "mountain of stars."* Westwards from Elbûrz the chain extends to the north-west, parallel to the shores of the Black Sea, at a distance of 20 or 30 miles, presenting in its eastern portion a series of granitic and porphyritic summits to the height of 7,000 or 8,000 feet. Further west the summits decline, and there are low, rounded, wooded hills, cut into valleys, with many perennial streams.

The Western Caucasus is called *Kuschkaa* by the Circassians, but by the Russians is named *Chernigor*

* Spencer's Western Caucasus, i. 111.

("black mountains"), covered as they are with dense forests. Towards the banks of the Kouban the mountain valleys open into a plain, a great part of which is covered with forests, the acclivities, glens, plains, and river banks being embellished with cypresses of the growth of centuries, palm-trees, plantains, maples, elms, firs, alders, and poplars. The right or northern bank of the Kouban presents a scene widely different, and contains a tract as wild, desolate, and woodless as can be imagined. The soil of the mountain valleys is rich and well watered, and needs only human industry to render it highly productive. To the north of the Kouban and the Terek extends a wide plain, the western part of which is unadorned by a single tree, but is botanically interesting, being luxuriant with grass and many varieties of beautiful flowers. To the east of the Terek, reaching to the Volga, is a saline, sandy, and barren steppe, occupied by a few wandering Tartars, and presenting the appearance of having been formerly occupied as part of the bed of the Caspian Sea.

The southern slopes of the Caucasus subside into two great valleys. Through one of these flows the river Kûr, and through the other the Rioni. These rivers are fed from mountains, most of which are of ordinary height, but some rise to an elevation of 10,000 feet. The great lake Gûkcha or Sivan is formed by this mountain country, on the southern side of the Kûr. Ali-Ghuz, one of these mountains rises to the height of 12,000 feet.

The whole of this great region, with the exception of a comparatively small portion to the north of the Kouban, forms one general government of Russia in Asia. The Governor-General resides at Tiflis, the capital of Georgia. This government includes several ancient kingdoms, states, and provinces, whose names and peoples formerly acquired historical celebrity:— viz., 1. Georgia; 2. Shirwan; 3. The Russian portions of Armenia and Azerbijan; 4. Imeritia, Mingrelia, and part of Gûriel; 5. Abassia; 6. Circassia; 7. Daghestan and Lesghistan; and, 8. The old Russian province of Caucasia. To speak of them in this order:—

1. *Georgia.*—The country comprises the basin of the Kûr, and is about 240 miles in length by 120 in breadth. The natural features are agreeably diversified with hill and dale. The temperature is mild, and the people cultivate wheat and millet, and a variety of fruits. The vine is abundant and of good quality. The Georgians boast of their management of bees. They have horses and cattle and sheep equal to the best European breeds. The language is radically different from every known tongue, but those who speak it affirm that they are descended from the same stock with the Armenians. The beauty of their women is not less celebrated than that of the Circassians, though their skin is not so fair. Unhappily many of them are exported to Persia and Turkey for the supply of the harems there. The men are well-made and active. Many of the inhabitants of the country live in huts

half-concealed in the ground, but in more advanced districts the houses are better; though, even then, generally inferior, and constructed of wood. In almost all the villages there are towers built to serve as places of shelter for the women and children against the attacks of the Lesghis. About two-thirds of the population are proper Georgians, and are attached to the ritual of the Greek Church. Armenians and Jews are also numerous. Georgia was formerly a feudal monarchy, subdivided among princes and nobles, the former of whom paid no taxes, but during war were obliged with their vassals to follow the king. Their lawsuits were all decided by the king. The nobles paid certain dues to both the king and the princes; and although they dwelt in thatched cottages, their pride was equal to their poverty and their ignorance. Under such lordship the mass of the people lived in deep degradation. They were sold, given away or pledged, like domestic animals. All who were capable of bearing arms were soldiers, each noble commanding his own vassals, and the king being commander-in-chief. The king's revenues consisted of the fifth part of the produce of the vineyards, fields, and gardens; with duties on all exports and imports, as well as on the yield of the mines, which were but little worked. Being protected by mountains, Georgia escaped the great Tartar devastations; but for the last three hundred years it has been the scene of almost constant warfare. Though now under the regular government of Russia, it is a most unquiet country, and so poor in its unsettledness that its public revenues are not sufficient to pay necessary expenses. *Tiflis*, the capital, stands nearly in the centre of the country, on the right bank of the Kûr. It is the residence not only of the Governor-General of Caucasus, but also of an Armenian and a Georgian archbishop respectively. It publishes four newspapers in the languages of Russia, Georgia, Persia, and Armenia. The inhabitants, including the Russian garrison, number about 30,000. The cathedral is remarkable for its antiquity, its extent, and its architecture, and the ancient citadel is an imposing mass of ruins. The other principal towns are *Doucheti*, 27 miles from Tiflis; *Gori*, 45 miles; *Ganjah*, 90 miles; *Telavi*, 35 miles; *Signakh*, 56 miles; and *Akhaltsike*, 110 miles. Beyond the last-mentioned town, which has a population of 13,000,—much less than formerly,—the country is quite volcanic, and miles further on there is a great fortress which was formerly occupied in the interests of Armenia, which is a complete city, and is hewn out of volcanic stone; there being, among other works, three large churches, entirely cut out of the rock, as also Queen Thamar's summer and winter palaces, some of the apartments having finely executed sculptures.

2. *Shirwan.*—This used to be a province of Persia; but is, and has always been, of uncertain limits. As restricted in the acceptation of the name it comprises the lower part of the basin of the Kûr, between that river and the mountains. The climate resembles that

of Georgia. It produces cotton, rice, grapes and fruits of various kinds. The inhabitants are chiefly Mahometan Persians. The soil is saturated with naphtha, black and white,—its chief sources being near Bakû. This being a region of fire, the ancient fire-worshippers of Persia found their way to it in large numbers, expecting that the pilgrimage would purify them from sin. The chief town is Bakû, in which there is an old palace of the Kings of Persia. It stands on the shore, and exports naphtha, and other products of the country. In itself the town contains about 4,000 inhabitants, and the district not more than 19,000, of whom at least a thousand are Turcomans. To the south of Shirwan, and divided from it by the river Kûr, the Russian territory includes a portion of the former Persian province of Ghilan; but it is of small importance in any sense.

3. The Russian dominion in *Armenia* and *Azerbijan* extends between Georgia on the north, and Mount Ararat on the south, being about 200 miles from north-west to south-east, and 130 in breadth. It is a great mass of mountains crowding upon each other, and filling up the whole space between the Black Sea and the Caspian. In the midst of these is the great lake *Sivan*, about 5,300 feet above the level of the sea. In breadth it varies from 6 miles to 21 miles, and to travel round it is 47 miles. There is an island in it called *Sevan*, which contains a monastery. The western border of this region is the boundary of the Russian territory, formed

by the *Arpa-Chai* ("barley river"); and, according to trustworthy testimony, it presents as little obstruction to the passage of an army as does the Tweed between England and Scotland—happily not now reckoned a barrier. It is therefore, to be hoped, that a wise policy, like the times we live in, will preserve peace between Russia and her neighbours. *Erivan*, lat. 40° 9′ 30″ N., long. 44° 33′ E., is the capital of Russian Armenia. It is situated in a rugged valley, on the eastern bank of the Zengue, which is the outlet of Lake Gûkcha. It is a small city without walls, but good houses, having about 12,000 inhabitants, including 1,800 Moslem and 700 Armenian families. About 12 miles west of the city is the convent of *Etchmiadzin*, the ecclesiastical capital of the Armenian Christians.

4. *Imeritia*, *Mingrelia*, and the part of *Guriel* which is within the Russian territory, occupy the basin of the Rioni,—the northern border being formed by the Caucasus, the eastern by the mountains of Kartalini, the southern by those of Akhaltsike, and the western by the Black Sea. The soil is fertile but not much cultivated. The lower part of the country is a dead, unvaried flat, full of swamps and marshes. The people are of the Georgian race, and number about 150,000. Imeritia is directly under the control of the Russian government, but Mingrelia and Guriel are possessed of princes of their own, who acknowledge the supremacy of the Czar. Yet their countries are filled with Cossack police stations. The state of the peasantry has been

considerably improved since the Russian ascendancy, and the sale of slaves has been discouraged. *K'houth-aissi*, the capital, standing on the Rioni, is an unhealthy town near the centre of the province. There are only about 2,000 people—half of them being Jews. The heights above the town are covered with the ruins of a former better state of things, in the remains of temples, churches, bridges, aqueducts, and towers. The ancient name of the city was *Cyta* or *Cutasium*, and it was the birth-place of Medea, celebrated in classic mythology.

5. *Abassia* or *Abkhaz* lies along the north-east coast of the Black Sea, between the shore and the summits of Caucasus. It is about 260 miles in length and 30 in breadth. It is possessed by wild independent tribes, who set Russia at defiance, although their territory is authoritatively claimed as part of the empire; but the Czar has command only as far as his soldiers can reach. The Abassians were formerly well known as pirates of the Black Sea. The chief towns and forts are *Anapa*, from which the Circassian girls, along with others from Abassia, used to be exported to Turkey; *Soujouk-Kaleh; Ghelenjik; Vadran;* and *Pitzounda*; at all of which the Russians have small forts for the purpose of overawing the population.

6. *Circassia* occupies the north side of the Caucasus, from the Sea of Azof to the Upper Terek; but, by the gradual progress of Russian encroachment, the independent Circassians are now restricted to the comparatively small region which lies between the Kouban

and the tops of the mountains. The rule of the Russian empire is here very imperfectly defined. The Circassians call themselves *Adeches*, but their neighbours, the Nogai Tartars, call them *Tcherkesses*, a name which signifies "to cut off the head," and which they have gained for themselves by the ferocity of their lives. From this word is derived their name of Circassians. They are divided into about a dozen tribes, whose habitat fluctuates by frequency of change from place to place. It is believed that they number about 272,400 males. There is much animosity among the tribes against one another. In religion they profess to be Mahometans; in morality, they are unscrupulous plunderers, who respect only those who are of their own tribe or lineage. In external appearance, however, the Circassians are a remarkably fine race, and their women are reputed the most beautiful of the Caucasians. They so harass and rob and murder the peacefully disposed all around them that it is the interest, if it be not the duty, of the Russian government to completely subdue them.

7. *Daghestan* and *Lesghistan* comprise the mountainous country which lies between the west coast of the Caspian Sea, and the summits of the Eastern Caucasus, as far west as the Koisou; and extends into Georgia as far as the Alazan, an affluent of the Kûr; along the coast reaches from the Terek to Abcheron, a distance of 260 miles, while its greatest breadth between the sea and Mount Teresh is about 100. The north-eastern portion of Lesghistan is included in this measure-

ment, but its southern portion extends beyond it, down to the northern slopes of the mountain. As its name implies, Daghestan is the country of mountains; yet the soil is fertile, and the climate mild. Daghestan abounds with rivers,—the Koisou being the principal, and its banks and the surrounding country very beautiful. The lowlands are inhabited by a mixed race, descended from Persian, Arabian, Syrian, Turkish and Tartar colonists, intermingled with the aboriginal Caucasians. The mountains are inhabited by the *Lesghis*, the most predatory and ferocious of all the Caucasian nations. They were conquered by Nadir Shah, and driven by his victorious arms in 1742 to seek the protection of Russia. Their language is peculiar, and has few analogies with any other tongue. They are Soonee Mahometans. *Derbent* is the principal town of Daghestan, and has 20,000 inhabitants. It was once larger, being an ancient city, and formerly was the key city commanding the side of the Persian empire on which it lies.

8. The *old province of the Caucasus* includes the whole territory to the north of the Terek and the Kouban, lying between the Caspian Sea and the eastern border of the government of Tauridia, and bounded on the north by the rivers Kouma and Manytsh. It is almost entirely a sandy steppe. It is occupied by various tribes whom Russia has not been able to subdue, but whose country they claim, and from whom

they exact such acknowledgment of supremacy as they can procure. Even official dispatches which have to be carried through these tribes require an escort of at least 150 men. In only a few villages in the valleys of the Terek on the military road to Georgia, is there anything like an acknowledgment of the power of the Czar. The Russians first took possession of this country in the time of Peter the Great, who extended his dominion along the Caspian Sea into Ghilan; but in the reign of the Empress Anne the military establishments were withdrawn to Kislar, and a line of forts was carried along the Terek, for the defence of the frontier. Mozdok was built in 1763, and from that point the line was extended gradually westward to the Sea of Azof, along the northern bank of the Kouban. In the history of the wars in which the Russians have been engaged with Persia and Turkey we find that they have been led again and again to the south of the Caucasus, anxious to establish their authority over the intervening tribes, who, when not reduced to subjection, are always troublesome neighbours. In the course of time such subjection may be accomplished, but hitherto the progress has been very slow. The towns in this province are, Stavropol, the capital,—a neat fortified town near the Kouban; Karass, a town at the "foot of the five mountains;" *Bech-tau*, remarkable for the presence in it of a colony of Germans and Scotch; and Kislar, an important fortress and a large town of 9,000 inhabitants, the greater part of whom are Armenians.

Some of these are very wealthy, and have built for themselves the finest church in the region of Caucasus, at an expense of £24,000 sterling.

2. SIBERIA.—Siberia is the name of that part of the Russian dominion which extends in length from the Ural mountains, on the borders of Europe, to Behring's Straits and the Northern Pacific Ocean, which separate it from America; and in breadth from the Arctic Ocean to the Altaï mountains, which form the borders between the Russian and the Chinese Empires. Its extreme length is more than 4,000 miles; and its breadth is about 1,870. Originally, Siberia was a small Khanat, or kingdom, founded by the Tartars in 1242, on the banks of the Irtish and the Obi, and which was called Siberia, from *Sibir*, its capital. The Russians invaded this khanat in the sixteenth century, and though vigorously opposed, conquered it by force of numbers, and annexed it to their own territory. As the Russian discoveries and conquests extended to the eastward, the name was vaguely applied to all the newly acquired countries, till at length it reached the farthest limits of Asia on the Arctic and the Pacific Oceans. It was even for a time extended to the kingdoms of Astrakhan and Kazan, on the west of the Urals; but it is now definitely restricted to the country east of those mountains.

Siberia is a vast plain, sloping upwards from the Arctic Ocean to the Altaï Mountains and the Urals; but the rise is so gradual that it is scarcely perceptible.

The Urals extend along its western border from near the Gulf of Karskaia to the River Ural, in few places exceeding an elevation of 5,000 feet. Immediately to the east is the basin of the great river Irtish. So low is this tract that at Tobolsk, 500 miles in a straight line from the Gulf or Sea of Obi, the lower portion of the town is only 128 feet above the level of the Arctic Ocean. Even the basin of the Upper Irtish, on the south side of the mountains, 1,750 miles from the ocean in a straight line, has been found not much to exceed 1,900 feet. The plain of Siberia consists almost entirely of steppes and marshes, intersected by large sluggish rivers. The steppes are different from each other in character and appearance. In some places they are like the American savannahs, covered with tall grass; in others, the soil is saline—the salt being mixed with the earth, or existing in ponds or lakes of salt water; but in general they consist of very loose soil, with many lakes, inasmuch as the waters stagnate from want of declivity or fall. This supposes that such spaces are not arid, as the name steppe would seem to imply. On the contrary, many of them are full of lakes, morasses, and rivers. In some parts the plain is a bog as level as the sea—here and there covered with grass or weeds, or patches of poplars and birches. Many of the smaller lakes are salt. In some of these regions a death-like silence obtains. In the neighbourhood of Irkutsk the country is agreeable, the soil fertile, and the agriculture good.

The rivers are the *Obi*, the *Yenesei*, the *Lena*, and the *Ural*, which is the boundary between Europe and Asia.

The great lake *Baikal* is about 360 miles in length, and from 20 to 52 wide, being thus about 1,200 in circumference. Its depth varies from 20 fathoms to 100, and at certain points is even 200.

The climate of Siberia is peculiar. It is not entirely that of a cold and frozen latitude, although it is such in no small measure, being a plain, and without shelter from the winds that reach it from the polar quarter. It is also excluded by the high mountains of Central Asia from the warmer breezes which would otherwise reach it from the equator. The winter lasts for nine months. It is thus a cold country for much of the year. But the summer heat, though short and sudden, is powerful. The growth of vegetables is almost visible. The animal and vegetable productions are, generally speaking, semi-polar.

Up to the year 1822 Siberia was under the rule of military governors, but at that date civil magistrates were appointed, and the country was divided into the provinces or general governments of Western Siberia— Omsk, and Tomsk, and Tobolsk, being included in that arrangement; and Eastern Siberia, to which belong the governments of Irkutsk, Yeniseisk, and Yatutsk, with the addition of the two governments of Okhotsk and Kamschatka, under slightly different arrangements.

The riches of the country consist chiefly of mines of

gold, silver, platina, copper, and iron. It will have been observed by the reader that the southern parts of Russian Asia yield little material profit to the empire. They are mere dominions, or alleged dominions, or the means and helps to aggression on other lands or other empires, or a protection from the encroachments of such empires on Russia proper. Such an instrumentality for the protection of great kingdoms is not to be despised. But while it is so in respect to the southern provinces, it is far otherwise with the northern and Siberian portion of this dominion in Asia. Siberia is largely used by Russia as a penal settlement, and to some extent such a settlement for such a nation may be a necessity, but it is also a source of abundant revenue. There are large forests of great trees in particular districts, so thick that the woodman has scarcely room to wield his axe, and from these much wealth is obtained. The yield of the precious metals is variable and precarious, though in some years considerable and even great. The copper ore is liberally productive, and the iron is spread over so wide a field that it must take many ages to exhaust it, while it lies so near the surface that the expense of procuring it is but small, and especially so when it is remembered that much of the labour is unhired, and exacted at the hands of persons sentenced to a penal servitude. There is an annual exportation of iron to the extent of 132,000 tons.

Till recently—the treatment of political offenders and criminals in Russia being now less severe—there were, on the average of every ten years, 70,000 persons sent to Siberia into exile. Except for crime, none, it is true, could be sent without their families. The lowest class are condemned to the mines; others are distributed among the distilleries; and a third section receive grants of land, for which a small sum is paid to the government. A strict police surveillance is placed over all.

In Russian Asia the population is about 7,000,000, in the Caucasian provinces 3,000,000, and in the Siberian division 4,000,000. The population of Russia altogether is about 75,000,000.

The government in all parts of the empire is an absolute and hereditary monarchy. The Emperor rules of divine right, and acknowledges no fixed law but his own will. Round his diadem is wound the pontifical tiara—for he is Head of the Church as well as King of Russia—and the titles which he bears, to speak with moderation, would at least fill one of these pages. He is now styled the Emperor most usually; in former times it was the Czar, or, more strictly speaking, the *Tzar*. Princes of the blood, and their sisters, are called Grand-Princes and Grand-Princesses, and among them the heir to the throne is designated the Czärowitz. Czärina is a title of the Empress. Princes, counts, and barons are the only titles of nobility. The orders of knighthood are seven in number. The officials in the service of the government are all classed as of certain *tchins* or ranks, and, nominally, there are fourteen.

There is, for the maintenance of the authority of the government, a Council of the Empire, which was established in 1810. The number of members is not limited, but it generally amounts to thirty-five or thirty-six. This council is divided into five departments—1. Legislation; 2. War; 3. The Church and Civil Affairs; 4. Internal Political Economy; 5. The Affairs of Poland. The Emperor himself is the real president, but the council has a permanent presiding member appointed by the Emperor for life. Each department has its own president and secretary, and the whole together have a common grand Secretary of State, who is the principal director of the Chancery, and the organ through whom the council makes known its decisions to the monarch. On receiving the Emperor's confirmation of the council's decisions, this grand secretary communicates them to the respective authorities upon whom their execution devolves. There are thirteen "Ministries" for the administration of justice and affairs. The religion of the State is the Greco-Russian —more popularly, the Greek Church. In Russia, however, there are certain peculiarities which distinguish it from what is usually styled the Greek Church. Here the Emperor is the head. This religion is professed by 49,099,717 souls. This Church separated from the Roman in 1054, and from the Byzantine patriarchate in 1587.

The army in 1822 consisted of more than 1,000,000 men; but since that time has not by any means been so large. The fact of its former immensity shows, however, what is possible in a case of emergency. At present it is supposed to number not fewer than 800,000, there being no special reason why it should be more. The navy has its principal station on the Baltic. It is not large. The principal naval station is Cronstadt, Sebastopol having been dismantled. There are some ships of war on the Caspian.

St. Petersburg, the capital of this great dominion, both European and Asiatic,—for Russians claim that the empire is one,—occupies more space than any other city in Europe, with the exception of London and Moscow. It is situated at the mouth of the Neva. It is 485 miles north-west of Moscow, and about 1,400 miles north-east of Paris and London. It is the seat of the court, of the senate, the holy synod, of a university, and of many public bodies besides, and for beauty and splendour surpasses every other city in Europe. The stranger wanders with admiration through the broad regular streets, surrounded with the most magnificent palaces, churches with gilded towers, and other massive and colossal structures, his eye resting everywhere on masterpieces of architecture. The Czar Peter the Great laid the foundations of the city in 1703, when he constructed a fort on an island in the Neva. Around this the city has grown. There are many most gorgeous palaces, marble without and with elaborately costly decorations within. But our purpose is not a history of European Russia or its capital. We name the capital because of its relation to the Asiatic provinces of the empire. Petersburg contains 115 churches for the established worship, and, other denominations being tolerated, 33 for other rites. The most splendid of these are Isaac's Church, and that of our Lady of Kazan. The latter is of great dimensions—the nave and cupola are supported by fifty-six granite columns, with bronze capitals; the pavement is of different kinds of marble; the steps to the choir of porphyry, with a silver balustrade. Among the towers, the most remarkable are that of the admiralty, and that of the fortress, of a pyramidal form, more than half being covered with plates of pure gold. Public worship is conducted in fifteen languages, and according to eleven different rites. There is no instrumental music in the Russian churches, neither are there seats in them. The worshippers come and go at pleasure. The climate is very severe, and sleighing continues nearly five months. The population is about 600,000. Such is the capital of the great empire of which Russia in Asia is a part.

In recalling the beginning of the connection of Russia with Asia, it is right to remember that this northern empire, now so great, sprang from a small nucleus, and in respect to Asiatic countries and nations was not the first aggressor. The nation originated in the union of a number of nomadic tribes, under the name of Scythians and Sarmatians, and inhabited the countries lying between the Don and the Dnieper. They were joined by others, and, from the fifth century, Alans,

Huns, Avars, and Bulgarians, made war with them and possessed their country, or joined them in a friendly manner, and thus there was formed a nation. In the north of what is now called Russia lived the Finns, wandering herdsmen and hunters; and these also, in the course of time, and after conflict, became incorporated. They built in their united state the two cities of Novgorod and Kiev; which, at a later period, became powerful by means of their commerce. At the first they suffered greatly from the Chazars. The various communities of which this one nation was composed became divided among themselves, and the surrounding rulers took advantage of their dissensions to invade their country. From 1223 the Mongols were the most dangerous of these neighbours. After a devastating war of fifteen years the Mongols occupied all Russia, Novgorod only being excepted by treaty. The Russians were, at that time, in a low state of civilisation, partly on account of the variety of tribes of which they were composed. Their military organization was also inferior. Commerce was chiefly in the hands of German merchants, who, since 1200, had entered the country. While the Mongols oppressed the Russians, the Livonians, Teutonic knights, and Swedes attacked them on the other side, and an annual tribute had to be paid to the Mongols.

But, in course of time, the tide, which had been at its ebb, began to flow. Ivan I. succeeded, after a struggle which continued from 1477 to 1481, in setting

s

Russia free from the Tartars. The wife of Ivan (Zoë, a Greek princess, through whom the double-headed eagle came into the Russian arms) did much good in Russia. Ivan established a standing army, made wars, met with many reverses, but began a career of conquest which has never since been abandoned.

Russia since it became great has ever been an aggressive and encroaching power. Even at the accession of the present dynasty to the throne of Russia, in 1613, the Russian dominions were very large. They included a map-space greater than that possessed by any contemporary power. From the time of Ivan the history of Russia has been one of uninterrupted encroachment, east, west, and south. At the north, her back was already against a wall of ice. Her first advance was along the northern latitudes of Asia. When Peter I. found himself sole Czar of Russia, in 1689, his dominions were immensely larger than those which, seventy-six years before, had come into the possession of his grandfather, Michael Romanoff; but he inherited the spirit of aggression which had already distinguished this empire. In him, however, this spirit of aggression developed itself in such a colossal degree, and was associated with such original force of intellect, that it is not uncommon to date the encroachments of Russia from his accession. His spirit has been bequeathed to his successors, and it has now come to be a commonplace of historical observation that Russia is, *par excellence*, the encroaching Power of the world. It has been truly said that, in regard to Russia, "History furnishes no other example of equal pertinacity in prosecuting, *per fas et nefas*, a predetermined course of aggrandisement. The crown of Russia has been transferred, by open violence or by secret crime, from one head or one family to another; but each successive sovereign, with hardly an exception, has made some progress towards the attainment of the hereditary objects." And there are reasons for this. It is natural in men who are poor to seek to become rich; it is natural in men who dwell in cold and barren regions of the north to press southward into warmer lands, of whose beauties they have heard, or which they have seen, and whose luxuries they may have tasted.

Peter made attacks on four out of the six Powers conterminous with Russia—namely, Sweden, Turkey, Persia, and Tartary. But it is not our present purpose to speak in general of Russian aggression, so much as of Russian aggression in Asia. There was, in 1717, an armed mission to the Khan of Khiva in Tartary, with a view to the establishment of relations with the Tartar natives, and, if possible, to seize a fabulous gold mine in those parts. The Khivans outwitted the mission, the members of which were got into separate parties, and cut to pieces. There was, thus, nothing gained. But the defeat has never been forgotten; and present complications with Khiva may not unreasonably be regarded as one of the results of it. In 1723-1725 there were aggressions made on the Caspian provinces of Persia, during the convulsed state of that country. These were in part successful, and temporary possession was gained of the whole western coast of the Caspian. In the reign of Catherine I., 1725-1727, and Peter II., 1727-1730, the Russians never ceased from interfering in Persian affairs, and continued to hold the Caspian provinces which had been seized. In the reign of Anne, 1730-1740, the Russians continued to prosecute their designs against Persia, and even came to an understanding with Turkey for the partition of the possessions of Persia lying between the Black Sea and the Caspian; but the genius of the great Nadir Shah restored the prowess of Persia, and both Turks and Russians were compelled to give up what they had gained. The accession of Catherine II., after the reigns of Elizabeth and Peter III., forms an epoch in Russian history. She boldly carried into practice what had been in the mind of Peter I., and communicated to Russia that impulse which has ever since carried her forward in a career of aggrandisement which, it is to be feared, is not yet terminated.

In 1768, six years after the accession of Catherine, Russian troops overran Crim-Tartary, Moldavia, and Wallachia, and prepared the way for encroachment and domination in more central and advanced parts; and in 1774 there was a carrying out of this policy by incessant intrigues with the small states and principalities south of Mount Caucasus, and in the country between the Black Sea and the Caspian, with the view of inducing those states to throw off their allegiance to Persia, and to come under the protectorate of Russia. These endeavours were successful so far that, in 1783, Mingrelia, Imeritia, and Georgia, submitted to the Russian protectorate, thus enabling Russia to dominate south of the Caucasus in the important isthmus between the two seas. In 1795-1796 there was war with Persia, arising out of an attempt by Aga Mahommed Khan, the Persian king, to recover Georgia and the other trans-Caucasian provinces. In this war the Russian victories in these regions greatly extended the Russian sway along the Caspian.

Paul I. came to the throne in 1796. At first he took part with the coalition against Bonaparte (1798), but afterwards sided with him (1800), and constituted himself the head of the northern union of states against British commerce, going so far as to project and fit out an expedition at Orenburg for an overland march to India through Tartary and Persia. About this time Georgia was formally incorporated with Russia, and ceased to be spoken of as under "protection."

Alexander I. became Emperor in 1801. There was continued and desultory war with Persia, carried on in the trans-Caucasian provinces, and the new territories in that region were all occupied by Russian generals. The war ceased, at the instance of the British, by the "Peace of Gulistan," in 1814, and Russia retained all her conquests from Persia, including Mingrelia, Imeritia, Georgia, Ganja, Derbend, Badkov, Kara-baugh, Sheki, Shirwan, Daghestan, and parts of Moghan and Talish. Persia at the same time surrendered the right of having ships of war in the Caspian. The effect of the treaty, as a whole, was to advance the Russian frontier along the whole Caucasian isthmus to the most southern point of the Caspian, leaving no population in that isthmus unsubdued except the brave Circassians inhabiting the mountains along the Black Sea from the Sea of Azof to Mingrelia.

Nicholas I. began his reign in 1825. There was again war with Persia in 1826, arising out of disputes as to the interpretation of the treaty of Gulistan, which was concluded by the "Treaty of Turcomanchai" in 1828, by which were ceded to Russia the rich provinces of Erivan and Nukchivan, the frontier of Russia towards Persia being thus extended to the river Arras or Araxes, while, by keeping possession of parts of Moghan and Talish, Russia retained a portion of the Caspian coast beyond that river, thus violating the boundary for Persia. In 1839-40, there was another expedition against Khiva, which failed.

Russian "aggression" has, during the time since the accession of Peter I., been without parallel. "The acquisitions of Russia from Sweden are greater than what remains of that kingdom; her acquisitions from Poland are equal to the Austrian empire; her acquisitions from Turkey in Europe are of greater extent than the Prussian dominions, exclusive of the Rhenish provinces; her acquisitions from Turkey in Asia are nearly equal in extent to the whole of the smaller states of Germany; her acquisitions in Persia are equal in extent to England; her acquisitions in Tartary have an area not inferior to that of Turkey in Europe, Greece, Italy, and Spain. The acquisitions she has made within the last sixty-four years (prior to 1836) are equal in extent and importance to the whole empire she had in Europe before that time. . . . In these sixty-four years she has advanced her frontier 850 miles towards Vienna, Berlin, Dresden, Munich, and Paris; she has approached 450 miles nearer to Constantinople; she has possessed herself of the capital of Poland; and has advanced to within a few miles of the capital of Sweden. Since that time she has stretched herself forward about 1,000 miles towards India, and the same distance towards the capital of Persia (Teheran). The regiment that is now stationed at her farthest frontier post on the western shore of the Caspian has as great a distance to march back to Moscow as onward to Attock on the Indus, and is actually farther from St. Petersburg than from Lahore, the capital of the Punjaub."*

Is the aggressive tendency of Russia exhausted? Has she reached the utmost limits of her spontaneous expansion? The man is absolutely fatuous who will say so. Russia is at present more aggressive, more voracious than ever. And her process is always the same. It invariably begins with disorganization, by means of corruption and secret agency, pushed to the extent of

---

* Sir John Macneill, "The Progress of Russia in the East," 1836.

disorder and civil contention. Next comes military occupation to restore tranquillity; and in every instance the " protection " has been followed by incorporation. Such have been the means by which Poland, the two Kahardas, Georgia, Imeritia, and Mingrelia, have been added to the Russian dominions. A careful observer will find that along the whole line of the present frontier of the Russian dominions, and even beyond that line, this preliminary process is just now, and has been for years, going on, and the fact which is indicated is that Russia has marked more victims and still more.

But why ought this to be allowed to go on unchecked? It is not for the interest of humanity at large that any great Power should go on ever enlarging its empire, and constantly absorbing into it new populations. The extension of Russian ascendancy beyond its present limits is not safe for the British Empire. Even if she cannot hope to dominate over Europe and dictate to England at home, there is still the possibility of a Russian invasion of India. The First Napoleon understood such possibilities, and he pronounced a Russian invasion of India to be not only practicable but one day almost inevitable. Speaking to O'Meara at St. Helena, in 1817, he said, "I do not think that I shall live to see it, but you may. You are in the flower of your age, and may expect to live thirty-five years longer. I think that you will see that the Russians will either invade and take India, or enter Europe with

400,000 Cossacks, and other inhabitants of the desert, and 200,000 real Russians. When Paul was so violent against you English (in 1800-1), he sent to me for a plan to invade India. I sent one with instructions in detail. From a point on the Caspian Sea he was to have marched on India." O'Meara observed that the distance to India was great, and that the Russians had not money enough for such a grand undertaking; but Napoleon answered, "The distance is nothing; supplies can be easily carried on camels, and the Cossacks will always secure a sufficiency of them. Money they will find when they arrive there. The hope of conquest would immediately invite armies of Cossacks and Calmucks without expense. Hold out to them the plunder of some rich cities as a lure, and thousands will flock to their banners."

But even on the supposition that the invasion of India by Russia is impracticable, it might be in the power of Russia to cause infinite trouble and expense to Britain by the extension of her sway in the East. Sir John Macneill says, "Every approach of Russia towards India lessens the difficulties, and, if once Persia were conquered, or became friendly, Herat would become the frontier, and there would no longer be any insuperable impediment. [Persia is in friendship with Russia now. Preparations are being made at the present moment for a visit of the Shah to the Court at St. Petersburg.] But were Russia established at Herat, the influence she would exert in India, even in time of peace, would be such as to render the government of that country much more delicate and difficult than it now is. Rebellions would become much more frequent and formidable. The revenue would in many places be collected with difficulty. The minds of all men would become unsettled, and every movement on the Indus or beyond it would assume a new character, from the connection it would or might have with the new and powerful neighbour to whom all the disaffected would have recourse." *

There are two modes by which Russia might penetrate to India; first, by the subjugation of Turkey, which would give her, as from a central citadel, the command of both Europe and Asia; and, second, by traversing the countries which lie directly between her Asiatic frontier and the north-western boundary of India.

As to the former of these we need here say but little—the point is not in present question. The great Lord Chatham said, "With the man who cannot appreciate the interests of England in the preservation of the Ottoman empire, I will not argue." The possession of the Dardanelles would give to Russia the means of acquiring an almost unlimited marine force. It would enable her to prepare her armaments in the Black Sea without the probability of interference, or perhaps of the knowledge of any European Power. Constantinople once in the possession of Russia, the passage to India is no longer a matter of difficulty.

* "Progress of Russia in the East," pp. 103-105.

The voyage from London to the ports of the Indian peninsula, and such as war ships and transports must take, is estimated at about sixteen or eighteen thousand miles; from Constantinople to Bombay or Surat, it is, at the utmost, three thousand, including a land carriage of four hundred miles from Trebizond to Mosul, through a country abounding with cheap means of transport, with the advantage of having Erzeroum lying directly in the route. And authority has declared that "there is no place, east of Constantinople, better calculated for assembling a large force than the plain of Erzeroum." *

The invasion of India by the traversing of the countries which lie between has been supposed by some to be impossible, because of the distance. But look at the matter. The countries known under the general appellation of Central Asia, and lying between Russia and England, are divisible into four—Persia, Khiva, or Kharesm, Bokhara and Cabul. Besides these there are vast regions which acknowledge no authority whatever. These countries present two lines of approach from the Russian frontier to India—the one by the subjugation of Persia, the other by the conquest of Khiva and Bokhara. It is a task of much difficulty for any foreign power to establish itself either in authority or good grace with the Uzbeks. But Russia has diligently laboured, sometimes by flattery, and sometimes by means of power, to be beforehand with the

* Colonel Kinneir, British Envoy at the Court of Persia.

other European Powers in the attempt. "The Russians," says Burnes, "have impressed the whole of the Uzbeks with high notions of their power, to the detriment of all other nations."

If Persia could be subdued matters would become much more easy, and every tyro knows how much Russia has hemmed in and narrowed the dominion and weakened the power of Persia during the course of recent years. Persia conquered first, or Khiva and Bokhara first subdued, the principal aim would then be to take possession of Herat, which is of all points on the frontiers of the Affghan country the most favourable to prepare for the invasion of India.

But even if Persia withstood all attempts at her overthrow, and resisted all endeavours even to draw her into an alliance with the northern empire against English rule in India, there are still other means of approach which are not impracticable. The possible routes are these: 1. From Orenburg, through the steppes of Khirgis to Bokhara, and thence by Balkh to Cabul; 2. From the Caspian at Manghishlak to Khiva and the Oxus; from the Oxus to Kilif near Balkh, from which to Cabul is only 250 miles. In both of these routes successive conquests might be necessary; but some have been accomplished, and others may be contemplated; 3. A *coup de main* from Astrabad through Khorasan to Herat, from which there are three practical roads to Kandahar, and from thence to the Indus. The entire distance is about 2,000 miles;

4. A rapid descent of the Euphrates to the sea on rafts from below Erzeroum, in the flooded season. Recent investigations have moreover proved the practicability of a passage along the banks of the Euphrates for the march of an army to the Persian Gulf.

Groundless alarm is weak; provision for an evil day is wise. Our great territory in India, ours now more than ever, though at great cost of life and treasure, must be sedulously shielded from the threatening of harm if that be possible. To "lock the door of the stable after the steed has been stolen" is not commendable policy. In this question all that affects the condition of Central Asia is of vast importance. The question may some day be, shall England encounter Russia with all Asia at her back, or oppose Russia with all Asia at her side?

Various attempts having been made by Russia against *Khiva*, and those attempts at the moment of our writing succeeded by another, which has been the subject of negotiation between Russia and the British government (such expedition being, indeed, already on its way), it may be well for us to refer to that country more particularly. *Khiva*, Kharesm, or Orgunje is an independent Khanat of Turkestan, in Central Asia. It properly comprises only a narrow strip of fertile land along the Oxus, in the lower portion of its course. It is but of late years that it has established a supremacy over the wandering Tartar hordes, and been able to hold Mervè (Murù) with its territory, which lies on the road between Khorasan and Bokhara. The dominion of the Khan extends between the 36th and 44th degrees of N. lat., and 52nd and 64th of E. long., having to the east the Karakalpac territories and Bokhara; to the south, Affghanistan and the Persian province of Khorasan; to the west, the Caspian; and to the north, the Khirgiz Steppe and the Sea of Aral. This territory had, for a lengthened period, been a sort of "no-man's land;" it was occupied by the Tartars, and was claimed by both Persia and Bokhara, and the claim was disputed by neighbouring great Powers, the tribes themselves maintaining their independence till but recently. The Oxus is the great fertiliser of the district through which it passes. The climate and products greatly resemble those of Bokhara. The summer is hot, the air dry, and the evaporation rapid. The winter is short, and lasts only a few days at a time. Various kinds of grain are cultivated. The vine thrives; but the inhabitants being Mahometans, little wine is made. The distillation of brandy, however, has been introduced by the Persians, and, except in the capital, is freely used. An intoxicating liquor made from hemp has also been brought into the estimation of the people, to their hurt. Many of the fruits are good. Wood is abundant; but all over the desert, as distinguished from the wooded parts, there are only a few stunted bushes. There are not many horned cattle; sheep, and goats, and horse-flesh forming the principal animal food of the people. Agriculture and cattle-breeding mostly occupy the settled population; but some cotton and silk stuffs and shawls are made by the women, and exported to the neighbouring countries. Camels are the ordinary beasts of burden, and almost every Khivan possesses one.

The most numerous race in the population in Khiva is Uzbek, as it also is in Bokhara. The Khan belongs to it. The rest of the people are Tartars of various tribes, Jews, Armenians, and Persians. The Tartars are altogether nomadic and live by plunder. The Uzbeks constitute the chief portion of the Khan's army. Many inroads are made by both Tartars and Uzbeks—it being sometimes difficult to distinguish the two—both into the Russian and the Persian territories.

According to Burnes, the Khivans are little better than an organized banditti, protected by the natural strength of their country. There are from thirty to forty thousand slaves; and many prisoners of war, taken in the constant broils of the Khanat with its neighbours, are detained in the utmost misery.

Travellers in the country generally express the opinion, some the hope and some the fear, that Russia will gradually take possession of Khiva. If it were for its own sake, and for the purpose of helping its people to a better civilisation, that Russia desired this possession, one could not but wish it success; but the history of Russia, which so much shows one point to have been coveted as a help to the reaching of another, is a lesson which tells the neighbours, nearer or more remote, of this great Power, to beware. The country is at a manageable distance, by no means a difficulty, from what is now the British frontier in India; and, moreover, it is strong as a means of defence if an attacking army were compelled to retreat.

The trade of such a country it is not difficult to describe. There are four routes for communication with Russia— one through the Khirgiz Steppe, west of the Aral Sea, to Orenburg; a second by way of Sarachak, on the Ural, also to Orenburg; a third through Sarachak to Astrakhan; and a fourth from Khiva to Karaghan, on the eastern shore of the Caspian, whence goods are sent by sea to Astrakhan. About 2,000 camels go annually to Orenburg, Astrakhan, and some towns of Cabul and Persia, with wheat, barley, silk, and cotton fabrics, and yarn; and about a dozen large boats come annually from Astrakhan to Karaghan and the Gulf of Manghislak, with the products of Russia and the West, to be exchanged for those brought by the caravans from Khiva. The chief imports are slaves, coin, iron and copper—wrought and unwrought—handkerchiefs, wax, honey, sugar, tea—which, as in Bokhara, is a favourite article—cochineal, spices, and hardware. The commerce with Persia is insignificant. The trade of Khiva is solely in the hands of Turcomans, Khivans, and Persians—none but Mahometans being allowed to transact business within the Khanat. No foreign merchant can go into the country with safety; when not openly robbed of a large portion of goods, the caravans are delayed by the Khan's officers, the bales of merchandise are opened, and much property has, at times, been extorted. The commercial duties realised by the Khan amount to, perhaps, half his revenue, which is roughly estimated at 2,000,000 roubles, the remainder of this sum being made up of one-fifth of the produce of every predatory excursion of his subjects, a family tax of three ducats a year, taxes on war-horses, and on land cultivated by slaves.

The government is despotic. In each town there is a judge, and in the capital a central court of justice as a last resort. The Khan can raise a force of 10,000 men, and ten pieces of ordnance. His troops are mostly cavalry. There are in the Khanat, besides Mervè, only two towns worth notice—Khiva, the capital and seat of government, and Orgunje, the chief commercial town.

Khiva is a picturesque town. The population is estimated at from ten to twelve thousand. These are very much mixed. The houses, even the palace, are of mud, the only stone buildings in the place being three mosques, a school, and a caravansery. The chief trade of the capital is in slaves. The way in which slaves and prisoners of war are brought into Khiva is described by a recent intelligent traveller, whose language presents a painful picture :*—"Next morning I really did see about a hundred horsemen arrive from the camp covered with dust. Each of them brought at least one

* "Travels in Central Asia," by A. Vambery, London, 1864.

T

prisoner with him, and amongst the number, children and women, bound to the tail of his horse or the pommel of his saddle. Besides, he had buckled behind him a large sack containing the heads of the slain. On coming up, he handed over the prisoners to the Khan or some other great personage, and then, loosening his sack, seized it by the two lower corners, as if he were about to empty potatoes, and then rolled the bearded or beardless heads before the accountant, who kicked them into a heap consisting of several hundreds. Each hero had a receipt given him for the number of heads delivered, and a few days later came the time of payment." For its own sake, such a country is not worthy of much consideration. If its possession is coveted, that may be from reasons of reprisal or revenge, or State policy on account of its position and natural features. If it be defended and its independence protected, neither can it be for its protection as a nation, so called; it must be, again, for State reasons, as arising out of its position and the character of the country. In judging of questions which connect themselves with the occupation or defence of any such people or territory it is needful to take into account the antecedents and probable motives of the States negotiating.

Sir Henry Rawlinson delivered a lecture on "Russian Advances in Turkestan," in the lecture theatre of the University of London, on the evening of the 24th of March, 1873; the Prince of Wales was in the chair, and the fine hall was filled to overflowing. The lecturer pointed to the fact that the Khanat of Khiva was the original seat of the great Aryan race, and that there was reason for believing that the astronomical science of Eastern Asia arose in Khiva, passing thence to China and India. In relation to Russia and Khiva, he stated that the great value of Khiva to the Russians would be a connection with the prolongation of the Oxus with the Caspian, the eastern shores of which were receding. Such connection might easily be formed. The attention of Russia had first been directed to Khiva at the beginning of the last century by exaggerated reports of the auriferous sands of Kara Su, which was spoken of as a sort of El Dorado. The Kara Su was a branch of the Oxus running north to the Sea of Aral.

The history of the intercourse of Russia with Khiva may be given in few words. The first expedition, to which we have referred in a former page, as having occurred in 1717, was practically destroyed. The next was, if we speak only of serious attempts, in 1839-40, and this also resulted in retreat with heavy loss. Since that date four Russian officers have visited Khiva, with the purpose of inducing the Khan to release his Russian prisoners and to conclude a treaty of friendship. Ten years later, when the Russians began their advance up the Jaxartes, they again came into collision with the Khivans. In 1854 a commercial treaty with Russia was concluded, but did not work smoothly. In 1859 Russia set forth a manifesto of the grounds of her quarrel with Khiva, complaining that her commerce was impeded, her merchants plundered, and her subjects imprisoned. In the spring of 1871 war was commenced, and all subsequent outrages by the Khivans must be contemplated in the light of retaliation on account of the Russian invasion of the country.

Count Schouvaloff, during his recent official visit to this country, assured her Majesty's Ministers that the design of the Emperor was merely the punishing of the Khivans for injury inflicted on Russia and the subjects of Russia; that that once done he would evacuate the country. Our government was satisfied, and so was the envoy. The force to be employed is said to be four columns, 4,000 men, with forty pieces of artillery; but the probability is that the force is larger. The length of the march will vary according to the points of departure and the points of attack on Khiva, from 480 to 1,000 miles. Khiva, altogether, contains only 500,000 people. If Russia retire after conquest the Orientals will despise her. Such a thing they cannot understand. If she remain, in opposition to her assurances to the contrary, her so doing must be at enormous expense, and cannot but lead to misunderstanding with neighbouring Powers and with England in particular. The plan of the campaign is—General Kauffman being in command— that each division shall be large enough to act independently, and that the chief force will skirt the north side of the Mura Tau, within the limits of Bokhara, and will cross the Oxus at Tünüklü. Once at Khiva success is certain, but the results only time can show. In Parliament, her Majesty's Ministers declare that "no difficulty is likely to arise." But these people have successfully resisted their enemies down to the present day. So that, if now, all that is said being believed, there be no threatening of difficulty, prolongation of hostilities may change the aspect of affairs, as may also a great success and a crowning victory.

It has been reported in this country that, at the eleventh hour, the Khan has suddenly abandoned his hostile attitude, and changed his policy of resistance into one of deprecation, and desires to make peace with the Czar, having executed his Prime Minister, and imprisoned some of his own relations and other members of the war party, sending the so-called Russian prisoners on their way to Orenburg. There is nothing improbable in the report, but it requires confirmation. Such a proceeding would be quite compatible with the politics of Central Asia. The Khan is not an amiable potentate, and would readily adopt any measures, however severe, which might seem to him likely to serve his present purpose. But if he has succumbed, his relenting has come too late. Russia has gone to great cost, and been at much trouble for years in the planning and organizing of the expedition. A march on Khiva has been the cherished dream of half a century. It has been the object of special preparations ever since the seizure of Samarcand made the Czar virtual master of Bokhara. To that end the Caspian coast was occupied, and the Russian frontier moved south to the borders of Persia. In order to find a way to this Khanate, which trusted in the remoteness and the breadth of the desert lying between a formidable enemy and his prey, Russian officers have ridden along and surveyed the practical routes, and continual activity has been manifested on Lake Aral. It is therefore not likely that such persistent ambition will permit itself to be easily frustrated. The grievances complained of are not new—they were formally stated more than thirty years ago. Muscovite griefs, aims and professions are precisely what they have long been. Will the Khan sign any instrument binding himself to a different line of conduct? Will he pay such indemnity as must be required even on account of money already spent? No. But even if he had changed his policy, Russia will not abate one jot of her designs. The independence of Khiva piques Muscovite self-love, and places an obstacle in the way of ulterior objects. Russia wants free admission to the Oxus and a material guarantee insuring its permanent freedom. The military party passionately desire conquest, and the harvest of honours its achievement will enable them to reap. They have so far had their way. Military opinion counts for something in all countries—in Russia for much, especially in all that relates to the remote regions of Central Asia.

In the House of Commons attention has again been called to these movements of Russia, and the note of warning sounded by members of that House whose opinions are of authority and weight. On the part of the Government assurance is once more given that no danger to the rule of England is at all apprehended.

The Khan has sent ambassadors to Fort No. 1, on the mouth of the Jaxartes, with power to make the best terms with Russia they can. He has done so under the advice of Lord Northbrook. But the Khivan commission was too late to find General Kauffman, and messengers were dispatched to await him at the rendezvous. This intelligence comes with authority from St. Petersburg. But no change has been made in the Russian plans; neither could there well be any—there has not been time. General Kauffman, accompanied by two Russian princes, was making his way, with a strong force, along a track never before traversed by any European soldiery; the Aral flotilla was steaming south towards the Delta, in order to prepare the means of crossing the river; and the troops from Orenburg had crossed the Emba, and were pushing onwards. By the time we write the junction of forces has been effected, and the general in command is in a position to say whether he will halt on the frontier, or not rest satisfied with anything less than an armed occupation of the offending Khanate. Much must depend upon his own discretion. General Kauffman is a highly-trusted servant, and no doubt his orders were framed in large terms. Much will depend on the concessions made by the Khan. At the same time, the princes and the general may feel that, having come so far, an entry into the city is absolutely desirable to exalt Russian prestige and gratify themselves. But if they can be satisfied by the concessions made the troops would be spared part of an arduous journey, and the question of withdrawing from Khiva, after it had been occupied, would be evaded. As we have said, much depends upon the concessions.

But the army of India is in good condition. England is mistress of the seas, and there are fleets of gunboats on the Indus. Affghanistan in the north-west is a kind of bulwark against any hostile approach from Central Asia, and beyond Affghanistan are countries as savage as their scenery, whom it has been the policy of England to regard and uphold as independent borderlands. The most important of these are the three Khanats of Bokhara, Kokan, and Khiva. Hence the importance to us of the present movement. Bokhara is the most important of these provinces, and joins on to that of Khiva.

Bokhara is a portion of the ancient Bactria, whose history runs back to the most remote periods. Its capital, Balkh, has frequently been named in connection with the expedition of which we have had occasion to speak. Balkh is one of the oldest of cities. Its ruins occupy a circuit of twenty miles. They consist chiefly of fallen mosques and decayed tombs. Of the territory and the capital of Khiva we have already spoken.

CHAPTER VII.

THE TARTARS.

INCIDENTAL references have been made in the foregoing observations to the Tartars and their various tribes; but they constitute a race so peculiar and remarkable, that it seems necessary in order to a correct conception of Central Asia and its people, that those tribes and several of their peculiarities should be more distinctly contemplated.

The old geographers were accustomed to speak of European or Little Tartary, and Asiatic or Great Tartary. The former, in their arrangement, comprised those countries round the Black Sea which were inhabited by the Nogai Tartars, and the Budshiac Tartars or Bessarabians, with part of the country lying between the Dnieper and the Dniester. But since these districts have been annexed to Russia, the name has gone out of use. Besides Tartars, the Russians have now in the governments which they have formed in these localities, Greeks, Germans, and Jewish colonists among their population. Asiatic Tartary, called, from its extent, Great Tartary, used to include part of what are now the Asiatic provinces of Russia, the borders of Persia, Thibet, and the Chinese Empire. But all this has been changed by time and conquest. The northern part of what some style Zagatai, or Independent Tartary, is partly governed by separate khans or princes, being occupied by nomadic tribes, differing considerably in their character and manners, being generally claimed, with their native rulers, as subject to Russia. The southern part is called Great Bucharia, in which, among other commercial cities, is Samarcand, once the residence of Timour. Little Bucharia is subject to China. The whole of Central Asia, to the west of Zagatai, is often styled Chinese Tartary, which is an error, and it has resulted from the confounding of the Mongol and Mantchoo tribes, who roam over those regions with the Tartars, but with whom they have no natural affinity.

The proper Tartars, or Tatars more correctly, are divided into many branches, and, under different names, occupy a large extent of territory, both in Europe and Asia. Their true name really is Turks or Turcomanns, *Tatar* being supposed to be a Chinese name for all the nomadic tribes of Central Asia; some, however, contending that it is the proper designation of a Mongol tribe. Once the terror of their neighbours, they are now for the most part subject to foreign masters, while a few tribes insist that they are still independent; most of these latter occupying regions too barren to offer any temptation to conquerors, or too remote to be easily accessible. The Tartar part of the population of Russia amounts to about three millions, residing chiefly in the southern Asiatic provinces—many of them dwelling in stationary habitations, and occupied with agriculture. There are also some Tartar colonies distributed among the Russian villages in the governments of Orenburg, Kasan, and Tobolsk, and several hordes besides who claim to be merely the independent allies of Russia. The Russian Tartars, as we have already had occasion to mention, consist of several branches. The Tartars proper, the Nogais, the Bashkirs, the Kirghises, Yakoutes, and Teleutes. The Tartars proper are descendants of the two great hordes which the successors of Genghis Khan established in Siberia and on the Volga. About one-fifth of these Tartars have embraced Christianity, the rest are Mahometans. The Nogai Tartars are Mahometans or heathens. The Bashkirs are wanderers. The Kirghises breed cattle and cultivate ground, though settled as their life is they live in tents; they are Mahometans. And the Yakoutes and Teleutes, who are fewer in number, are in a purely nomadic condition, and worship idols. The Bucharians, under the protection of Russia, live in cities and villages, and are industrious workmen.

These people, being dispersed throughout the countries of Western and Central Asia, are widely different from the pastoral tribes of the desert (the Bedouins), and are more than equally removed from resemblance to the ordinary inhabitants of the towns.

Persia is largely occupied by tribes of this character; indeed, their chiefs are the princes and nobles of that country. These tribes, now inhabiting Persia and Turkey, are the descendants and relatives of those warlike pastoral races formerly and now inhabiting the regions beyond the Oxus, and who have been great conquerors at former periods of their history, having placed their chiefs on thrones in all the countries from the Ganges to the Adriatic Sea. The descendants of these chiefs are still sovereigns, really or in name, throughout the same extent of country. The great Mogul and the principal inferior princes of India were of Tartar descent. So are the kings of Persia, and the great lords of their empire; and so is the Sultan at Constantinople.

Many tribes of them have entered Persia at different times, and under various circumstances. These seem to a stranger to be one people; and, as distinguished from the other inhabitants, such they are; but, among themselves, they are divided into distinct tribes, each of which has a name of its own, and which has little connection with any other, except when several tribes take the same side in cases of civil war. The tribes differ greatly in numbers and power. Each has its own chief, who has the title of "khan," or lord. But this designation is not restricted to the chiefs of tribes; in fact, there are no precise rules in regard to the use of this title. On the one hand, it is a title which kings have been content to bear, the great Genghiz Khan, for example; and on the other, it is frequently bestowed at the present time on persons of no great consideration. The king may bestow it. The title descends from father to son, except in the case of the chief of a tribe, who is khan not merely because his father was khan before him, but because he is chief. The designation "lord" is sometimes used equally loosely among ourselves; others than peers of the realm—all the sons of dukes, and the eldest sons of marquises being so styled. The dignity of chief of a tribe generally, however, does descend from father to son. But even the king himself, who is a Tartar chief, knows that if any considerable number of tribes were to unite for the purpose, they could deprive him of his crown, and confer it upon another of their chiefs. Although for a thousand years Persia, when independent, has never been governed except by a native king, yet those kings have always been either native Tartars or Arabian princes. Every chief of a powerful tribe feels that he has about as good a right to the throne as the reigning sovereign. Hence, when an opportunity occurs, some chief either seizes the throne and declares himself king, fighting with the actual ruler, or with other chiefs who also desire the crown. In the end the strongest obtains the coveted position. The Persian king reigning at present is but the third monarch of his family.

For a number of years past the Tartar tribes have

been held in moderate check by the government, but they have not forgotten their own old exploits in robbery, and are fond of reciting those of their ancestors. True, all the tribes are not alike in this particular; but most are actuated by the same spirit. Those who are in the neighbourhood of large towns are obliged to be more orderly than those who are distant from the control of the government. Travellers can nowhere go far from their camps if they would not lose their horses and their goods. Those who are hired as escort or guard are generally faithful to the trust reposed in them. Some tribes are considered robbers, but not thieves; some are thieves and not robbers; and others are both. Generally speaking, they like better to be considered robbers than thieves.

The great lords do not generally live with their people, or move with them from place to place. The explanation is this:—Among the expedients of the kings for the keeping of the tribes under control, one is, the requiring of certain young men, usually of the families of the chiefs, to be sent to the capital, as hostages for the good behaviour of their fathers. These young men acquire habits less rude than they would otherwise have possessed, and are not, therefore, disposed to resume the life of the tribe; besides, as they advance in years, they obtain appointments in the military and civil services of the country, and so also are detained in the city.

A tribe does not continue to live in the same place.

One place would not afford sufficient pasture for their cattle. Moreover, for this and other reasons, the tribe is divided into sections; and while the chief is over the whole tribe, each of its branches is presided over by a person called an "elder." This is a designation of office, not of age, and usually descends from father to son. As a rule, the elders are related, more or less remotely, to their chiefs; and they are the officers of the tribe in time of war, and its magistrates in peace. When the chief does not reside with his tribe, he appoints one of these elders to act as his deputy. Chiefs and their deputies have very great authority in their several tribes. In ordinary cases which call for judgment, the chief or his deputy decides the matter according to his own individual judgment. In graver matters the whole of the elders of the tribe meet as a council, and the decision is given by the majority of their number. A criminal is seldom put to death by the mere sentence of the chief ruler, even when he deserves to die. If it be thought that he ought to be capitally punished, he is given up to the party he has wronged, who may either kill him, or require him to redeem his life at a price, or pardon him. In order to preserve the peace of the tribe, the chief and council always endeavour to persuade the party who has been wronged to make up the difference for a price. Where life is exacted for life lost or taken away, great and fierce feuds frequently occur among the survivors. Such a case is not frequent, but it sometimes does happen that one who has committed murder throws himself upon the mercy of the murdered man's family. In such circumstances, the murderer ties a sword to his neck with a black cord, and goes to the nearest of kin to the deceased, and tells him that he has come to receive his doom from him. The avenger may kill him if he choose; but it is a point of honour among the tribes—and it is seldom violated,—that a man is not to be put to death who sues for mercy in so humble a manner.

We have spoken of the Tartars as "wandering" tribes; at the same time we have referred to them as occupying particular districts, and as being under the authority of recognised chiefs. There is no contradiction in these statements. Each tribe has a large space which it holds as its own, and within which it moves from place to place, and beyond this territory they are not expected to go. How they severally came into possession of these lands is not always apparent. It seems as if each tribe, when it came into the country, had an allocation of land made to it, on which it might graze its flocks. It may not have been intended that these should be retained as an absolute and perpetual property; but long possession came to be held as a right of prescription with which others must not interfere. There is abundance of room for the whole of these tribes in a country so large and so thinly peopled as Persia, and many of them have a range which includes much land, extending over several valleys and mountains. Disputes between tribes in regard to boundaries, or particular springs, or wells, or murders, sometimes lead to much bloodshed, and are maintained for generations. The right to these lands is not that of owners. The tribes are at liberty to feed their flocks, to cultivate ground where it has not been cultivated by others, and even to build villages and towns within their districts. For such privileges they do not pay money; but are obliged to furnish a certain number of horsemen to serve the king in his wars. They also pay a small tax on their flocks. This is paid in sheep, butter, cheese, and such other produce as their mode of life supplies. The wealth of a chief consists in his flocks, and in contributions from his people, which contributions, being voluntary, vary according to his popularity or his power.

A tribe changes its particular place of abode when the flocks have consumed the grass in the previously occupied locality. The change must, of course, be always within the prescribed domain. The elder appoints the time of removal; and the distance of the next settlement is regulated by the facility or difficulty which may be experienced in the finding of suitable pasture. It is also affected by the season of the year. Some tribes remain in tents all the year round. These are easily moved. Others occupy small wooden houses, which may be carried almost as readily as tents; while others build huts to which they return in the winter. In the last-mentioned instance, a certain amount of grain is sown previously to the summer migrations, and a few aged persons are left behind to attend to it. In the removals camels are sometimes employed, but, more frequently horses, mules, or asses. The sheep, goats, and other cattle are driven separately and by short stages that they may feed by the way. They are *led*, rather than driven—led by well-known shepherds who are followed by sagacious members of the flock, familiar with the shepherds, and these are followed by the great body. The people generally go on foot, with the exception of the infirm and weak, or those who have the care of little children, and for the use of these advantage is taken of unladen beasts of burden. The men on foot are well armed, with guns at their backs, daggers in their girdles, and sticks in their hands, ready to defend their families and property from danger.

They generally form their encampments near some rivulet or stream, and, if they are not strong, they pitch their tents near the foot of mountains, that they may be within the reach of a place of safety when danger arises. The tents are usually pitched in squares. When the party is large, and there are many tents, they do not pitch them all together, but form them into groups at a short distance from each other. They can thus keep their individual flocks separate, and each obtains its due proportion of forage. At the same time, the different parties are within call of each other in case of danger.

They live almost entirely on what their flocks

produce, for the animals themselves they very rarely kill. They weave a coarse cloth for their own use; and when they want anything which they cannot provide from their flocks, they take cheese and butter, or sheep, goats, kids, cows, horses, asses, or camels to the towns for sale. They thus supply the cattle which the settled inhabitants require, and receive in return corn, cloth, money, and articles of hardware.

The men spend their time in riding, military exercises, and the chase. One of their chief pleasures is derived from sitting in the shade, smoking their pipes, and listening to songs and tales, or in witnessing the tricks, grimaces, and practical jokes of looties, or buffoons. These looties are sometimes well skilled in their art, and take pains for the purpose of making themselves so. The women are most frequently engaged in their domestic duties, in making butter and cheese, or in weaving cloth and carpets. These women never complain of the hardness of their work. But this practice of making drudges of their women is common among all wandering peoples, and all savage nations.

The chiefs and other great men have more than one wife as a rule; but they are obliged to be careful in their whole conduct, lest they should give offence to the principal wife. It is a pitiful picture of domestic life where a man must show respect to one wife by slighting the others, and where a father is afraid to notice his own son, he being the child of a mother whose rank is secondary.

The marriage ceremonies among these people are almost identical with those which are represented in the Sacred Scriptures. In religion they are professedly Mahometan, but their consciences are not particularly burdened. There are no stated religious teachers among such tribes. Occasionally, a priest finds his way from one village to another, and calls the people to prayers; but there is no regular or systematic instruction among them. There is no point of their religion as to which they are particular, unless it be in the matter of restriction in regard to certain kinds of animals as to food. Hares and pigs, and all beasts which do not chew the cud, and also divide the hoof are professedly abominated, and yet the practice is far from strict.

There are Tartars whose winter encampment is in the plains of Antioch, and who have habits of their own. They are a nomade people, and yet, to a certain extent, they have become agriculturists. It is said that the attention of this tribe was drawn to agriculture by a chief whose acquaintance with other nations enabled him to see the advantages which were to be derived from the cultivation of the soil. Still, their principal riches consist in cattle. These people do not pay the usual miri, or land-tax, to the State for the ground which they occupy, nor is there any direct rent. But they render a tribute to the governor of the province for the occupation of their lands. And besides, they are subject to the obligations of military service.

They are divided into minor tribes or clans, and each has its own chief. The head of the most important of these is, in a certain sense, the head of the whole tribe; but he does not interfere in the internal affairs of the other clans. Much depends upon his personal character. Where he is respected, his influence is great. The ties of tribal connection are seldom strong. This renders a chief more cautious and studious of popularity. These Rhyaulu Tartars do not pitch their tents in any large number together—only to the extent of five or six. They are frugal in their habits, having usually but two meals in the day, and these very moderate. The women do not hide themselves even before strangers. They are industrious like those of all the wandering tribes. They marry at fourteen or fifteen, the girls at about thirteen. They are robbers like their kind. They also profess to be Mahometans.

There are also bodies of Tartars occupying positions in the region of the Caucasus. They are not all Mahometans. Within the Ottoman territory these people are everywhere treated with at least ordinary moderation. Their professed Mahometanism is a kind of protection to them. But the strong arm of Russia is against them wherever they are found. Between Russia and them there is no bond of common faith, and their utter extirpation seems to be the aim of the policy of that Power. Doubtless, the same spirit is the animus in the present Khivan expedition. With respect to the Tartars, and the matter here in hand, it may be observed that the Emperor himself, bent on his purpose, visited Caucasus in 1839. In 1840 Schamyl became conspicuous. He was born in 1797, of Tartar blood, in a family of obscure condition, as well as in a province not distinguished, Dargbestan, on the S.E. of the Caucasus, along the Caspian. Schamyl in early life gave no signs of distinction. Under one Shelal Eddin he studied Arabic philosophy. In that he found a resource from which he drew a new religion. That resource was Sufism. According to the doctrine of the Sufis, man has to reach four stages in order to rise to celestial blessedness. The first step is set by those who follow the outer law of the faithful (Sharyat), and observe its instructions respecting prayers, fasts, pilgrimages, almsgivings, self-purification, the love of truth, honour. Then comes the second stage, another step on the way of perfection (Tarykal), when, in contrast to externalities, he diligently and reverently worships God in the depth of his heart. When this adoration becomes so habitual and deep as to carry the worshipper by rapt meditation and intimate communion with nature into the essence of things, so as to give him extatic intuition of what is heavenly, then he has ascended to the third stage, which bears the name of truth (Hakykal). In the fourth and last stage of knowledge (Maarifat), the condition has been so sublimed that man enters into immediate personal union with God. This old mystical philosophy has been revived by Schamyl, under whose hands it has received the following practical application; the lowest stage is occupied by the common people, who, not sufficiently cultivated to guide themselves, require a governor who may lead them to the outward and ceremonial observance of the law. The second stage is occupied by the better sort of people, the disciples, or murids, for whom the outer law is superfluous, since every one who seeks truth is good, because he knows that goodness only leads to truth. A higher class stands on the third step to the heavenly temple, and the murshid alone reaches the fourth. The murshid is the Caucasian Pope. The chosen ones of the second degree are his naibs, princes, or cardinals; then come the bishops of the third class; and, finally, the people whose principle is passive obedience, and whose only duty is to observe the commands of religion, and to defend and promote its interest by the sword.

The ground of this spiritual despotism was laid by Kasi Mullah, who prepared the way for the hero of the Caucasus; but Schamyl gave it consistency and practical application. In particular, he applied it to two great purposes. He made it the bond of union, and so gained unity, after others had striven for it almost in vain, and in which lies the inexhaustible and unconquerable strength of the Caucasians. He also made it otherwise a source of power. Here was a new religion to fight for; a religion neither Christian nor Mohammedan, though partaking of qualities found in both, and which consequently could be enforced against all the populations of the Caucasus, that sympathized with Russia, no less than against Russia itself. The time in which Kasi Mullah put forth his system was one of danger. Jermolow, one of the best Russian commanders, had obtained so much power that the final conquest of the country seemed imminent. In 1824 the new Sufism began to spread. The cry "Moslem, war against the infidels, and ruin on the Giaours," ran like wild-fire from aul to aul (village), until in Daghestan it fell on the ears of the Russian. When the movement reached the north, Schamyl was living as a priest at Hinery. He attached himself to the side of Kasi Mullah. The Russian sent an army and carried the apparently inaccessible pass which led to Hinery, and besieged Kasi Mullah. All fell. Kasi Mullah was killed. Schamyl fell, pierced with two balls. He appeared covered with blood in the council, as it met to deliberate on the choice of a new leader. He was elected, and he drove the Russians back. Subsequent events showed in this man great nobility of character; but the enemy was more than able to cope with him, and, after a prolonged struggle, he and his fellows were compelled to succumb. The massacre of 1860-62 was a deep disgrace to its agents.

We have thus before us a people, scattered over a

wide space, distinguished by many peculiarities; in former times having great qualities, but characterised by many evil habits and customs, and who, in many parts, are being driven from their fastnesses, and whose power for good to their fellow-men is but small.

CHAPTER VIII.

BRITAIN IN INDIA.

BRITAIN in Asia—India—is so large a subject that in any general work it cannot be written upon exhaustively. This is to be regretted the less as many books exclusively devoted to this one theme are within easy reach of the reader. But, even if our notices be but few and cursory, Asia, with its peoples, cannot be fairly judged of without including India.

India lies between 7° and 35° N. lat. and 67° and 97° E. long. The greatest length from north to south, or from the Himalayas in Cashmere to Cape Comorin, is 1,870 miles; and the greatest breadth, from the Hala mountains to Scinde to the eastern extremity of Assam, nearly along the 27° N. lat., is about 1,800 miles. The superficial area comprises about 1,250,000 square English miles, with a sea-coast line of 3,622 miles. The boundaries of India are remarkably well defined. The origin of the name is uncertain. The general aspect of the country includes great varieties. The Himalayas

extend along the whole of the northern and northeastern frontier, with a continuous series of snowy peaks. These are extended by a region of mountains. To the south of them are the great plains of Hindustan. But the most remarkable region is the Great Desert. This extends to a distance of 350 miles, from the western base of the Hala mountains to the western base of the Aravulli, and from the Runn of Cutch to the Sutlej, upwards of 450 miles. The surface has no covering of turf, nor any closely contiguous roots; but there are various kinds of plants whose berries, leaves or fruit are fit for food.

The Gulf of Cutch, the Gulf of Cambay, the Gulf of Manaar, and the Gulf of Bombay, are the principal inlets from the sea.

The distance between Ceylon and the Continent is 62 miles; and the sea-passage is narrow and difficult.

The great rivers are the Indus and the Ganges. The *Indus* is formed in Balti, or Little Thibet. The principal affluent is the Cabul river.

The *Ganges* is reckoned the principal river of India. At a distance of 500 miles from the sea the channel is 30 feet deep, when the stream is at the lowest. About 200 miles from the sea begins the Delta of the Ganges. The branches of the river are here called by different names, the two which are most westerly being known as the Cossimbazar and the Jellinghy rivers, which unite and form the Hooghly, which passes

Calcutta, and is the only branch commonly navigated by sea-going vessels.

The history of British dominion in India reads like a romance. "The fair land of the East" was to our forefathers, even from the time of the Crusades, like a gorgeous dream, and, in their imaginations, that was a country of marvel, and mystery, and untold wealth. Sir Thomas Myddelton, and the Shirleys, and Sir Thomas Roe returned from it with glowing descriptions of Eastern magnificence and glory. In the steady progress of British trade with India much of the hope which was excited was realised. Reckless adventurers, portionless younger brothers, went forth, and after years of absence and silence returned with wealth so vast, that our sober, plodding great-grandfathers were absolutely bewildered.

But the progress of British power in India was, nevertheless, very slow; and we cannot repress our astonishment when we find that, not a hundred years ago, the representatives of that power were borne with on mere sufferance. It is to Clive that we owe the foundation of our mighty empire in the East, and there was much of romance in his career. And romantic incidents, often of the wildest kind, have marked almost every subsequent event in the history of British India. The story of the late war, connected as it was with intrigue, and massacre, and stern retribution, is a strange and exciting tale, but solemn and complete as a Greek tragedy. In recent years, and not many before the Sepoy outbreak, the public mind at home was startled by the intelligence that the British troops had been defeated by hordes of barbarians, and an army utterly annihilated in the terrible Koord Cabul Pass; and then, in a few years only, there came after the war in Affghanistan what was even more appalling, in the form of the wide-spread rebellion.

The history of that event throws light on the establishment and character of British authority in India. The story of the greased cartridges no doubt connects itself closely with the outbreak; but we find in that only one of many occasions of dissatisfaction on the part of the people and the native soldiery. For many years that dissatisfaction had existed, even if it but smouldered. A handful of Englishmen had obtained the mastery of a vast empire through their indomitable courage. They trusted confidingly in their legions of native soldiers, and discovered when it was too late that little reliance is to be placed in hirelings. These mercenaries were the dupes of a few designing men, who had filled their minds with suspicions, and by their tales and whisperings had worked them into a state of frenzied panic. It is true, many innovations were constantly being introduced; the ancient landmarks were being one by one broken down and destroyed, and all classes were disquieted and perplexed by fear of change.

Lord Hardinge had defeated the Sikhs, and had annexed the Cis-Sutlej Provinces. Henry Lawrence, acting as Colonel of the Bengal Artillery, accomplished much in most difficult circumstances connected with these operations and changes. A great, good man, and a good soldier, Sir Henry devoted himself to the task of conquering the turbulent and troublesome, but he also sought to regenerate the country. It was, however, too much for his strength. He was obliged to relinquish his post in 1847. Lord Hardinge also quitted the shores of India at the same time. He was succeeded in the early part of 1848, at which time Lord Dalhousie commenced his brilliant career as Governor-General of India. Everything seemed to promise permanent peace. The country wanted railroads, and the people education, and there was good hope that Lord Dalhousie would provide both. But before May war had broken out in the Punjaub. The murder of two British officers at Mooltan, and the rebellion of the Dewan Moolraj, formed the appropriate prelude to the second Sikh war, and led to the annexation of the "Land of the Five Waters." Lord Dalhousie was not to blame for this war. He could say with truth, "I have wished for peace; I have longed for it; I have striven for it. But if the enemies of India determine to have war, war they shall have; and on my word they shall have it with a vengeance." And he kept his word. The Government put forth its power. After a lengthened campaign, and a struggle severe and anxious, the Sikhs were utterly defeated, the Affghans were driven with ignominy through passes of the mountains, and the Punjaub became a British province. But this success was like the first taste of blood to the lion's whelp—the ambition of territorial aggrandisement set in. Hostilities with the Court of Ava occurred, and the province of Pegu was annexed. There were disadvantages connected with these annexations. True, they eradicated hostile powers which were in the midst of the British territories; but they dissatisfied the Sepoy soldiery, inasmuch as they were by this means frequently removed far from home, and had imposed upon them the irksome tasks of a military police.

A new law was framed which gave great offence. It was enacted that if a prince died without a male heir, his dominions, "by right of lapse," should be declared and held as forfeited to the paramount power. This was held to be a great grievance. Both Hindoos and Mahometans attach much importance to the having of a son, natural or adopted, to perform the funeral obsequies of his father. The right of adoption is, therefore, held to be a most sacred privilege. The new law abolished this; and, as there could not, it was believed, be any resurrection to eternal blessedness without the suitable funeral rites, it may readily be supposed that the change was received with much disfavour. Sattarah was, by this means, annexed. So also the principalities of Nagpore and Jhansie passed under the British rule. The two titular sovereignties of the Carnatic and Tanjore also became extinct during Lord Dalhousie's tenure of power, adequate pensions being, however, settled on the two families of the deceased princes. The Government also resumed, on the death of the ex-Peishwar, the enormous stipend that had been guaranteed to that fallen prince; but this act bore the bitterest fruits. The deceased Badjee Rao left three adopted heirs, one of whom was Dooadoo Punt, afterwards notorious as the Nana Sahib, the instigator of the massacre of Cawnpore. This man never forgave the wrong which he believed had been done him. The kingdom of Oude was subsequently appropriated. That it was shamefully misgoverned is true, but the British connection with it was in part the occasion. On the 4th day of February, 1864, Wajid Ali was deposed, and the annexation of Oude was completed. Not a blow was struck in defence of the native dynasty.

New arrangements were made everywhere in regard to the collecting of the revenue. The revenue was farmed. The peasants were ground down to the dust, and an upstart plutocracy suddenly became rich. A social revolution of the most sweeping description was thus accomplished. Many small and poor proprietors of land were ruined.

Among the sufferers were the Brahmins, who had been in a great measure supported by revenues from lands which the English Government now resumed and taxed. This excited the enmity of these priests towards the Government. Besides, there were other causes combining to raise their hostility against the unbelieving foreigner. By means of the influx of Western learning and ideas, "a new generation was springing up, without faith, without veneration; an inquiring, doubting, reasoning race, not to be captivated with absurd doctrines or by grotesque fables." If this spirit of scepticism and inquiry were permitted to spread, not only would Brahminism be overthrown, but the Brahmins themselves would be reduced to destitution. The spread of secular education, the introduction of railroads, electric telegraphs, and other scientific improvements, the emancipation of women, and the re-marriage of Hindoo widows, were all heavy and fatal blows directed against the exclusivism and monopoly of idleness. Every monstrous lie exploded, every abominable practice suppressed, was a blow struck at the priesthood. The murder of women on the funeral pile, the murder of little children in the Zenana, the murder of the sick and the aged on the banks of the river, the murder of human victims, reared and fattened for the sacrifice, were all religious institutions, from which the priesthood derived either profit or power, or both. Nay, even the wholesale strangling of unsuspecting travellers was sanctified and ceremonialised by religion. But all the foul superstitions which nurtured the Brahmins were fast disappearing from the land. A stand must therefore be made.

They had still the means supplied them by caste. The great institution of caste was an ever-present reality. It entered into the commonest concerns of life. It was intelligible to the meanest understanding.

x

Every man, woman, and child knew what a terrible thing it would be to be cast out of the community of the brotherhood, and compelled to live apart, condemned of men and forsaken by God. If, then, the people could only be persuaded that their English rulers entertained an insidious intention of depriving them of their caste, and of sinking them to their own pariah level, a universal uprising might be counted upon almost to a certainty. The Brahmins, therefore, were on the watch for a fair and plausible opportunity. At length they found one. It had been the practice to allow prisoners to cook their own food, but the liberty was abused, and was therefore abolished. Prisoners were then divided into messes, then rations issued to them, and cooks appointed to prepare their meals at stated times. If the cook chanced to be of a lower caste than the prisoner the food was contaminated, and all who partook of it were defiled. There were, therefore, riots in several gaols. An attempt was made in some prisons to remove the *lotahs*, or drinking-vessels of the inmates, but so great was the excitement that it was deemed expedient to yield and restore them. The Mahometans have no caste to lose, but among their customs none are more dear to them than circumcision and the seclusion of females. A report was spread that the Government was about to prohibit both. The lie was readily credited, and thus Moslem and Hindoo were joined in an unholy alliance against the common enemy of their respective faiths.

Sagacious men, therefore, expected an outbreak. "There stands our future enemy," said the Hon. James Thomason, one day in 1852, pointing to a Sepoy. "There is no doubt," wrote Sir Henry Lawrence, "that whatever danger may threaten us in India, the greatest is from our own (native) troops."

Fancied slights and injuries were supposed to be inflicted on both Hindoos and Mahometans. As we have said, the latter had no caste to lose, but his beard was sacred in his eyes, and his ear-rings had been given him at his birth, and dedicated to his patron saint. To both the hat was an abomination; for it was in part made of leather prepared from the skin of the cow or the hog. These changes, the hat for the turban, and the abolition of ear-rings and beards gave much umbrage. Fakeers became numerous. They went about the forts jeering the soldiers, and telling them that they would soon be Christians to a man. Looking at a stock, they would say, "What is this? It is leather! Well!" Then they would look at his belt and tell him that it made a Christian's cross upon his person. Within the forts and outside of them men of all classes were to be found talking about the forcible conversion to Christianity which threatened them. Another story was that Christian churches were to be built in every town and village in the land; that all worshipping of images was forbidden; and that no one was to be permitted to enter a pagoda.

The whole story of the greased cartridges took its

rise in a careless blunder in the Ordnance Department. The mixture of wax and oil which had been previously used to lubricate the cartridges for the two-grooved rifle, not being found suitable for the new Enfield rifled ammunition, a mixture of stearine and tallow was substituted in its place. But sufficient care had not been taken that only mutton fat should enter into the composition of the tallow, and there is no doubt that beef fat was sometimes used, though it does not appear that hogs' lard was ever employed for that purpose. But these new cartridges were being made in the first instance for the European troops only, and in no case were ever given out to the native Sepoys. While these fabulous cartridges were exciting terror and disgust among the native regiments, fables of similar import were diligently circulated among the industrial classes. It was said and believed that the officers of the British Government, under command from the Company and the Queen, had mixed ground bones with the flour and the salt sold in the bazaars; that they had adulterated all the *ghee* (clarified butter used for cooking purposes) with animal fat; that bones had been burnt with the common sugar of the country; and that not only bone-dust flour, but the flesh of cows and pigs had been thrown into the wells to pollute the drinking-water of the people. . . . . All classes, it was believed, were to be defiled at the same time; and the story ran that the "burra sahibs," or great English lords, had commanded all the princes, nobles, landholders, merchants, and

cultivators of the land to feed together on a particular day upon English bread.

The mysterious circulation of the chupatties increased the excitement. So little was known about these means of communication that the mere absence of knowledge was an additional reason of apprehension. A messenger would arrive in hot haste at a village, deliver one of these cakes to the headman, desiring him to make others like it, and send them to the other villages in his neighbourhood. For a time, these chupatties were flying in all directions. Strange events were manifestly at hand; and, no doubt, political intrigues were rife; and there is good reason to believe that Doondoo Punt (Nana Sahib) and the adherents of the King of Oude were especially busy.

The first mutiny of the Bengal army dates as far back as 1764, when it was barely seven years old. Thirty of their leaders were condemned to death, and blown away from the guns. A far greater danger threatened the British Government when the Army of Retribution was about to enter the Passes of Affghanistan after the disasters at Cabul. Both Sikh and Brahmin emissaries took advantage of the hesitation of the Sepoys, and tampered with their fidelity. The Affghan war was followed by the annexation of Scinde, and this led to the mutiny and disbanding of the 34th Regiment of Native Infantry. And various individual regiments have mutinied from time to time. But the great rebellion, latest and greatest, over which so many families at home mourn because of their loved ones left cold and stiff on the Indian plains, seems to have led to such a mastery of the land by the British as to induce the hope that now the rule of England is at last firmly established.

Once begun, the rebellion rapidly spread throughout the Bengal presidency. In Oude, at Delhi, Lucknow, Jhansi, Cawnpore, and other places, the mutineers rose upon the Europeans and perpetrated the most horrible atrocities, murdering all whom they encountered under circumstances of the utmost cruelty and ferocity. At Cawnpore, on June 27, 1857, there was a most melancholy episode, and yet it was not permitted to stand alone; the massacres at Jhansi, Delhi, and elsewhere were not much behind it.

There were immediate and heroic efforts to check and suppress this mutiny. But the European soldiers in the country were few compared with the rebellious troops. Still they had indomitable energy. It was but a small force that was commanded by Sir H. Lawrence; but they defended themselves until Sir H. Havelock, with a mere handful of men, captured Cawnpore, and fought his way to their relief, which he effected in conjunction with Sir James Outram, though the siege was not raised. Sir Colin Campbell, afterwards Lord Clyde, being appointed commander-in-chief, arrived at Cawnpore, and in November advanced against Lucknow, stormed and captured the approaches, and opened a communication with Sir James Outram. The besieged and exhausted garrison were then liberated—there being many women and children—and were removed to Cawnpore; but the good and gallant Sir Henry Havelock died on the 25th of that month—November—suffering from anxiety and from his wounds.

In the year 1858 there were many successful operations of the British forces, by means of which the rebellion was thoroughly subdued.

In 1858 the Government of British India was completely transferred from the East India Company to the Queen. By the terms of the Act of Parliament, all the powers of the Company are exercised by her Majesty, and all revenues and tributes are to be received and discharged in her name. The Executive is invested in a Secretary of State for India, with a Council of fifteen members, seven of whom are elected by the directors of the East India Company from their own body, and eight are nominated by the Crown, vacancies among the nominated members being filled up by the Queen, and other vacancies by election of the Council. It is, however, provided that the major part of the Council must consist of persons who have resided ten years in India, and have not left it for more than ten years before their election. There is a salary of £1,200 a year for every member, payable, as is also that of the Secretary of State, out of the revenues of India.

The Government is administered by the Governor-General and a Supreme Council of eleven to fifteen members at Calcutta, under direction, or at least approbation, of the Secretary of State.

Under the new form of government affairs have prospered in every way; education has been promoted among the natives; railways have been constructed; electric telegraph lines opened; roads improved, and new roads made. Trade and commerce have also greatly increased. In 1863 there were 10,566 miles of Government telegraph line in the country, worked by 2,973 persons. In 1865 there were ten railway companies guaranteed by Government, and one not guaranteed. In addition to these there are other lines designed or executed, the expense being more than £100,000,000.

From the earliest times, the commercial enterprise of Europeans has been directed to India. Vasco da Gama landed in Hindostan in 1498. The earliest East India Company was that of the Portuguese; but they were not successful. The next was Dutch, and their commercial enterprise and perseverance gained for them establishment and profit; and after them the English. The history of the English East India Company may be divided into four sections. During the first fourteen years its members were in a great measure independent. In the following ninety-five years they were restricted in their operations by the superiority of the Dutch in the Indian seas, by the civil wars at home, and particularly by the calling in question of their exclusive privileges, which were extended to them by a Royal grant, and not by Act of Parliament. For the next forty

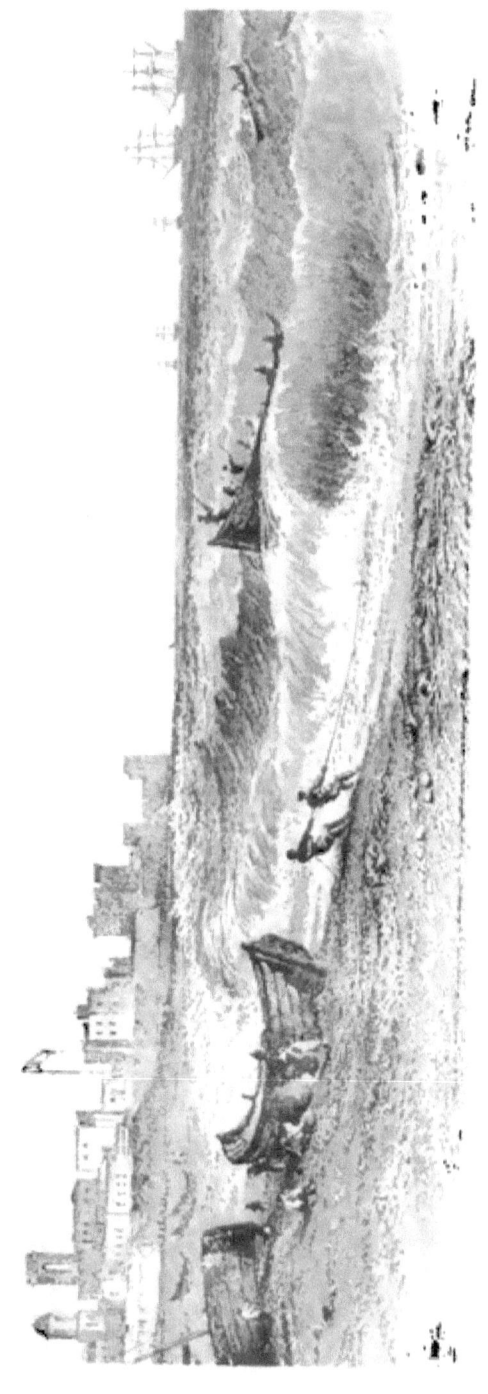

years their privileges were undisputed, and based on Parliamentary authority. And, finally, during the subsequent seventy years, in which time they possessed political power as well as commercial rights.

1. The first period extended from 1600 to 1613. The original capital was £30,133. Their profits were large, amounting on eight voyages to 171 per cent.

2. The second period extended from 1613 to 1708. Their trade was chiefly with the states of the Great Mogul, and it was most successful. Cromwell attempted to make the East India trade free, but this was found to be impracticable. During the wars of the Revolution, such were the embarrassments occasioned that the company was not able to meet its liabilities, and Parliament granted a charter to a new company in 1698. Great contentions ensued between the two companies, and it was found necessary to unite them in 1708.

3. The third period ran from 1708 to 1748. The business of the company was now managed by twenty-four "directors." The affairs in India were very much entrusted to three Councils in Madras, Bombay, and Calcutta. It was needful to have the charter renewed in 1732, and this was obtained with difficulty. The Company therefore deemed it advisable to advance £1,000,000, at an interest of three per cent. for the service of the Government, in consideration of an extension of their charter till 1780.

4. The fourth period. The political power of the British in India began in 1748. The French had already

set the example. In 1740, a French battalion had destroyed the army of the Nabob of the Carnatic, and soon after the French officers succeeded in training Indian troops according to the European method. The Company imitated their neighbours; and by-and-by complaints were heard in respect to violent oppressions of the people, and of ambitious projects against the princes. A partial reform was accomplished. Burke was prominent in the impeachment of Hastings, who was hanged, justly or unjustly. The great orator alleged of the Company "that it had sold every monarch, prince, and state in India, broken every contract, and ruined every prince and every state who had trusted them." The high officers in India were all blamed. After an incomplete reform in 1773 there came the famous East India bill of Fox. Pitt introduced another measure, and a Board of Control was established. The Company's charter expired in 1813, but an extension of time was obtained; while the trade was also opened to the public on certain conditions. The Company's commercial character ceased on the 22nd of April, 1834, and after that date, closing its accounts as speedily as possible, its functions were to be wholly political. Up to 1854 this arrangement had effect, but in that year it was enacted that, time being permitted for discharge of obligations, all the property of the Company should become vested in the Crown. A dividend of $10\frac{1}{2}$ per cent. was guaranteed, but this might be redeemed by Parliament any time after April, 1874.

The population of such a country can only be guessed at with probability. Under the direct rule of Britain, and of the few remaining princes who still claim a kind of nominal sovereignty, but who are under British control, there are about one hundred and forty millions; Europeans, about fifty thousand.

The French, Danish, Dutch, and Swedish establishments in India never were of great account in any way in regard to the country. They have ceased to exist with the exception of the Swedish Company, which restricts its trade to China.

The Government revenue in British India is greater than that of any European State, unless France and Britain be excepted. The particulars of the budget have just reached this country by telegraph, and from these it appears that the past year has been financially the most prosperous since the present form of government was established. It was necessary to impose extra taxes on account of the expenses of the war; but Lord Mayo had begun the task of remission and retrenchment before his lamented death, and Lord Northbrook is disposed to carry out the same policy. The revenue for the year is about £50,000,000, which last year left a considerable surplus. We are informed that "no great public works have suffered by means of the disturbances and taxation incident to the war." In further prosecution of the system of late years, it is intended that, in 1873-74, the Government shall spend £4,000,000 on new railways.

Calcutta is the capital of Bengal, and of the whole of British India. It is situated on the Hooghly, a branch of the Ganges, on which the largest East Indiaman may come quite up to the city. The place was formerly an insignificant village, but rose in the course of last century to be a great city; the population has been estimated very variously at from 500,000 to 1,000,000. The probability is that, at present, it may number about 800,000. Within a range of twenty miles the country is very populous, and in all likelihood is not less than 2,500,000. The British occupy a separate part of the city. Their houses are of brick, generally comfortable, many of them elegant like palaces. They are separate buildings, with verandahs for shade, and lofty and airy apartments within. With this quarter the "black town," which is the district of the native population, forms a striking contrast. It has extremely narrow and crooked streets, interspersed with gardens and innumerable tanks. The houses differ greatly from each other, some of them being built of brick, some of mud, and others, the majority, of bamboo or straw mats. Fort William is in the neighbourhood. It is a magnificent work, was begun by Lord Clive, has bomb-proof roofs, and can accommodate 10,000 men. It is too large for purposes of defence, and would require 600 pieces of cannon for the works. There is a great plain between Fort William and the city, and there, as on a vast promenade, Hindoos, Europeans, equipages of all sorts, and palanquins, mix together in a motley crowd. On the western side of this stands the new palace, built by the Marquis of Wellesley, at a cost of £1,000,000. The old fort is now a custom-house, and the infamous "black-hole" has been converted into a warehouse. An obelisk fifty feet high stands at the entrance, and bears the names of the unfortunate captives who, in 1756, when the city was taken and plundered by Suraja Dowla, fell victims to the most inhuman cruelty. There are eleven places of Christian worship, with many mosques and pagodas.

Barrackpore is ten miles above Calcutta, and, as its name signifies, is the head-quarters of the troops. There is here a country-house for the Governor-General.

Patna is a large city on the Ganges, 400 miles north-west of Calcutta, and it contains about 300,000 inhabitants.

Benares is the sacred capital of Hindûism, and is a great city on the left bank of the Ganges, 53 miles east of Allahabad, which is 475 miles west-north-west of Calcutta in a straight line, 820 by the course of the river. Benares has a population of 400,000. It is surrounded by many villages. In the city itself there are scarcely any inhabitants besides Hindoos, of whom many are Brahmins. The principal place of worship is a pagoda, called Visswisshor, which, though small, is elegant, and contains a stone, black and cylindrical, which represents Siva, the Mahadeo or Great God. There are numerous mosques and temples besides.

The number of pilgrims who come to worship this idol is very great.

Agra, which gives its name to the government or province, stands on the Jumnah, 830 miles from Calcutta. It was formerly one of the capitals of the Mogul empire, and still contains 96,576 inhabitants, two-thirds being Hindoos, and the rest Moslem.

Delhi was for long the capital of the Mogul empire. It is 137 miles from Agra. It is one of the most ancient cities of India. It used to occupy a space of twenty square miles, but great part of its area is now covered with ruins. This city was the scene of some of the saddest events of the late war. The king was sentenced to perpetual banishment, having been guilty of the most barbarous cruelties, and the city itself was dismantled, but not ruined. There are still contained in it many remains of its former rude magnificence and splendour.

Ajmeer is a beautiful and flourishing city, in Rajpootana, and was formerly the capital of one of the provinces of the Mogul empire.

Madras is the capital of the province whose name it bears. The principal part of the city is Fort George, a handsome and strong fortification. The population of the city is estimated at 450,000.

Bombay is the capital of another province, a picturesque city of 230,000 people.

Surat is situated on the Tuptee, with a population of 600,000.

Poonah is occupied by 70,000 people, contains a college, and is in many respects an important town.

Allahabad, 820 miles from the sea, by the course of the Ganges, is a large city, which bears an unenviable name for turbulence and insubordination. The population is 80,000.

Nagpore is a town of about 80,000.

Trevandrum is the capital of Travancore, and is a large town.

Of *Districts* and *Provinces* we can furnish only the names,—Assam, Arracan, Agra, Madras, Bombay, Bengal, Hyderabad, Nagpore, Travancore, Mysore, Sikim, Oude, Bundelcund, Bhurtpore, Dholpour, Bhopal, Holcar, Guicowar, Cutch, Rajpootana, Scinde, Daoudpootra, Lahore, Nepaul, Bhotan, and others. Of the beautiful island of Ceylon we cannot speak,—"the jewel of the Eastern seas." And there are other islands besides. More or less under British influence are also the Birman empire, the kingdom of Siam, the empire of An-nam, the country of the Laos, and the Malay States. It will thus be seen how vast is the territory of Britain in Asia, in India, how enormous is the population which is under the rule of England, and how deeply interested this country must ever be in all that affects the welfare of Asia.

The possessions of France in India are very small, and form the single government of Pondicherry; the Danish territory is restricted to the narrow limits of two small establishments at Tranquebar, on the

Coromandel coast, and Serampore in Bengal; and the Portuguese have only Goa on the west coast, Damaun in Gujerat, and the island of Diu on the south coast of Kattiwar. All besides is under the control of England. The responsibility is immense,—the vigilant defence of the frontier should be unflagging,—and the care of so many millions having been placed in British hands, the welfare and progress of the people ought to weigh heavily on the parent State at home. It had been well, while we watch the encroachments of other Powers on territory which is not theirs, if our own hands had been clean in respect to every fresh enlargement of our own dominion in India.

About nine-tenths of the people are professors of Brahminism; but with many shades of difference and in numerous sects. There are five sects, each of which worships only a single deity, and one which recognises all the five deities which are worshipped by the others. The Saivas, who worship only Siva; the Vaishnavas, who worship Vishnu; the Sauvias, Surya, or the Sun; the Ganapatyas, who worship Ganesha, the god of wisdom and policy; and the Sactis, who worship Bhovani or Parvati, the wife of Siva. The sixth sect is the Bhagavatis. Vishnu and Siva are the most common objects of worship; while Brahma, the first of the triumvir of gods, has only one temple,—at Poshkur, near Ajmeer. Vishnu is believed to have frequently appeared on earth, but the most deeply venerated incarnations are those of Krishna and Rama-chandra.

We need not enter into the follies of these idolatries. Bishop Heber says, "Of all the false worships which I have heard or read of, the religion of the Hindoos appears to me to be the worst in respect to the degrading notions which it gives of the Deity, the endless round of its burdensome ceremonies, which occupy time and distract the thoughts without instructing or interesting its votaries; in the filthiness of its acts of uncleanness and cruelty, not only permitted but enjoined; and in the total absence of any system of morals, or any single lesson by which the people may be taught to live virtuously, and to do good to each other." With the Hindoos everything is mixed up with their religion; their sciences, their arts, are all revealed from heaven. Their doctrines and precepts are contained in Scriptures called the *Puranas*, of which there are eighteen. *Buddhism* appears to have once been extensively prevalent in India. This is pre-eminently the religion of reason, while Brahminism depends entirely on tradition and authority. The Maghs of Arracan and the inhabitants of Bootan are now the only Buddhists on the continent of India; but this is still the religion of Ceylon. The *Jains* are to be found in Central and Western India and Mysore,—a numerous sect, professing to believe in one God, having little respect to the Hindoo gods, and hating the Brahmins. The *Mahometans* number about 15,000,000, and are spread over the northern and central provinces. In Malabar and the Carnatic there are about 220,000 *Syrian Christians*. *Armenian*

Y

Christians are to be found in most of the great towns. The Portuguese are all *Roman Catholics*. The Europeans of other nations are all professedly Christian, and most of them *Protestant*. The hill tribes, if they are anything,—the Bheels, Ramoosies, and Koolies,—are Brahmins. The Brahminical religion is very accommodating, and can admit of various customs in different circumstances. India is infested by religious devotees, who prey upon the community. They are a numerous class of sturdy beggars, being both Hindoo and Mahometan. The festivals of the Hindoos in honour of their gods are numerous. The European officers are expected to do honour to the great public occasions of the natives, of all classes. There is a great festival of the Mahometans, *Mohurrum*, which they must regard; and also the Hindoo festival of Dûrja-puja; both of these being specially religious seasons, each lasting ten days. This is felt to be a severe tax on the patience of those who have no sympathy with the celebrations. During the last seventy years efforts have been made by various societies in England to convert the people to Christianity, and, although unpromising at first, such efforts are now being crowned with much success. There were many most noble specimens of Christian character exhibited in the history of the late great war.

Coal extensively occurs in the southern slope of the Himalayas. *Fossil salt* is to be met with in large quantities in the range of hills which crosses the bed of the Indus, extending from Suffeid-koh to the Jhylum,—

and elsewhere, as in Rajpootana, by evaporation. *Iron* is worked in the Carnatic, and with considerable profit. *Talc* exists in such abundance in the Mahabaleshwar hills that it is used instead of glass.

The vegetable productions of India are cotton, indigo, sugar-cane, cajeput oil, caoutchouc, rice, wheat, barley, pepper, ginseng, sandal-wood, spikenard, and gigantic bamboos and palms. The wheat grown is good. Potatoes have been introduced and thrive. The grape is healthy in most parts. Culinary vegetables as at home now crowd the bazaars. Coffee, tobacco, hemp, and opium are luxuriant in many districts. Timber is everywhere abundant, the forests being numerous and covering a large extent of country; the woods for export are teak, ebony, and other kinds. The most remarkable vegetable production of India is the banyan tree (*ficus Indica*), the branches of which send out shoots, which fall to the ground fixing themselves there, and in time becoming large trunks, forming a grove around the parent stem. A famous banyan tree is mentioned as growing on an island in the Nerbuddah; and one in Mysore is said to cover an area of 100 yards in diameter.

Of animals India produces many varieties. The elephant is domesticated, but in some parts is to be found in large herds, wild,—in Assam particularly. There are also the camel, the deer—of many varieties— antelopes, wild boars, hyenas, jackals, foxes, hares, squirrels, and others. Bears abound in the wooded mountains; wolves in the northern provinces; wild dogs in the Himalayas; the buffalo in large herds; and several descriptions of beeves, the most common of which is the sacred humped species; the wild ass exists in several varieties; the native horse is small and vicious; the goat of Cashmere has long been celebrated for its wool. There are several varieties of sheep. But of all the animals of India, those of the feline tribe are the most remarkable; lions, tigers, leopards, ounces, panthers, in great beauty and strength, abound in the jungle, and are the great objects of pursuit with European sportsmen.

Birds are, in many cases, splendid, and they are numerous. *Reptiles* abound. Serpents are frequently to be found in the gardens, and sometimes even in the houses. Some are innocuous; but the bite of others is quickly fatal. Alligators are not rare either in the rivers or on the banks. The shark infests the mouths of all the rivers. There is a large variety and an abundant supply of fish in the rivers and on the coast. The insect tribes are innumerable, and many of the varieties are most troublesome.

The exports *from India* to the United Kingdom average £50,500,000, and the imports of home produce *from the United Kingdom*, £20,002,241, annually.

For the sake of security there has been a large augmentation of her Majesty's forces in India. There were at the last computation, 79,174 Europeans, and 126,713 native soldiers.

Agriculture has always been inferior in India, and the celebrated manufactures of former times are rapidly being superseded by British production. Yet, on the whole, the industries of the empire increase rather than otherwise.

BORNEO is a large island, 800 miles long, and 600 broad, with a population estimated at from three millions to five millions. It forms part of the great East Indian Archipelago, and is situated long. 109° to 118° E.; lat. 7° N. to 4° 20' S. The territory is in part mountainous, and in part marshy, while there is a large extent of cultivable ground, yielding grain and other produce. The population consists of Malays, Javanese, and Arabs, subject to many despotic princes. Mahometanism is the prevailing religion. But of religion or morality there is little. The Dutch have endeavoured to form settlements on the island, and have partly succeeded; but Sir James Brooke, or Rajah Brooke, has done more for the good of the population than had previously been accomplished by any European. He has had the countenance and encouragement of the English Government. The coast population used to be much addicted to piracy, a tendency which of late years has been largely repressed.

SUMATRA is another great island in the same seas. It is about one thousand miles long, and, on the average, one hundred and sixty-five broad. The surface is varied as to height and depression. There are two large and beautiful lakes. The soil is generally fertile.

The population is thin. The Malay is everywhere spoken. The English have settlements; but the power of the Dutch is paramount. Attempts have been made at various times by the latter-named Power to subdue the whole island, but the native chiefs have resisted. Even in the new circumstances which political changes in Germany have thrown around the Netherlands and all neighbouring countries, it has still been the effort of the Dutch to subdue Sumatra. No doubt the end will be success; but while we write, the population of *Acheen*, a province and capital, are in revolt, and special means are required to keep the island in subjection. The people are devoted to their native chiefs, and are jealous of the interference of foreigners.

CHAPTER IX.

CHINA.

AS in regard to India, so also it may be said of China, that its immensity forbids us from entering into minuteness of detail. The empire is so large, and, in its characteristics, is so peculiar, that one is apt to think of it as standing by itself, and as not to be included in any formal geographical division of the world. And, indeed, it is so important a section of the earth's surface, and contains so many millions of people, that it can be fully dealt with only when taken by itself. Still, as constituting so large a portion of Asia it is desirable that we present a general idea of this empire and its population.

The Chinese Empire, including the tributary states, and those under its protection, consists of about 5,250,000 square miles, and 420,000,000 inhabitants.* China proper, "the centre of the world," contains 1,298,000 square miles (lat. 18° 37'—41° 35' N.) with

* *North China Herald.* Customs Returns.

146,280,000 inhabitants, of whom 2,000,000 are supposed to live on the water. There are 31,000 sailors, 822,000 foot-soldiers, 410,000 horsemen, and 7,552 military and 9,611 civil officers. Subject to China are Mantchou, 726,800 square miles, Mongolia, 1,935,910 square miles, and Tourfan, 578,275 square miles. Under the protection of China are Thibet, Bootan, Corea, and Loo-choo, containing together 726,202 square miles. This empire has extended its conquests over the greater part of what was formerly called Independent Tartary—the inhabitants of which, however, are not Tartars, but Calmucks and Mongols,—while Russia has advanced on the other side into Siberia, and thus Russia and China have come into contact, on a line extending from Lake Paleati to the mouth of the river Amur. While the Chinese dominions extend to the confines of Asiatic Russia, they reach over the immense regions of Thibet, and almost join the English territories in Bengal. Thus the greater and stronger empires have been enlarging their spheres of rule, and annexing and absorbing the smaller kingdoms and tribes all over Asia,—and the process still goes on, if not on the part of one, most surely on that of some of the others.

The great cities of the empire are,—*Pekin*, the capital, about twenty miles in circumference. There are really two cities, the Tartar and the Chinese towns. The streets are long and wide. The city is walled, and some of the gates are lofty and strong. There is a large assortment of fine shops. The finest buildings are the temples, which are spacious and magnificent, adorned with columns and stairs of white marble. There are probably 2,000,000 of population. In the neighbourhood of the city is the imperial summer palace, which consists of a large number of buildings, and is gorgeously splendid. The gardens extend to about sixty thousand acres, diversified with artificial hills, valleys, lakes, canals, rocks, and islands.

Nankin, by its walls, encloses a larger space than Pekin. It was formerly larger than it now is. It is the seat of considerable manufactures, and also is known as the patron of learning.

Canton is a very ancient city. The European factories have long established themselves here. Gutzlaff says that these are unquestionably the most elegant buildings in the empire. There are about six hundred streets in Canton, but none of the houses are imposing. The population is about 1,000,000.

Hong-Kong is a sort of British colony in China. It was ceded to England by the "Elgin" Treaty in 1858. It is an island, and, since the date of the treaty, large additions have been made to the original grant. It is healthy, and many natives are to be found mixing and preponderating in the population.

Shanghai. This is really a foreign settlement on the mainland of China, adjacent to a city which bears the same name, but which is perfectly distinct. The name signifies "upon the sea," but the settlement is now

25 miles from the coast. Nowhere in China have the natives such faith in foreigners as in Shanghai. It is a great mart of foreign trade. On the average there are imports to the extent of £18,000,000, and exports reaching £8,441,557 a year. The principal mission establishments are at Shanghai, and here is an hospital supported by the London Missionary Society for the gratuitous cure of poor patients. There are two daily newspapers, one twice a week, two weekly, and one fortnightly. The oldest of these is *The North China Herald*, a reliable authority in all matters that affect the empire.

There is nothing specially characteristic in the physical aspect of China. It is not what we should call Oriental, neither does the scenery resemble our own. It has a character peculiar to itself. It bears the appearance in many places of a well-watered plain. Green rice-fields form the main feature, with here and there hills and trees, the fields being without hedges, walls, or any boundary line, except what may be afforded by streams of water, ditches, or sign-stones. There are no meadows or pasture-lands covered with flocks; no country mansions, pleasure-grounds or parks. Pagodas appear instead of the tall church-spire; and water-communication, by means of numberless streams and canals, supersedes the use of high roads and coaches. Forests and waste places are rarely seen. Every available part is cultivated by the hoe and the plough for the exclusive use of man. The people cannot afford to consume flesh, except in small quantities; hence the absence of pasture and graminivorous animals. Pigs, geese, ducks, and fowls are brought up in the farmyard. Buffaloes and sheep are fed in stalls with grass cut from the hill-sides. The energies of the agriculturist are chiefly given to the cultivation of rice, maize, cotton, and wheat. By the most careful manuring and irrigation two crops of rice and one of vegetables may be obtained from the soil every year. The success of the rice crops depends upon the supply of water from the tropical rains; if that is deficient there is a failure; if absent, a famine—a famine to such multitudes! The Chinese are industriously laborious, and yet the living which they obtain is usually but scanty,—two or three basins of rice twice or thrice a day, with a little pork, fish, and vegetables. The rivers and streams are ordinarily well-stocked, and supply the principal article of animal food. But nothing comes amiss; everything that can be used for food is so used. All animal life is spared of course by Buddhists; but, with the exception of priests, nuns, and women who have taken vows not to touch animal food, there are not many who are strict vegetarians. Such being the diet of the Chinese, the estimated number of the population need not be considered as exaggerated. The Coolies shipped by private parties for South America and other places have usually been the very refuse of society. The Chinese are fond of making money, and they do not spend it in display of any kind. Their houses do not exceed two storeys, and are close and uncomfortable. The female apartments are always separate from the others; and the women even take their meals apart from the men. Young unmarried women are guarded with the greatest care. Young persons are betrothed while they are yet children; indeed sometimes an agreement is made before they are born; but, in any case, they are entirely passive, and quietly submit to any arrangement of the kind which is made for them. The parties do not meet till their marriage. Polygamy is permitted by the law, and is practised by many, especially by the mandarins or magistrates. The funeral ceremonies of the Chinese are most expensive, and a kind of worship is presented by children at the tombs of their parents.

Education is cheap, but inadequate. Mathematics, the natural sciences, and the languages of other nations do not form any part of the curriculum of even the more advanced, and there are no examinations such as correspond to those which are requisite in this country for the B.A. and M.A. degrees. There is no school supported by the public funds for the education even of boys, and women are precluded from learning. It has been said that "the Chinese are the most reading people in the world." They are not so. Any good knowledge of letters is confined to the literati, who are a small class; and among the busy and labouring portions of the community there are few to be found with education sufficient to the understanding of the commonest book. Yet books are both abundant and cheap.

The usual subjects are the history and topography of China, comments on the writings of the ancients, ethics, poetry, novels, medicine, astrology, agriculture, and military tactics. No books of great age are to be found in the country. The paper is very perishable, and, being exposed to worms and insects, whole libraries of Chinese books are soon eaten up. Standard works, therefore, require to be reproduced from time to time. The printing is from square blocks of the wood of the pear tree. The language is monosyllabic. Every word consists of one syllable only; but words may be combined, as in English, *e.g., welcome, welfare;* every syllable, however, is significant, and is itself a word. The difference between the oral and the written language is so great that they can be acquired and used separately. The Chinese cannot be called a moral people, and yet they are in advance of many pagan nations.

The common crimes are treason, piracy, street brawls, housebreaking, swindling, forgery, and debt. Deliberate murder is not frequent. Poisoning on a large scale was attempted a few years ago at Hong-Kong; but that was a rare act of fanaticism and retaliation on account of the destruction of life and property by the British forces at Canton. Capital punishment is inflicted by the sword or scimitar, and when many criminals suffer at the same time the scene is most revolting. The bodies are buried, and the heads fixed in cages as a warning at various points throughout the city. Much crime escapes detection.

There is nothing more remarkable in the social state and moral condition of the Chinese than the wonderful influence which the writings of Confucius have exerted upon them for upwards of twenty centuries. They are the basis of its laws and institutions, and they have moulded the mind and character of the whole nation. Who was Confucius? He was born in the northern province of Shan-tung, about 650 years before the Christian era. One of the literati says "he taught on four great subjects: 1. Polite literature; 2. Conduct, or the practice of virtue and benevolence; 3. Fidelity, or the discharge of every duty; and 4. Sincerity, or strict integrity without deceit." His writings compose the famous ancient books known as the "Five Classics." His immediate followers composed four other books, which are, in the main, digests of the works of their master, and which are called the "Four Books." These nine volumes have been explained and amplified by many commentators.

Socrates, Plato, and Aristotle, are names familiar to every school in Europe. The moral legislator of China and the surrounding countries, though born only a little earlier than these great men, is regarded with but little interest. Yet in his own country his writings are revered with a respect similar to that which is paid by Christians to the Sacred Scriptures. He seems to have been considered too good to be placed among the gods whom the people feared; but his image, or some representation of him, is found in every school of the empire, and every scholar performs an act of obeisance before it daily. Probably his great influence is to be accounted for—1. By the adaptation of his teaching to man's moral instincts of right and wrong, and his showing that the course of virtue is the best and wisest, and that the root of all virtue is the practice of filial piety; 2. A family is a prototype of the nation; the patriarch of the family represents the emperor, and the well-ordered family, the empire; and the principles of dependence and subordination of children to their parents, and inferiors to their superiors, is the moving spring of his whole system. This last-mentioned principle of Confucianism has strongly commended it to all the governments of China. The supreme rulers saw that the adoption and prevalence of such doctrines would give them sway. They therefore early embodied them in their laws and institutions, and had them instilled into the minds of the young, so that they have become the basis of the moral sentiment of the Chinese empire, and have served to hold together the largest associated population in the world. Benevolence, uprightness, politeness, wisdom, fidelity, and the duties of the human relations are strongly enforced by the Confucian ethics upon all classes. But it is much as if the tale of bricks were exacted without the necessary straw—no help is provided by the system for poor human nature; neither is there any scheme of rewards or punishments to stimulate to virtue and to deter from vice. Confucius taught a philosophy entirely practical. He was a state officer and a state reformer, and his teachings are such as might be expected from such a man. With this he has united much misty speculation about the origin of the world. More than two thousand years have passed since his age; but he has never ceased to live, nor ceased to rule; people, nobles, and emperors of China, to this hour, submit to his undisputed authority. A noble principle of this philosophy is that every man is regarded as merely one of a vast community, and for that community he must live—the child for the parent, the elder for the younger, the subject for the sovereign, and the sovereign for the sake of the sublime law of order; society is to be perfected whether the individual members of it be happy or not, this is a great principle—that personal happiness is to be sought in ministering to the welfare of others. That were a poor patriotism which should not be strong to suffer. Even in our schoolboy-days we are taught to feel that

"Dulce et decorum est pro patria mori;"

and surely such a sentiment as this among the Chinese gives good promise of the success of a better faith among them, and inspires the hope that this people will, by-and-by, favourably receive the Divine confirmation of the teachings of their own sage—" Look not every man on his own things, but every man also on the things of others"—" none of us liveth to himself."

On the origin of our own war with China we cannot enlarge. The result has been the opening up of the empire to Western and Christian influences to a much wider extent than before, and can lead only to much good in the end. Opium is the bane of the people, and one cannot wonder at the exasperation which, on the part of the Chinese, goaded them on to such atrocities as they inflicted on the European merchants, whom they regarded as the agents of an illicit traffic in an article which they saw to be so much abused and so deleterious. England felt, however, that humanity has its claims; but it would have been to her honour if she had been called to espouse a better cause. Still, as we have said, great good has been the result.

The late Chinese rebellion or revolution was characterised by strong and remarkable peculiarities. From the earliest times the peace of the empire had been open to disturbance from without. There were frequent hostile inroads made by the Tartar tribes to the north and the west, and in such inroads originated that remarkable wall which extends over eighteen hundred miles of territory, crossing mountains and rivers, and furnished at intervals with gates and towers. It was built about two hundred years before the Christian era, by the founder of the Tsin dynasty; which is supposed to have originated the name Chin, or China. It is related of this emperor, that having resolved to make his dynasty last from the beginning to the end of time, he not only caused the wall to be built, which demanded the labour of every third man in the empire, but that he also "collected together and burned all the records of past ages, and buried alive 460 learned men, desiring to make posterity believe that the dominion of the world commenced with himself as the first universal Emperor of China." The internal history of the country presents little that is interesting. A succession of contests for the sovereignty, and frequent changes of dynasty, make up nearly the whole from the earliest times down to the last conquest, and the establishment of the present reigning family, about two hundred years ago.

But the late rebellion, which has faded away and resulted in very little, was as much a surprise to the ruling powers in China as it was to all the rest of the world. It was something entirely new in the experience of all. And although it has subsided it was but feebly met. The Pekin journals first noticed the rebellion in August, 1850. Discontent and a cry for reform had been widespread for years before, and a sort of freemasonry among the disaffected had enabled them to mature their plans without suspicion or hindrance. The leader of the insurgents, "the Prince of Peace," professed to have revelations from Heaven, and the whole movement presented a sacred aspect, many Christian doctrines being professed, and New Testament phrases being employed in all the proclamations which were issued by the party. This fact can be accounted for only by recollecting the earlier and later Gospel instructions which have been attempted among the Chinese. Every difficulty seemed, at first, to give way before the rebels; but they paid little regard to the places which they subdued, and took no measures either to retain them or defend them. There was much fanaticism in their entire proceedings. Greater wisdom and an ordinary amount of proper policy would have made a wide difference in the history of China for all time to come. In the course of 1851, more than seven hundred of them were executed in Canton alone.

Allusion to the religious character which was borne by this movement makes it natural for us to revert to the subject of religion in China. Confucianism is not so much a religion as a morality—not so much a theological creed as a system of ethics. The ancient religion of the Chinese seems to have been a pure theism, soon perverted, however, by human traditions. After that came a kind of polytheism, which is only a particular expression for pantheism—God is everything, the sun, the moon, the stars, all nature idolised and worshipped as emanations of Deity. Buddhism was later, and was introduced as an importation. The former two are ancient and contemporaneous. The Confucian sacrifices are thank-offerings rather than expiations. The incarnations of Buddha were not for the purpose of atonement, but for instruction and example.

The Roman Catholics have done much to introduce the knowledge of Christian truth—so far as they retain it—to the Chinese. Since the days of the

Apostle Paul, no man has been found more capable of "forgetting the things that are behind" than Francis Xavier. It was he who planned the missionary expedition of the Jesuits to China, and, although he died within sight of its shores, the work which he contemplated has been prosecuted by others down to the present time, and, notwithstanding many interruptions and much defect, it continues its operations. The efforts of Protestants in behalf of the Chinese are comparatively recent. The agents of the London Missionary Society have, for the most part, been men of a high order of ability. The names of Morrison and Milne, as the first in the field, and those of Medhurst and Legge, as their successors, are worthy of special honour. Others have followed such examples—various Christian denominations both in England and America; and their efforts, combined with those of the British and Foreign Bible Society, which has distributed millions of copies of the Sacred Scriptures, cannot fail to affect the minds of this vast multitude. These, with the breaking up of old forms of thought incident to the insurrection, taken in connection with the late war with England and France, and the freer intercourse of the people with the West, must tend to the accomplishment of many changes, and to the introduction into China of a still higher civilisation, and a true and spiritual religion. "The land of Sinim" was not unknown to the inspired prophet, and the time may not be remote in which his visions shall be realised.

CHAPTER X.

JAPAN.

AT the eastern extremity of Asia, between 31° and 49° N. lat., is the empire of Japan, which consists of a number of islands. Three of these are very large: 1. Niphon, which is 700 miles long, but which is so narrow that its breadth in the centre is only 48 miles. It is divided into forty-nine provinces, of which the principal cities are Meaco, the residence of the dairi, or spiritual chief, and in which all the coins are struck, and all the books printed; Jeddo, the capital of the secular emperor, or cubo, whose palace is five leagues in circumference, and forms of itself a considerable city; and Osacco, a rich commercial city: 2. The second island is Ximo, or Kiusiu, 180 miles long and 66 broad, consisting of nine provinces: 3. And Xicoco, or Sicop, 84 miles long and 46 broad, containing four provinces. Surrounding these great islands there are many others which are smaller, some being fertile and others bare rock, and which have the appearance of having been separated by some convulsion of nature. The superficial contents of the whole islands is estimated at 266,500 square miles, and the population at 45,000,000.

The islands of Japan are mountainous, like the opposite coasts of the continent. The principal summit, called *Fusi*, is covered with snow the whole of the year. There are also many volcanoes. It is only the great industry of the people which has made the sterile soil productive; but that industry is so diligent that even the steepest mountains are cultivated. Agriculture is prescribed as the principal employment by the laws of the State. Goats and sheep are banished from Japan, the former being regarded as prejudicial to agriculture. Cotton and silk supply the place of wool. Swine are to be found only in the vicinity of Nangasacki, one of the large cities. In general there are but few quadrupeds, with the exception of dogs, which are abundant. The whim of a sovereign, with whom dogs were favourites, has prescribed the breeding of them by a law of the empire. They are supported at the public expense.

Japan was not much known to the ancients. Christianity was introduced by the Jesuits, and it is alleged that about the year 1616 one half of the population were nominally Christians. The Portuguese had established a trade with the country, and they favoured the work of the Jesuits; but the Dutch supplanted the Portuguese, and both Portuguese and Jesuits were banished "for ever" from the empire in 1637. There was a long-continued persecution of the Catholic religion, and it is believed that seven millions of persons were sacrificed. The Dutch and the Chinese were afterwards, for many years, the only nations whose ships were allowed access to Japan. The Dutch were subjected to many restrictions, and yet they found the trade profitable.

There is but little trade between England and Japan. Russia has repeatedly of late years tried to form a commercial connection with the country, but with small success. The Japanese are well situated for commerce. Formerly their ships covered the neighbouring seas. Their silk and cotton cloths, their porcelain wares, and their lacquered tin ware, with raised figures (japanned ware), are well known, and in much demand, and their steel work is superior. The recent visit of the Japanese ambassadors to this and other European countries is an indication of the desire of the nation to enlarge its knowledge of humanity, and the promise of competition by the Japanese at the Vienna Exhibition is a proof of self-consciousness in respect to those arts in which the people excel, which must procure for them the respect of more privileged communities.

The Japanese are a mixture of the Malay and Mongolian races, like the Chinese, from whom they have probably derived their civilisation. Their language is a dialect of the Mongolian—the Chinese is the learned language. They are the most civilised and refined nation of Asia, a noble, proud people, intelligent, docile, and desirous of instruction. They are active, cleanly, and laborious, cheerful and contented, but sensual and revengeful.

The government is despotic and severe, and the laws very strict. The people in general are poor, the landlord exacting from the peasant a most inordinate portion of his earnings. The law holds every one responsible for those with whom he is connected—the father for the children, the master for the servant, and even a neighbour for his neighbour. All crime is punished, not in any case by fine, but by imprisonment, and banishment, or loss of limb or life; and every punishment is inflicted with inexorable rigour on high and low.

The high priest of Japan is still called dairi, which was the title of the emperors, while they possessed spiritual and temporal powers united. A revolution in 1185 deprived them of the secular power, and Yori-Tomo was appointed supreme ruler of the nation. The dairi is visible only to those who wait upon him. He lives in a fortified palace. Where he was born there he lives and dies, and never goes beyond the precincts of his residence. All orders are issued in his name. He has a rich income. The secular emperor resides at Jeddo. Under him are the princes, who are responsible to him. He acknowledges the superiority of the dairi, but he himself, the cubo, rules the empire with the assistance of a council of state consisting of six aged men.

The religion of the Japanese is of Hindoo origin, and in adherence to it there are many sects. They worship many inferior divinities, whose statues are placed in the temples of the great deities. There is a numerous priesthood, with many monks and nuns who live in a multitude of monasteries, under the superiority of the dairi. The Hindoo religion has nowhere been more changed by superstition and additions of various kinds than in Japan. The Sinto, or Confucian sect, is philosophical, like the sect of the learned in China, and despises the folly of the popular belief. There is free toleration granted to all religions. Christian missionaries have laboured with considerable success, and there is at present a large addition being made to their number.

In the time of peace the army of Japan consists of 100,000 men, besides 20,000 horsemen. Their arms are bows, muskets, sabres, and daggers. They have very heavy cannon. Besides this imperial army the separate provinces maintain, in the aggregate, a force of 368,000 infantry and 33,000 cavalry. The navy, which formerly consisted of large vessels in large fleets, is now insignificant.

CONCLUSION.

ASIA has been the battle-field and the grave of great nations. The most gorgeous displays of kingly grandeur have been, and even now are, to be found within these territories. If Asia were taken out of the map of the world, all history would be rendered enigmatical. And the future of the history of man is largely dependent upon the position of this great central continent.

The great mental conflicts of the informed and reflective classes have here had their field. In certain instances they have not originated in Asia; but it is on this ground that ancient controversies have fought themselves out, and have most widely affected the population. Judaism and Christianity here contended. Gnosticism, Arianism, Pelagianism, did not take their rise within these bounds; but in this limit they all had their fiercest struggle. The diversity of opinion, in regard to ceremonial observance, which separated the Greek Church from the Roman, more deeply affected

Asia than any other part of the world, and, indeed, was the means of alienating multitudes from the Christian faith altogether. And now there are perpetually being carried on here, in one part or another, the battles which are natural and inevitable between Christian truth and the ancient systems of the idolatrous and mythological races.

The question, politically, is important—what shall become of Asia? The great Powers which rule the world have been more, and still more nearly approaching each other on this field. Trace the history. Who can give assurance that there shall be no collision? The *prospects* of Asia are as those of a troubled sunrise. No man can forecast the day. Turkey can scarcely hold its own; Persia is effete; China, mighty as it is in extent, cannot cope with European arms; Russia gradually goes on to increase of territory, and so does Britain. If the mighty enginery which moves along the same line from opposite termini should one day meet, the collision cannot fail to be disastrous. There are great battle-fields, in this continent, almost as if prepared, by the absence of all but wandering tribes, to be the arena in which shall be settled the world's destiny. Some say that, as here the Gospel of peace was first proclaimed, so here also shall be first and most distinctly manifested its most conspicuous results—that here is preserved the sacred and fertile land sanctified by the tread of the Redeemer's feet; but into such theories we cannot enter—theories they are, and nothing more.

The look of things in Asia seems to say that, as in the past, so in the future, for some little time to come, the weak and the scattered must give way to the strong and united, and that the great Powers shall thus possess the entire land. What the result of such possession may be none can predict. It is better to espouse another's quarrel than one's own. Hence the importance of preserving the independence of the small border kingdoms. If the boundaries of vast empires were closely contiguous, it might, as experience has elsewhere shown, be less easy to preserve the peace. Yet this partition of its soil seems to be the prospect of the "unappropriated" parts of Asia.

The religious "faiths" of Asia are dormant if not dead. The force of the Christianity which, in this continent, took its rise, is exhausted as indigenous to the country, and if any good end would be reached in the Christian name, the means must be imported. Judaism is a dead letter; Brahminism and Buddhism do not master and dominate the people; and Mohammedanism is equally inefficient. The great temples and mosques are all old. There is no freshness of life or enterprise in any of these religions. The future of Asia must therefore be moulded and characterised by Western and Christian modes of thought. In order to succeed in this work, the great Christian nations are especially called upon for consistency of policy and conduct with the principles which they profess to honour. England and America appear to be the great civilising and evangelising Powers of the world. Both are zealous in seeking the good of Asia; and their efforts have not been unsuccessful. In China, among the Caucasian tribes, and in India, the people have been taught, in large numbers, to understand their relation to the human brotherhood, and many have been led to a true belief in respect to Him who is the Father of all. Keshub Chunder Sen, the well-known leader of the Brahmo Samoj, in India, notwithstanding the peculiarity of his own views, says, in one of his recent addresses—"The spirit of Christianity has already pervaded the whole atmosphere of Indian society, and we breathe, think, feel, and move in a Christian atmosphere. Native society is being roused, enlightened, and reformed under the influence of Christian education." When this state of things really prevails in all parts, then will have arrived the day of emancipation for Asia.

THE END.

PRINTED BY VIRTUE AND CO., CITY ROAD, LONDON.

www.ingramcontent.com/pod-product-compliance
Lightning Source LLC
Chambersburg PA
CBHW020305240426
43673CB00039B/711